TRACING YOUR SCOTTISH ❦ ANCESTORS ❦

A GUIDE TO ANCESTRY RESEARCH IN THE NATIONAL ARCHIVES OF SCOTLAND

THE NATIONAL ARCHIVES OF SCOTLAND

DEFINING MOMENTS IN HISTORY

BIRLINN

ISBN 13: 978-1-84158-743-1

This fifth edition first published 2009 by
The National Archives of Scotland and Birlinn Ltd,
West Newington House, 10 Newington Road,
Edinburgh EH9 1QS
www.birlinn.co.uk

First published 1990, revised edition published 1997,
third edition 2003, fourth edition 2007

British Library Cataloguing in Publication Data

A catalogue record for this is available from the British Library

❧ **Contents** ❧

❦ Illustrations ❧

ꙮ Maps ꙮ
of ScotlandsPeople Centre
and West Register House

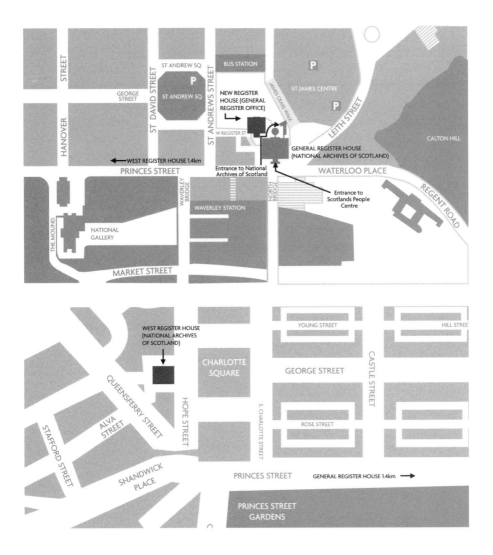

∽ **Preface** ∽

There are many books on Scottish family history. The one you are holding is unique because it is an insiders' guide, based on the combined knowledge and expertise of the people who look after the records. With the distilled experience of generations of archivists and record keepers, it is equally of use to the novice and the expert family historian.

This is the fifth edition of this book, which is the best-selling publication of the National Archives of Scotland. You will find more information about NAS records than ever before, including new chapters on the ScotlandsPeople Centre, and about occupations such as lighthouse keepers, labourers, slaves and artists. There are also helpful updates on our developing electronic resources for readers.

In the two decades since this book first appeared in 1990, access to and use of records and archives have changed considerably, but interest in family history has continued to grow steadily. Among the customers using our historical search rooms, two-thirds are doing family history, and the proportion is even higher among our Internet users.

The computer and the Internet have made family history research quicker and easier. Of course, nothing can beat the sheer excitement of using original records, of seeing the documentary traces of our ancestors and of learning to "listen" to what they have to say. But if you cannot easily reach Edinburgh to use the great treasures of the National Archives, the General Register Office and the Court of the Lord Lyon, remote searching of documents is now possible via the ScotlandsPeople.gov.uk website. The entire NAS catalogue is also searchable via the Internet (*www.nas.gov.uk*), allowing researchers to plan visits and to request copies remotely.

For those who can come to Edinburgh, the new ScotlandsPeople Centre at Register House is an essential destination. It is described in a special new chapter. All the important records for the Scottish family historian are in one place, in magnificent surroundings and with expert staff on hand to help. Millions of images are available at the click of a mouse, and for those who want to dig deeper, the adjacent NAS search rooms provide access to huge resources of original records. Across Scotland a number of local authorities are opening or planning similar centres, encouraging visitors to see the places from which their ancestors came.

I would like to thank Duncan Macniven, Registrar General for Scotland, and David Sellar, the Lord Lyon, for the assistance provided by their colleagues in the writing of Chapters 4–6.

Whether you come to search personally in the records, or work remotely from your home, this book will be an indispensable guide.

GEORGE P MACKENZIE
Keeper of the Records of Scotland

↷ Tracing ↶
Your Scottish Ancestors

∞ 1 ∞
Introduction

They trace his steps till they can tell
His pedigree as weel's himsell
Robert Fergusson

1.1 You want to find your Scottish ancestors. This book is written specifically to help you to trace those ancestors who are mentioned in the documents preserved in the National Archives of Scotland, a primary location of records for family research.

The National Archives of Scotland

1.2 The National Archives of Scotland is the government department responsible for the custody and preservation of the records of the government of Scotland. It also has taken responsibility for and custody of the records of many non-government concerns, including church records and the records of some private families and businesses. Most of these records may be consulted by members of the public.

1.3 The National Archives of Scotland occupies two buildings in the centre of Edinburgh, close to the railway and bus stations. One building is General Register House, at the east end of Princes Street, opposite the Balmoral Hotel and the former General Post Office. A statue of the Duke of Wellington ('the man on the horse') guards the entrance to this building, which now gives access to the ScotlandsPeople Centre and the shop. To reach the NAS search rooms you must use the Garden Entrance at the rear. Turn up West Register Street on the west side of the building (on the left as you face the front), proceed through the courtyard, and follow the signs for the National Archives of Scotland, which literally lead you up the garden path.

1.4 General Register House contains two NAS public search rooms: the Legal Search Room and the Historical Search Room. Searching for your

Family group, 1910, private collection.

ancestors is regarded as historical research, so you will use the Historical Search Room. Doing historical research is free, but you must do your own research. The staff will advise you and try to answer all reasonable questions, but the rest is up to you. Hence this book!

If you want to see any of the records for a legal purpose, then you will need to use the Legal Search Room and pay a fee for the records to be produced.

1.5   The second NAS building, West Register House, is situated in Charlotte Square, less than a mile away from General Register House. It also contains a search room, the West Search Room, in which you may do historical research. The same rules, regulations and procedures apply to both Historical and West Search Rooms. Both are open from Monday to Friday, 09.00–16.45 hours, apart from certain public holidays. Please check the NAS website (*www.nas.gov.uk*) for details.

1.6   New Register House, which is adjacent to General Register House, is not part of the National Archives of Scotland. It houses the General Register Office for Scotland (GROS) which administers the official records of births, marriages and deaths and census records. These records are of paramount importance to the family historian, and are available through the ScotlandsPeople Centre (see Chapters 4-5).

1.7   The ScotlandsPeople Centre occupies parts of both General Register House and New Register House, but the three partners bodies, the NAS, the GROS and the Court of the Lord Lyon all continue to provide their non-family history services in the two buildings.

About this book

1.8   The first six chapters are introductory ones, which you should read before planning a visit to or writing to the National Archives of Scotland. The remaining chapters describe records in the National Archives of Scotland that might be of use to you in your search for your ancestors. In a sense, all records which name individuals may provide genealogical information, but we have tried to select and describe those which will be most useful. Chapters 8-13 concern records which should be of interest to all ancestor hunters: records of baptism, marriage, death, inheritance, land-owning and tenancy. The remaining chapters describe records which concern particular activities or professions or situations; records which are less likely to specify relationships, though they may, but will add foliage to your family tree.

1.9   An attempt has been made to lead the reader step-by-step into the records, particularly those records described in the earlier chapters which should prove the most profitable. The intention is to enable you to do your research with decreasing reliance on the advice of the staff. Descriptions of procedures in the later pages of the book will assume that you have become familiar with the techniques of searching records.

1.10   As this book is intended specifically to help genealogical researchers, it does not cover all the records in the National Archives of Scotland or deal with all aspects of those records described. Legal concepts may be simplified in their description.

1.11   Do bear in mind that you will be using records which were drawn up for particular administrative or legal purposes. You will be using them for a different purpose (genealogy) so do not be disappointed if the information you are seeking is not available in the form in which you would like to find it. Perhaps we should warn you that any sort of historical research can be addictive and after a little practice you will find yourself becoming familiar with words and concepts from the world of your ancestors.

1.12   While reading this book, you may encounter unusual words. There will also be unfamiliar words in the records which you are going to search. It is useful get into the habit of using a dictionary, such as *The Concise Scots Dictionary* (Polygon at Edinburgh, 1999). You will also find in the records expressions which seem to us now to be pejorative, such as 'bastard' or 'lunatic'. Please try not to be offended by such phrases. However much we may dislike this today, these were the terms in use at the time and there is no point, for example, in referring readers to a 'register of psychiatric patients' when the record is called 'Register of Lunatics'.

1.13   Most of the published works we mention in this book should be available in the United Kingdom through a local library, perhaps by inter-library loan. The names of publishers are placed in brackets after the titles of recently-published books, but not out-of-print ones.

1.14   In our use of personal pronouns, we have described your ancestors as if they were all male. This is a matter of convenience and we apologise to those who are rightly offended. However, it is a sad fact that men are more likely to be named in the records than women.

1.15   Throughout the rest of this book, the National Archives of Scotland will be represented by the initials NAS. All paragraphs in the book are numbered and a reference to a paragraph from elsewhere in the book will be by its number. A reference to this paragraph would be simply **1.15**.

Enquiries from a distance

1.16   This book is designed to help people to do their own research in the NAS and get the most from using our online resources in advance of a visit. The NAS website contains guidance on researching remotely, including how to search our online catalogue (or Online Public Access Catalogue - OPAC) and guides to important series of records. We hope that the book will also help and guide those who are unable to come to Edinburgh, but who wish to trace their Scottish ancestry. NAS staff will provide advice and will answer specific enquiries, but cannot carry out research on behalf of enquirers. If you are unable to carry out your research yourself, you may wish to consider employing a professional searcher. NAS staff will send a list of those currently working in Scotland on request, or you can find information about them on the website, or by contacting ASGRA (see Appendix A).

1.17   Please do not send any payment unless and until you are requested to do so.

1.18   All correspondence should be addressed to

The Keeper of the Records of Scotland
The National Archives of Scotland
H M General Register House
2 Princes Street
Edinburgh EHI 3YY
Scotland

The telephone number is 0131–535 1314 and the fax number is 0131 535 1360. The website address is *www.nas.gov.uk*.

E-mail enquiries should be sent to *enquiries@nas.gov.uk*.

⚶2⚶
First Steps in Family Research

2.1   The NAS will not be your first port of call when you decide to find out who your ancestors were. First ask your Aunt Jessie. In other words, begin with your own living family. There is usually at least one elderly relative who is interested in the family and acts as the family memory, though that memory may be reliable for only a couple of generations back. (Be wary of romantic family traditions that claim descent from the disinherited child of a nobleman or from the owner of a castle.) Some of your relatives may have preserved old family letters and documents such as birth certificates and wills. Also, if the family has lived in the same locality for some generations, it will be worth looking at gravestones in the local kirkyard or graveyard.

2.2   From this information, you will have a basis on which to build. If you live in Scotland, a visit to your local library is recommended. Even if you live in another country, your library may be able to obtain useful books for you. If your ancestors stayed for a long time in one area, familiarise yourself with that area, by means of studying local maps, e.g. Victorian large-scale Ordnance Survey maps; reading parish histories; checking if the local library has any street directories.

2.3   If your ancestor was genuinely a product of a noble or landed family, you should look at *The Scots Peerage* or *Burke's Peerage, Baronetage and Knightage* or *Burke's Landed Gentry*. Useful guides to printed sources on particular families are *Scottish Family History* by Margaret Stuart and Balfour Paul and *Scottish Family Histories* by J P S Ferguson (National Library of Scotland). Miss Ferguson has also produced a *Directory of Scottish Newspapers* (National Library of Scotland), which will tell you which Scottish libraries hold copies of a particular local newspaper. Similar information may be found in *NEWSPLAN: Report of the NEWSPLAN italics project in Scotland* (British Library). If an ancestor was a local dignitary, there may be an obituary of him in a local newspaper. The annual volumes of

Wedding photograph 1930, private collection.

the *Edinburgh Almanack* name office holders throughout Scotland since the mid-eighteenth century.

2.4   To find out information about an ancestor, you must know in what part of Scotland he lived. You must also have some knowledge of the administrative areas into which Scotland was divided. For centuries, the basic units were the parish, burgh, county and sheriffdom, and you should try to find out in which of these your ancestors may have lived. The General Register Office has produced a useful *Index of Scottish Place Names* (various editions), which lists the then inhabited places in Scotland, showing the county and parish in which each was located. If this publication is not available or you cannot find a place-name in it, try a pre-1975 gazetteer or a nineteenth-century edition of the *County Directory of Scotland,* which gives the nearest town and sometimes the county of inhabited places. A useful index of parishes, showing the related counties, sheriffdoms, commissary courts (see Chapter 8) and burghs is obtainable from the compiler Mrs A R Bigwood, Flat B, The Lodge, 2 East Road, North Berwick, EH39 4HN. Another alphabetical list of parishes, showing the sheriffdom, diocese, presbytery and commissariot of each is printed in *An Historical Catalogue of the Scottish Bishops* by Robert Keith (Edinburgh, 1824) and in *In Search of Scottish Ancestry* by Gerald Hamilton-Edwards (Phillimore). As the boundaries of parishes and other administrative areas did not remain the same throughout the centuries and human beings are often mobile, you should note the names of adjacent parishes and other areas in case you need to extend your search to them. There was a particularly significant alteration of county and parish boundaries in 1891.

2.5   If you want to find out about the history of your surname (as opposed to that of your family), look at *The Surnames of Scotland* by George F Black (New York Public Library). However, names can be a snare sometimes, as it is only in comparatively recent times that we have spelled names consistently.

2.6   An ancestor may have had the same surname as you, but spelled it differently. Clerks writing this surname down in official documents might spell it in yet other ways. Even with forenames, you have to be canny: e.g. Patrick and Peter used to be interchangeable names. But with forenames, you have a marvellous advantage in the Scottish practice of naming almost every child after a relative. Thus, it is reasonable to expect that an eldest son is named after his father's father, the second after his mother's father, the third after his own father, an eldest daughter after her mother's mother, the second after her father's mother, and the third after her own mother, and younger children after available uncles and aunts. A practice less convenient for us, however, was the naming of infants after elder brothers and sisters who had died: another snare for the genealogist.

2.7 Your preliminary investigation complete, you will probably now want to consider the resources available to the genealogist on the internet. See the next chapter for guidance. If you do not have access to the internet, it is perfectly possible to carry out research in the traditional manner. If you are in this position, you may wish to skip the next chapter and move to Chapter 4.

⌒3⌒
Tracing Scottish Ancestors on the Internet

3.1 We should start this chapter with a warning. The Internet has created expectations that with its help information can be found almost instantly, but this is not always the case. By using the web, the fortunate family historian can find descriptive catalogues that lead to images or transcripts of original documents. While this is not true of every record group, work is constantly advancing, in Scotland as elsewhere, to make copies available in this way to assist historical research. But that is only part of the Internet's value.

3.2 As this book describes, there are many papers, registers, and volumes, files and photos – together simply described as 'records' – of great potential to Scottish genealogists. Such is the accumulation of records preserved from generations past that catalogues of great numbers of collections have yet to appear online. This is despite the mass of relevant material already available in that way. Also, the genealogist is one of many users, although an important one, to be considered when resources are being allocated to increasing access to records online. Then there are practical and legal reasons that prevent many records from being displayed on the web. It is sadly the case that, sometimes, gaps exist in collections. In such circumstances the Internet again comes into its own. It helps to track down alternative sources from which we may glean information. It acts as a tool for individual family historians to plan what it is realistic for them to do in exploring the resources of the archives, libraries and record centres of the world and in our case Scotland. The downside is that the freedom of the Internet itself creates a form of chaos, for example in the inevitable duplication of information that one finds on different gateways providing hundreds of links to other sites.

3.3 In some circumstances the suggested outcome of your search for genealogical information on the Internet would be a visit to Scotland. For advice on conducting a search from a distance see the NAS website at *www.nas.gov.uk*. If a visit is impractical, one option is to use a professional record searcher to do the work for you. Contact details for some searchers are found on the NAS website and Cyndi's List of Genealogy Sites on the Internet—*www.cyndislist.com/scotland.htm*. Members of family history societies in areas of interest to you may help you in exchange for any assistance you can provide for them in return. It may be worthwhile becoming a member of a family history society in Scotland, and benefiting from advice and tuition, or work already done by fellow members via a society's register of members' interests. For information about other family history societies see the Scottish Association of Family History Societies—*www.safhs.org.uk*.

3.4   A reference to a website in this publication is not in itself an endorsement. Please note that some websites mentioned below make charges for the services they offer. In this short chapter we aim to give a flavour of what can be found and can do no more than mention a selection of sites. We have selected those created or supported by government bodies and Scottish archives and libraries; gateways giving family history links by category; and a further selection of sites to demonstrate a variety of record types and services on offer. Given the developments taking place here at the NAS, we are only too aware that information on particular websites and webpages can change, as can web addresses, and that sites come and go. Keep an eye on our website, *www.nas.gov.uk*, for developments in our own family history services.

The Scottish Archive Network

3.5   The Scottish Archive Network (SCAN) is a major co-operative venture of relevance to the family historian. The SCAN website (*www.scan.org.uk*) is maintained by the NAS and provides a convenient gateway to the records of more than fifty archives throughout Scotland. The key point about the SCAN online catalogue is that it gives general information about the extent and content of collections held in Scottish archives. You would not search it by personal name for individual ancestors, but once you have exhausted the indexed sources, such as census returns etc, you can turn to the SCAN site to find out what other records survive for a parish or county or burgh from which your ancestor came. Or, if you are planning to visit a Scottish archive, you can browse the holdings of that archive to see whether there are records of potential interest for

Web page from the Scottish Archive Network site.

your family history research. The site also provides an online directory of archives in Scotland, with contact details. Other useful parts of the SCAN site include a knowledge base on many aspects of Scottish history, a glossary of legal terms found in Scottish records (especially wills and testaments) and a gazetteer of Scottish places, which allows you to familiarize yourself with the old administrative units of counties, parishes and burghs.

Scottish public registers, census records and wills

3.6 The official government source of genealogical data for Scotland is *www.scotlandspeople.gov.uk*. The NAS, the General Register Office for Scotland (GROS), and the Court of the Lord Lyon are partners in the ScotlandsPeople, the major Scottish family history service. The site is already one of the world's biggest genealogical resources, giving online access to the Scottish old parish registers (OPRs), statutory registers of births, marriages and deaths, and census returns (up to 1901). For a full description of these services see Chapters 4 and 5, and visit *www.scotland-speople.gov.uk* or *www.scotlandspeoplehub.gov.uk*.

3.7   The ScotlandsPeople website also contains the index to Scottish wills and testaments to 1901. Colour images of the documents are available to buy, save and download (*www.scotlandspeople.gov.uk*). For fuller information on wills see Chapter 9.

Other government records and court and private records held by the NAS

3.8   The NAS Online Public Access Catalogue (OPAC) can be found on the website *www.nas.gov.uk*. It is a descriptive catalogue of NAS collections and covers the whole range of records we hold, other than uncatalogued material. A significant part of what is in the catalogue is not of direct relevance to the family historian. Nevertheless it is constantly developing and is a most important tool. Used in combination with the information described in the following chapters covering the records, the catalogue may help you identify NAS references for sets of records, or in many cases the call-up references of individual items or files. Some records are described in the briefest of terms, while in other cases fuller information about the contents of single documents, or of series, is found. Detailed information extracted from criminal trial records is included in the catalogue (see **15.2**). The catalogue does not take you into images of the records themselves, so, as discussed in **3.3**, you may well need to follow up on what you have found online.

National Library of Scotland

3.9   Summary information about the NLS's extensive manuscript collections can be found through the Scottish Archive Network website *www.scan. org.uk*. The NLS's own website features online catalogue descriptions of some collections, as well as several databases dealing with the activities of Scots abroad. One is an important database of emigrants' correspondence and papers, and contains other material relating to emigration, all from manuscripts collections in the NLS. See *www.nls.uk/catalogues*.

Public registers, census and government records held in England, Wales and Northern Ireland

3.10   These may be of relevance if you are searching for ancestors who have moved to or from Scotland, even temporarily, and therefore may be recorded in the registers of births, deaths and marriages, and census returns, outside Scotland. Such records also relate to government and public bodies whose holdings are of relevance to the whole of the United Kingdom.

3.11   Access to the records of births, deaths and marriages for England and Wales from 1837 is now via the online General Register Office website *www.gro.gov.uk/gro/content/certificates/*. The BDM registers are not open to public inspection, but entries can be bought online in the form of certificates. Information on this service can also be found via *www.familyrecords.gov.uk/frc/* or *www.gro.gov.uk/gro/content/certificates*. The Family Records Centre in London, which formerly provided onsite access, closed in 2008.

3.12   The website of The National Archives (formerly the Public Record Office), *www.nationalarchives.gov.uk*, takes you into its own vast online catalogue The National Archives' series of information leaflets has been incorporated into this. A growing number of searchable databases linked to images of the records can be explored through the TNA website or related pay-per-view websites. They now include the 1911 census for England and Wales. Other records held include registered wills and administrations proved in the Prerogative Court of Canterbury, 1384-1858.

3.13   The TNA site also leads you into the Access to Archives (A2A) database, containing a number of catalogues submitted by archives in England. A2A's database of hospital records gives information on the existence and location of records of hospitals in the UK, but does not reproduce the catalogues in detail.

3.14   The Public Record Office of Northern Ireland (PRONI) is the main source for family history records in Northern Ireland and is the official place of deposit for all public records there. For information see *www. proni.gov.uk*. Unfortunately almost no nineteenth-century Irish census returns survive, although census returns are available for 1901. RASCAL (Research And Special Collections Available Locally) is a gateway to research resources in libraries, museums and archives in Northern Ireland – *www.rascal.ac.uk*. The General Register Office (Northern Ireland) – *www.groni.gov.uk* – has an online service for birth and death certificates from 1864 and marriages from 1845.

3.15   The FamilyRecords consortium website *www.FamilyRecords.gov.uk* provides guidance in finding the government records and other sources you need for your family history research. The partners are: Access to Archives (A2A); British Library – India Office; Commonwealth War Graves Commission; General Register Office; General Register Office for Scotland; Imperial War Museum; Llyfrgell Genedlaethol Cymru/ National Library Wales; The National Archives; National Archives of Scotland; Public Record Office of Northern Ireland; Scottish Archive Network. The site contains some useful links to other sites of interest to the family historian

The Republic of Ireland

3.16 If you are searching for ancestors who lived in the Republic of Ireland, visit the National Archives of Ireland at *www.nationalarchives.ie/index. html* and the General Register Office for Ireland at *www.groireland.ie*

Other archives, libraries and local research centres

3.17 The Scottish Archive Network, through its directory at *www.scan.org. uk/directory*, gives contact information on partners in the Network and many others, including links to websites. Familia – *www.familia.org.uk* – is an essential guide to genealogical resources in public libraries in the UK and Ireland. Other gateways directing you to websites and services in the different parts of Scotland include *www.cyndislist.com* and *www. genuki.org.uk*. The gateway to descriptions of archive collections held by UK universities and colleges is the Archives Hub – *www.archiveshub. ac.uk*. In the main, collections are described only briefly on the Hub, but where possible there are links to complete catalogue descriptions. A splendid search tool is provided by the Hub for you to explore its indexes of subjects, place names, personal and corporate names. This quickly reveals the diversity of university and college archives, including much relating to the country's industrial and commercial heritage.

3.18 The range of help offered online to genealogists by archives, libraries and others serving different parts of Scotland and different specialist interests, varies widely. On the one hand you may find genealogy research services as offered by the Angus Local Studies Centre, which specialises in researching Angus ancestors and can be commissioned to do this – *www. angus.gov.uk/history/archives/*. On the other hand, some hard-pressed organisations may offer you no more than an email address to write to. When you e-mail them, in some cases you may receive only a leaflet or a standard response. It is likely in such circumstances that detailed work

cannot be done in looking into records for you. The best advice about
e-mails is to keep them brief, focussing on one or two precise points of
real importance to you, which will give you the best chance of getting
good advice back.

Other large genealogy websites

3.19   The Family History Library of the Church of Jesus Christ of Latter-day
Saints has the largest collection of genealogical materials in the world.
These include copies or information drawn from many of the records
referred to in **3.6**. Go to *www.familysearch.org* or visit your local LDS
family history centre to get access to the resources of this genealogical
service. *Ancestry.com* is another Internet giant. It provides a subscrip-
tion service for access to a huge collection of genealogical data. The
large free genealogy site *RootsWeb.com* is one of its associates in the
MyFamily.com, Inc. network. Also see *www.findmypast.com/* and *www.
origins.net/*.

Family and local history societies

3.20   There has been real benefit to Scottish culture in the gathering together
and preservation of records and other evidence from the country's past
and, best of all, information about ordinary people, by genealogists and
local historians.   One example of this is in the wealth of information
held by the Scottish Genealogy Society – *www.scotsgenealogy.com* – in
its Library and Family History Centre. Another is the enterprises of the
Aberdeen & N.E. Scotland Family History Society, such as its growing
list of transcriptions of north-east Scotland graveyards – *www.anesfhs.org.
uk*. A third is the Glasgow & West of Scotland Family History Society's
large projects, including co-operative ventures such as the indexing of
poor law records for Glasgow, Lanarkshire and Dumbartonshire – see
www.gwsfhs.org.uk and *www.glasgowlibraries.org*. For links to other family
history societies see the website of the Scottish Association of Family
History Societies – *www.safhs.org.uk* – or *www.genuki.org.uk* and *www.
cyndislist.com*.

Clan societies and associations

3.21   Clan links are not usually the most useful ones with which to start family
history research. Clan genealogies found in print, in manuscripts and on
the web often relate to the grander families in the clan and shared family
names of clan members do not mean that the latter are related, though

some may well be. However membership of societies or associations may lead to the discovery of rewarding information and contacts. In that respect it helps that particular clan names are locally common in relatively small areas of the Highlands and Islands. It is also beneficial that many societies have active membership or fellow societies in other countries where Scots have settled. Such is the case, for example, with the great Clan Chattan (pronounced 'Hattan') confederation, with its constituent clans and many septs – see *www.clanchattan.org.uk*, which acts as a gateway to these. Other sites carrying links to Scottish clan societies include Electric Scotland – *www.scotsearch.org* – and *www.scotlandsclans. com*. There is also a good list in *http://clan-maccallum-malcolm.3acres.org/ ScotClanFamily.html*. The webpage of the Library, Study and Genealogy Centre, at the Clan Donald Centre at Armadale on the Isle of Skye – *www.highlandconnection.org/cdltstudy.html* – is instructive. The Centre, which assists people to research West Highland ancestry, and not just Macdonald ancestry, is an example of what can be achieved when clan enthusiasm is part of the effort deployed.

Emigrants from Scotland

3.22 A salutary exercise when setting out to search for records of emigrants will be to have a look at the very fine work of the Immigrant Ships Transcribers' Guild (*www.immigrantships.org*). It can be dispiriting to find that there is often not enough information recorded in the lists to iden-tify your ancestors with certainty. A gem to be found on the Scottish Archive Network's site is a searchable index of passenger lists, 1852-57, of the Highlands and Islands Emigration Society – *www.scan.org.uk/ researchrtools/emigration.htm*. In those years the Society, which was set up to relieve destitution after the potato famine, assisted almost 5,000 people from western Scotland to emigrate to Australia. The SCAN 'knowledge base' entries on emigration, passenger lists and passports give sensible practical advice. *Ancestry.com* includes immigration and emigration databases. For another interesting source see details of the NLS databases at **3.9**. Online searching and guidance would certainly have to be supplemented by referring to the passenger lists and emigra-tion records that have been published in books, particularly in recent years.

Immigrants to the UK

3.23 For a useful introduction to this subject, see: *www.familyrecords.gov.uk/ topics/immigration_1.htm*.

Occupations and social groups

3.24 One of the biggest challenges on the Internet is to track down records for occupational and social groups, such as paupers, prisoners, fishwives, members of craft incorporations and guilds, soldiers, handloom weavers, miners and steelworkers. Searches of online catalogues are an obvious option. Visits to websites with relevant local and social interests – see **3.17**, **3.18** and **3.21** – would be a priority. Specialist online directories can be very helpful, for example people in business as booksellers, publishers, bookbinders, printers and in other book-related trades before about 1850, are to be found in the Scottish Book Trade Index at *www.nls.uk*. Directories of British artists' suppliers, picture restorers and framemakers are newly-available through the National Portrait Gallery website (*www.npg.org.uk/research*).

3.25 It is of course always worth checking for links using the big gateways mentioned above, including those which *www.genuki.org.uk* gives to sources on 'United Kingdom and Ireland occupations'. On a variety of websites military records figure quite highly among the occupation groups considered. The Scottish Archive Network's 'knowledge base' contains answers to questions frequently asked in Scottish archives, with a directory of where to find historical records. Advice is provided on topics including poor relief, policemen, school admission registers and log books, scholars, prisoners and suffragettes.

3.26 The following chapters will not answer all the questions you have about your ancestors. But the richness and variety of what is described in this book is something that is not yet generally found on the web. In other words the latter has some way to go before it fully serves the purposes that books do now.

∽4∾
The ScotlandsPeople Centre

4.1   ScotlandsPeople makes available digital images of some of the most important records for Scottish family history which are held by the General Register Office for Scotland, the National Archives of Scotland and the Court of the Lord Lyon. You can consult the digitised records either on the ScotlandsPeople pay-per-view website *www.scotlandspeople.gov.uk*, or by visiting the ScotlandsPeople Centre in Edinburgh. There are also plans to make the ScotlandsPeople resources available in local family history centres around Scotland.

4.2   The records which you can see are:

Census Returns	1841–1901
Old Parish Registers:	1553–1854
Births & Christenings	
Banns & Marriages	
Deaths and burials (only available on the website, but due in the Centre in 2009)	
Statutory Registers:	
Register of Births	1855–current
Register of Deaths	1855–current
Register of Divorces	1984–current
Register of Marriages	1855–current
Register of Corrections, etc.	1855–current
Register of Civil Partnerships	2005–current
Wills & Testaments	1513–1901
(from the National Archives of Scotland)	
Coats of Arms	1672 to 100 years ago
The Public Register of All Arms and Bearings in Scotland (from the Court of the Lord Lyon)	

Minor Records detail the register of births, deaths and marriages that have taken place outside Scotland where it appears that one of the child's parents or the deceased person was usually resident in Scotland. They comprise:

Air registers of births & deaths	1948–current
Consular returns	1914–current
High Commissioner's returns	1964–current
Marine registers of births & deaths	1855–current
Registered events in foreign countries	1860–1965
Service Records	1881–1959
War Registers	1899–current
Foreign marriages without the presence of a British consular officer	1947–current
Marriages solemnised by army chaplains	1892–current

These records are described in the next Chapter. Information can also be found at the ScotlandsPeople websites at *www.scotlandspeoplehub.gov. uk* or *www.scotlandspeople.gov.uk*.

Visiting the ScotlandsPeople Centre

4.3   The Centre is open Monday to Friday from 9.00am to 4.30pm. Closures for some bank or public holidays are listed on the website *www. scotlandspeoplehub.gov.uk*. The Centre contains four search rooms, a shop, a café and an exhibition/seminar facility.

4.4   The Centre is based in General Register House (GRH) and New Register House (NRH) at the east end of Princes Street, opposite the Balmoral Hotel. See the map on page ix. The main entrance to the Centre is on the (south) front of GRH, behind the equestrian statue of the Duke of Wellington. You need to climb the steps to enter the reception and shop area. If you have difficulty climbing steps, you may proceed to the north-west corner of the building where there is a stair hoist (ring the bell), or walk along the ramped pathways and enter the Matheson Dome (GRH) or Dundas Room (NRH) directly. Wheelchair access is by the latter route.

4.5   The shop leads to the impressive Adam Dome, named after the architect, Robert Adam who designed General Register House. The Adam Dome has 36 search places and is primarily used for introductory taster sessions.

The central search room is called the Reid Room, after its architect Robert Reid, and offers 43 search places. The next search room, which leads to the garden, is called the Matheson Dome after the architect Robert Matheson, and has 39 search places. The Dundas Room in New Register House is primarily for season ticket holders, but its search places are used if the other areas are full.

4.6 The free introductory 'taster' sessions are aimed at people who have not used the system before. The supervisor in the search room will give you a short introduction to using the ScotlandsPeople Centre. You will be searching the indexes in order to call up digital images of records. Two sessions run daily, 10am-12pm and 2-4pm. Once you have had one taster session you need to purchase a day search ticket in order to continue searching.

4.7 You pay a statutory fee for a full or part-day search place in the ScotlandsPeople Centre (currently £10). You can reserve a day search seat or pay in advance by calling 0131 314 4300, e-mailing *bookings@scotlandspeoplehub.gov.uk*, or by calling in person between 9am and 4.30pm. Although it is not necessary to book in advance, you are advised to do so if you are travelling to Edinburgh, because seats are in great demand, particularly during the summer months and the school holidays. If you pay for a search seat in advance it is allocated to you for the day, so you can go straight to it when you arrive. Booked seats that have not been pre-paid are reserved only until 10am.

4.8 If you plan to carry out prolonged research, you can also purchase quarterly and annual season tickets.

4.9 Please note that certain restrictions apply in the Centre. Access to the records is not allowed to anyone under the age of 12. Children of 12 or 13 may be allowed access only if accompanied by their parent or legal guardian. Children aged 14 to 16 may be allowed access unaccompanied provided they can show written parental or guardian consent to their searching the records. Normal fees are payable in all cases. No food or drink is allowed in the search rooms, but a café is available in New Register House.

4.10 If you have a disability which might make it difficult for you to use the search facilities, contact the Centre in advance. Each search room has a 19" (48cms) computer terminal with zoom text facilities, and three of the search rooms have adjustable desks for customers in wheelchairs or with walking sticks. Two disabled parking bays directly outside New Register House can be booked in advance by ringing 0131 314 4300.

Opening and using your account in the Centre

4.11 When you book in at the Centre you are allocated a user name to allow you to log into the system. You can request any username, but if it has already been allocated to someone else you may need to alter it to make it unique. You then set up your own password to establish your own account, which allows you to search the records. You can use your account for subsequent visits.

4.12 If you want to make copies or electronic 'saves' of the historical records, you need to pay money into your account at the supervisor's desk in the search room. You can then make prints or 'saves' provided there is sufficient credit in your account. To save records you may only use a USB pen. Historical records are defined as registers of births more than 100 years old, marriages more than 75 years old, and deaths more than 50 years old. More recent records are deemed to be 'modern day', and you cannot print them or save them electronically. Instead you need to order an official Extract certificate.

4.13 Official Extract certificates of the statutory records can either be ordered directly from GROS by visiting New Register House, or by ringing 0131 314 4411, Monday to Friday 9am to 4.30pm. Further details can be found on the GROS website *www.gro-scotland.gov.uk*. Alternatively, it is possible to order official certificates in the ScotlandsPeople Centre, but for priority service you are best to visit the public counter in New Register House.

4.14 You can save images of the Public Register of All Arms and Bearings in Scotland for a fee, but you need to order prints specially.

4.15 There are more than 50 million entries digitised. Some of the digitised images of statutory registers may be difficult to read because they were created from microfiche rather than the original record. If you encounter problems with legibility when using the Centre, you can ask to view microfiche or microfilm copies, which will be brought to you.

4.16 The computer systems serving the Centre and the pay-per-view website are completely separate. One major difference is that in the Centre you can view modern day statutory records (see **4.12**) that you cannot view online. Another is that a transcribed version of the 1881 census and images of the original census record are available on the website, but at the Centre you can only see images of the 1881 record. More generally, the records available may vary slightly if new record sets have been added to one system ahead of the other.

4.17 You should bear in mind that county boundaries have changed over the years, so if you do not get a result it may be worth checking adjacent counties. Also, the boundaries of many registration districts in Scotland have changed, as there are now fewer than the original 1,027 districts.

Searching the ScotlandsPeople records

4.18 The computer system at the Centre is very similar to the pay-per-view ScotlandsPeople website: both have 'soundex' and wildcard facilities when searching for names (see **5.7**).

4.19 Tracing a line of descent back to 1855 can be a fairly straightforward task, provided you start with some reliable details about more recent members of your family. A simple search form will appear on the screen asking you to input the name of the person you are looking for, together with other details if known. Unless you are searching for an unusual name, it is always helpful if you know the approximate year of the record and/or the county or district that the event took place in order to reduce the number of results that you need to review. A good tip is to omit a middle name, and instead be more precise about dates and counties in order to limit the results. The example on the next page is for John Logie Baird, whose birth was registered with his middle name spelled 'Loggie'. You would not find him by searching using 'Logie', the name by which he is generally known.

4.20 Once you click the search button, a list of index entries matching the criteria you have chosen will appear. You then select the record that you are interested in by clicking on the person's surname. A digitised image of the register or record page containing that person's entry will appear, from which you can take notes.

4.21 If the record is deemed to be historical you can print a copy, or make an electronic 'save' if you have enough credit in your account (see **4.12**)

Top: screenshot of search for birth of John Baird.
Bottom: register of births entry for John Logie Baird.

ScotlandsPeople Centre reference library

4.22 In addition to the digitised records, if you have paid for a day search fee, you have access to the following resources to aid your family history research:

- a reference Library of approximately 4,400 books, maps and microfiche publications;
- an e-Library of digital publications on the Centre's network;
- access to useful genealogy related websites at each computer terminal;
- and two stand-alone computers in the Dundas Room and Reid Room for databases and CD publications.

4.23   The library includes gazetteers, maps, guides to occupations and surnames, medical terms, transcripts of pre-1855 birth, death and marriage records held in other archives, monumental (or gravestone) inscriptions for burial grounds, post office directories for the four main cities, Statistical Accounts of Scotland, church history and a small collection of family and clan histories.

4.24   If you have the name of a place but do not know what parish it is in, there is a collection of directories, gazetteers and maps in the library to assist you. To preserve the original OPR volumes from overuse, consultation of the registers is from digital images or microfilm, and not the originals.

ScotlandsPeople pay-per-view website

4.25   For those unable to visit the ScotlandsPeople Centre to research their family history, ScotlandsPeople pay-per-view website (*http://www.scotlandspeople.gov.uk*) provides access to all of the indexes of the records listed earlier.

4.26   The site provides a free search to give you some indication of how many entries you will find on the site for a particular name. However, to search further, you will need to pay an access fee (by credit card, through a secure payment mechanism) which will give you a certain number of 'credits', allowing you to download a given number of index entries or digital images.

4.27   You can buy images of all the wills and testaments, census records and coats of arms for the dates shown at **4.2**, for a prescribed fee, but only the images of the historical statutory records can be viewed and saved. These are births more than 100 years old, marriages more than 75 years old, and deaths more than 50 years old. See **4.12-13** for how to obtain copies of more recent records.

4.28   Having downloaded index entries or images to your own PC, you are welcome to print or save them for personal use.

4.30   If you encounter poor images you can report them so that the original register can be scanned and the new image transferred into the records. Some of the original entries may be too faint for the image to be enhanced completely.

5

Statutory Registers, Old Parish Registers and Censuses

The General Register Office for Scotland

5.1 Most of the original records that are now available digitally through ScotlandsPeople are actually held by the General Register Office for Scotland (GROS), a Government department. Under the direction of the Registrar General for Scotland, the GROS administers the registration of the statutory records, namely the births, deaths, marriages, divorces and civil partnerships. The adoption register is also maintained by GROS (for adoption records see **8.15**). The Registrar General is also responsible for the taking of decennial censuses of the population of Scotland. The GROS is located in New Register House, conveniently next door to General Register House (see plan). For most family history purposes you will not need to use GROS services, although you can obtain Extract certificates of modern records directly from GROS (see **4.13**).

Births, Deaths and Marriages since 1855 – the Statutory Registers

5.2 In Scotland compulsory civil registration of births, deaths and marriages began on 1 January 1855 under the Registration of Births, Deaths and Marriages (Scotland) Act 1854. It is likely that you will want to start your family search in these registers, unless your ancestors left Scotland before 1855.

5.3 Within a few months of any birth, death or marriage being registered in Scotland, the 'event' is added to the ScotlandsPeople network. Events registered since 1855 can be looked up on the computer, but the computer indexes were in the main prepared from paper indexes compiled at the time, so their contents vary.

5.4   The *birth indexes* give details of the child's name; the year of registration; registration district name and number; and register entry number. From 1929 onwards the mother's maiden surname is also given, unless the person was adopted (see **8.15**).

5.5   The *death indexes* give the deceased's name; age at death; the year of registration; registration district name and number; and register entry number. From 1855 to 1865 the age at death was not recorded in the old paper indexes, but some have been added to the computer indexes. You can search for both female married names and mother's maiden names, but maiden names were not consistently entered for all persons. From 1974, the mother's surname is generally included for both male and female deaths. Ages given by informants may be only approximate, particularly in the early decades of registration, and in the cases of persons born before compulsory civil registration began.

5.6   The *marriage indexes* give each party's name, the year of registration; registration district name and number; and register entry number. From 1929 onwards, the spouse's surname is also given.

5.7   There are a number of points to note about the indexes. First, the spelling of names may be unusual, particularly during the earlier period of registration. The indexes record the names as spelt by the registrar at the time, irrespective of present-day spelling. To help overcome these variations, a 'Soundex' facility has been incorporated into the indexes, and this can be used to identify alternative spellings or similar sounding surnames. Secondly, names beginning 'Mac' and 'Mc' are indexed separately. You should therefore check both if you have difficulty in finding the entry you are looking for. If you use the wildcard facility, e.g. entering 'm★c', the system will look up *all* Mac and Mc surnames. This may result in too many index entries for the system to show, unless you restrict your search by area or a range of years. In the Centre, if you are searching for a surname containing an apostrophe, replace the apostrophe with a question mark. For example, if you are looking for O'Hara then you need to enter O?Hara into the search box. If you are searching the website, you can search using the normal spelling.

5.8   Entries in the statutory registers of births from 1861 include: name, date, time and place of birth; sex; father's name and profession; mother's name and maiden name; date and place of marriage; signature and qualification of informant, and residence if out of the house in which the birth occurred.

5.9   Entries in the registers of deaths from 1861 include: name; rank or profession; marital status; spouse's name; when and where died; sex; age;
father's name and rank or profession; mother's name and maiden name;
cause of death; signature and qualification of informant, and residence if
out of the house in which the death occurred.

5.10   Entries in the register of marriages from 1861 include: when, where and
how married (e.g. after banns, according to the forms of the Church
of Scotland). For both bridegroom and bride are given: name; rank or
profession; marital status; age; usual residence; father's name and rank
or profession; mother's name and maiden name. In the case of regular
marriages, names of the officiating minister (or registrar from 1940) and
witnesses are recorded. In the case of irregular marriages, date of conviction (to 1939), decree of declarator, or sheriff's warrant is given.

5.11   You will find that there is some variation from the above in the information registered between 1855 and 1860. The first year of civil registration
in Scotland, 1855, is particularly good, with fuller details recorded about
individuals and their families. If you are lucky enough to find an ancestor
who was born, died or married in this year, the additional information
supplied can be very full indeed and may include some of the following
details.

5.12   *In the registers of births for* 1855: name; whether informant present at birth;
baptismal name (if different) or name given without baptism; sex; date, and
time of birth; where born; father's name and rank, profession or occupation, age and birthplace; when and where married, and any previous issue,
both living and deceased; mother's name and maiden name, how many
children she has had, age and where born; signature and qualification of
informant, and residence if out of the house where the birth occurred.

5.13   *In the registers of deaths for* 1855: name; rank, profession or occupation;
sex; age; where born and how long in district; parents' names, and rank,
profession or occupation; if married, spouse's name and names and ages
of any children; date of death and time; where died; cause of death,
length of illness, by whom certified and when they last saw the deceased;
burial place, undertaker by whom certified: signature and qualification
of informant.

5.14   *In the registers of marriages for* 1855: when, where and how married; (and,
for both bridegroom and bride) signatures; present and usual residences;

age; rank and profession; relationship of parties, if related; marital status; children by any previous marriages, whether living or dead; where parties were born; the date and place of registration of birth; parents' names, rank, profession or occupation; if a regular marriage, signatures of officiating minister and witnesses; if irregular, date of conviction or decree of declarator and court pronounced.

5.15   Corrections or changes to the registered particulars – for example, in the cases of divorce or change of name – are recorded in the *Register of Corrected Entries,* or *Register of Corrections Etc.* The entries in the registers of births, deaths and marriages are cross-referenced to these.

5.16   Minor records consist of the indexes and images of the series of records of births, deaths and marriages which occurred outside Scotland, but which relate to Scots. For a full list see the table in **4.2**. These records are in some cases patchy and incomplete. You search for an entry as if they are part of the main registers, e.g. by searching the indexes of Births from 1855.

5.17   The statutory registers of births, deaths and marriages are all duplicated, one copy being held centrally by GROS and a second copy held locally. The majority of local registration offices have on-line access to a system called DIGROS, which gives access to all the digital images and indexes of census returns (except the 1881 census), and of the statutory registers, that are available in the ScotlandsPeople Centre. Before you visit a local registration office it is advisable to telephone first to ask about their facilities.

Births, Deaths and Marriages before 1855 – the Old Parish Registers

5.18   If you have been lucky enough to get back beyond the year 1855, and have not come to a dead end during your search of the Scottish statutory registers – which may happen if, for example, your ancestors came to Scotland from Ireland – then the old parish registers (OPRs) may take you further back beyond this date. ScotlandsPeople provides access to those that survived, which were deposited under the Registration Act of 1854 to form a splendid continuity with the statutory registers.

5.19   The OPRs are the registers of the established Church, the Church of Scotland, which record births and baptisms; proclamations of banns or marriages; and deaths or burials, up to 1854. The parish ministers or session clerks of some 900 parishes kept these registers until their formal transfer to the GROS. The surviving registers number approximately 3,500, but they are far from complete. Though the oldest register relates to baptisms and banns in 1553 for the parish of Errol in Perthshire, for some parishes the earliest registers date from the early nineteenth century, while for others there may be no registers at all. A lot of parishes do not have any burial or death registers. The standard of record-keeping varied considerably from parish to parish and from year to year, and most entries contain relatively little information in comparison to the statutory registers.

5.20 You should therefore set out with optimism tinged with realism when tackling the OPRs. Remember also that although registration in the Church of Scotland's registers was in theory compulsory for all denominations, it was both costly and unpopular. Members of other churches, such as the Free Church of Scotland or Roman Catholic Church, may not be recorded, though with luck you may be able to find some (see Chapter 8 for alternatives). Also, as populations shifted and cities started to develop in the nineteenth century, religion began to lose its hold, and as few as 30 per cent of 'vital events' may be recorded for certain urban parishes.

5.21 Indexes for the registers of deaths or burials are available on the ScotlandsPeople website, and are due to be added to the ScotlandsPeople Centre records in late 2009. The records can be consulted on microfiche or microfilm at the ScotlandsPeople Centre. The OPRs have been added to the Genealogical Society of Utah's International Genealogical Index (IGI) and to its FamilySearch family-history software, which is also available for reference in the Centre, but this is not so up-to-date.

5.22 The OPR computerised indexes contain some seven million birth, baptism and marriage entries. You can search either the whole of Scotland for a particular name, or just a specific county.

5.23 The *births and baptism indexes* give details of the child's name; the father or both of the parents' names; date of birth or baptism; and the reference number and name of the parish where the baptism took place.

5.24 The *banns and marriages indexes* give the name of the person who was married; the name of their spouse; date of proclamation or marriage; and

Registration of the baptism of George Something, son to What-ye-call-him, 1704.

the reference number and name of the parish where the marriage took place.

5.25 There are no hard and fast rules about the details given in the OPR pages themselves. These vary from parish to parish, and the information can be very thin. In the case of baptisms, aside from the name of the child and the date of the baptism, you might hope to obtain the names of both parents, their place or parish of residence, and perhaps the occupation of the father. On some occasions a list of witnesses may be supplied. For marriages, you might expect to find the date on which the marriage took place or was contracted, the names of the parties and their place or parish of residence. If you are lucky enough to have an ancestor with a relatively uncommon surname, this can be useful when attempting to identify the correct entry from the indexes. Unfortunately, remote parishes such as those in the Highlands are notoriously difficult, with the same combinations of forenames and surnames common to particular localities. These names may crop up again and again, for example, John Mackay; Kenneth Mackenzie; Mary Macdonald; Ann Ross; Margaret Fraser.

Census Records (1841–1901)

5.26 Census records can make an excellent bonus for the family historian. They can both fill out information about families already traced in the registers of births, deaths and marriages and other sources, and lead you to ancestors or family members whom you had not previously identified.

5.27 The ScotlandsPeople facilities allow you to search the indexes of over three million personal names enumerated for each census year from

1841 to 1901. The Centre holds catalogues from which you can identify the census districts and their reference numbers. For the census years 1841 to 1901 the districts are arranged alphabetically within counties.

5.28 The decennial census of the population of Scotland was taken for 1841 and every tenth year thereafter, except for the wartime year of 1941 when no census was taken. The records of censuses taken after 1901 are still confidential and are not available for searching or extracting until 100 years after the date of each census. For these records the districts are simply arranged alphabetically.

5.29 Census records open to the public are of the censuses held on 7 June 1841, 31 March 1851, 8 April 1861, 3 April 1871, 4 April 1881, 5 April 1891 and 31 March 1901. The records consist of the transcript books prepared by the census enumerators after the census schedules were collected from individual households within each parish.

5.30 The census books generally contain particulars such as name; age; sex; marital status; relationship to head of the household; occupation and birthplace of every member of a household present at that address on census night, including servants, lodgers and visitors. However, details do vary from census year to census year. It is worth bearing in mind that nineteenth century households could include many people who were not actually part of the family as such, including servants or apprentices. Also, places such as hotels and lodging houses counted as one household, and if the person for whom you are searching was staying at an hotel on census night, he or she will be recorded with this 'household' rather than with their family, as you might be expecting. Institutions such as prisons, workhouses and hospitals were enumerated separately from other households in their area.

5.31 The returns for the 1841 census year are the least detailed. Marital status and relationship to head of the household were not recorded. Birthplace details confirm only if an individual was born within the Scottish county being enumerated or not. If the person was born outwith that county, unfortunately no other county name is given and, if born outside Scotland, only the initial letter of the country of birth is given: for example, 'E' for England; 'I' for Ireland; 'F' for France. Also, the ages given may not always be accurate. In some cases enumerators may have recorded the actual age given, but they were instructed to round down ages for persons over the age of 15. For example, a person aged between 15 and

20 can be recorded as aged 15, or someone aged between 25 and 30 appears as aged 25.

5.32   By the year 1851, marital status; relationship to head of the household; and fuller details of birthplace, including place and county of birth were added. Details of whether a person was blind or deaf and dumb are also noted. By 1861, additional details such as number of children attending school; and numbers of rooms with one or more windows are also recorded, as from 1891 was the fact of a person being a Gaelic speaker. These will help you to build a more detailed picture of your ancestors, their family circumstances and the accommodation in which they lived.

5.33   The entries in the census books were not indexed by the enumerators. Street indexes are available for certain large urban areas and the bigger towns. These identify the census books for each small 'enumeration district' in which addresses are recorded, and are invaluable particularly for the cities, which cover many books. At the front of each enumeration book you will find a short description of the area it covers. When searching census records, therefore, you should start out with enough information to identify positively the person or family you are looking for, including their town or parish of residence. This can be accessed on the browse system of the census.

∽6∽
The Court of the Lord Lyon

6.1   The Court of the Lord Lyon is situated in New Register House, beside the General Register Office for Scotland and the ScotlandsPeople Centre (see plan). If your ancestors were members of the nobility or large landowners you may have cause to use their services. The Court of the Lord Lyon is responsible for the administration of the system of heraldry in Scotland which has evolved into a precise science. The Public Register of All Arms and Bearings in Scotland, established in 1672, the Public Register of Genealogies and Birthbrieves in Scotland, and considerable genealogical material is in the custody of the Court of the Lord Lyon, which also maintains a large private library.

New Register House.

6.2 Coats of arms were originally used for military purposes and consisted of an actual coat bearing a distinctive design which was worn over a suit of armour. This enabled the knight to be recognised. The design was also displayed on his shield. On his head he wore a helmet and in time this was surmounted by a crest which identified the wearer from a distance and was used particularly during tournaments. As the military use of coats of arms declined they were adopted for civilian purposes on seals and to identify property. See the website for more details.

6.3 Most personal coats of arms consist of a shield, helmet, crest and motto. Supporters, the figures or beasts standing on either side of the shield, are only granted to particular groups of people, including clan chiefs, peers, and senior knights in orders of chivalry.

6.4 Companies and other corporate organisations such as civic councils, schools, universities, sporting clubs and charities can also have a coat of arms and while some may have shields, crests and mottoes many only have a shield.

6.5 The ScotlandsPeople Centre and the ScotlandsPeople website at *www.scotlandspeople.gov.uk* both provide access to digital images from the Public Register of All Arms and Bearings in Scotland from 1672 up to 100 years ago. As mentioned in Chapter 4, you can save images of the Register for a fee, but you need to order prints specially.

6.6 The staff of the Court of the Lord Lyon do not undertake genealogical research, and if you request a search in the Public Registers you will pay a search fee.

6.7 Heraldry, although allied to family research, is a fascinating and special-ised field in its own right, much of it outside the scope of this book. Further information and guidance can be found in the Lyon Court website *www.lyon-court.com*. Enquiries regarding genealogical materials held in the Court of the Lord Lyon should be made in writing to: The Lyon Clerk and Keeper of the Records, Court of the Lord Lyon, H.M. New Register House, Edinburgh, EH1 3YT, or by email to *bruce.gorie@ gro-scotland.gsi.gov.uk*.

∽7∾
At the National Archives of Scotland

7.1 You are now ready to visit the National Archives of Scotland. Try to be clear in your mind what information you are seeking and what records you want to see. Before your visit, especially if you do not live in Edinburgh, please contact us to find out where and whether the records you want to see may be consulted. This will also enable us to inform you if records are unavailable, perhaps because they are undergoing conservation treatment, or are on exhibition. This is most important to prevent you from making a wasted journey, particularly if you are travelling from a distance. Records may be in General Register House or West Register House, or in a local archive elsewhere in Scotland (see Appendix A). Some NAS records are stored in our suburban repository, and consequently a day's notice will be required before you can see such records in a search room. As records are sometimes transferred from one location to another, the present location of most of the records is not specified in this book. However, you will probably go first to General Register House, as the records currently held there include the legal registers, wills and church records. Please also give advance notice if you are disabled. Seats in the Search Rooms cannot be booked in advance.

7.2 On your first visit, bring two official means of identification, one containing photographic identification, such as a driving licence or passport, and one containing proof of address. You must also bring two recent passport-sized colour photographs. You will not be able to obtain a reader's ticket without all of these items. When you arrive at General or West Register House, tell the duty staff that you have come to do research in the Historical (or West) Search Rooms, and they will direct you there. On your first visit you will have to complete a visitor's form. Remember to bring a pencil with you every time, as ink of any kind is banned from the search rooms (in case of accidental damage to the records). You will be asked to leave your outer garments and bag in a cloakroom locker (£1 coin or token). Remember to take your identification, pencil, and notebook or laptop with you.

7.3 You have arrived in one of the search rooms on your first visit to the NAS. A member of staff will speak to you, issue you with a reader's ticket and a copy of the search room regulations, show you where the catalogues and indexes are kept, and give you preliminary advice. Your reader's ticket will be valid for up to three years. Keep it carefully, as you will need to bring it on subsequent visits to gain admittance to the search rooms. It entitles you to see the records without charge. You will be asked to hand it over every time you order out any records.

7.4 Though staff are on hand to advise you further and to answer reasonable questions, you will be the person carrying out the research. The records are divided into various groups, each with its own reference code, consisting of letters, e.g. AD for Lord Advocate's Department, CH for Church records, E for Exchequer, GD for Gifts and Deposits. They are listed in the paper Summary Catalogue of all the records, and can also be found in the electronic catalogue. Each document has its own unique reference (or call) number, consisting of a group code followed by a series of numbers (e.g. AD14/53/203). When searching the electronic catalogue, the letter codes are a handy means of narrowing down multiple hits, for example if you are looking only for precognitions in AD14 you can select only catalogue entries beginning with the letter A.

7.5 The guides to the records take various forms and some are easier to use or more thorough than others. Each group of records has its own catalogue which supplies the date, description and reference number of each document or set of documents. There are indexes to some collections, but many records are not indexed. Perhaps a quick word of explanation on the difference between a catalogue and an index would be helpful: a catalogue is a descriptive list of records, containing entries such as 'Letter from Sir Walter Scott to the Lady of the Lake' whereas an index is an alphabetical list of names, places etc, that refers to catalogue entries eg 'Scott, Sir Walter, letter from, to the Lady of the Lake, GD999/1'. Indexes vary tremendously in quality and style. Pre-twentieth century manuscript 'indexes' may not be indexes in our understanding of the word, sometimes being a contents list, and sometimes alphabetical only as far as the first letter of each surname.

7.6 Also available are source lists that gather together catalogue entries from various record groups relating to particular subjects, e.g. Canada, coal-mining, military records. These were compiled before the advent of computer cataloguing. As such, they are incomplete and have been largely superseded, but they can still prove useful if you are researching a particular subject.

7.7 The National Archives of Scotland catalogues are available electronically, both in the search rooms and online (*www.nas.gov.uk*). In consequence, some of the advice on searching the records which follows below may be avoided by searching the electronic catalogue, which is mostly referred to in this guide as the catalogue. However, the procedures for searching have been described in detail, because the electronic catalogue may not always carry specific information on every item in a series of records. In addition, some readers still prefer to search paper catalogues where these are available, and very occasionally the electronic catalogue is temporarily unavailable.

Online catalogue entry for New Luce kirk session minutes, CH2/700/1.

THE NATIONAL ARCHIVES OF SCOTLAND
DEFINING MOMENTS IN HISTORY

Catalogue search - internet

| Welcome | Browse | Search | Results summary | [Results] | Help |

You are in: Catalogue search> Search results > Overview   Tuesday 9 June 2009 11:12

Page options:

🖨 Print this page
✉ E-mail this page
↩ Previous page

Records updated:
8 June 2009

Search results overview sorted by reference.

Simple search for catalogue records where any field contains all the words **new luce**, including undated records

Jump to: All A B C D E F G H I J K L M N O P Q R S T U V W X Y Z

< previous	Records 1 to 10 of 89	next >	Explain Access status

Reference	Title	Date	Access status
AD14/36/138	Precognition against John Muir for the crime of forgery and uttering a forged writing at Glen**luce**, Old **Luce**, Wigtonshire	1836	
AD14/69/177	Precognition against Agnes Morgan for the crime of murder at **New Luce**, Wigtown	1869	
AD14/71/237	Precognition against Margaret Kelly for the crime of assault and murder at Hard Croft, **New Luce**, Wigton	1871	
AD15/09/173	Precognition against Donald Spence Stewart for the crime of rape, or contravention of 48 and 49 Vict., c. 69, s. 5 (Criminal Law Amendment Act) at Quarter, **New Luce**, Wigtownshire	1909	

Reference	
CH2/700	**New Luce Kirk Session 1694-1995**
CH2/700/1	Minutes 1694-1741
	Contribution for bell and steeple 1730 1694-1741
CH2/700/2	Minutes 1725-1770 (Perhaps scroll)
CH2/700/3	Minutes 1742-70
	Minutes 1803-21
	Accounts 1803-26 (poors' fund) 1742-1826

Top: online search hits for New Luce; bottom: paper catalogue of CH2/700.

7.8   Whenever a group of records or series of documents or individual document is mentioned in this book, its reference number will be given in brackets, eg GD1/99. You may find it helpful as you go through this book to note down the references of records classes which sound promising.

7.9   Once you have a document reference, to see the document, order it using the Electronic Ordering System (EOS). You may usually order a

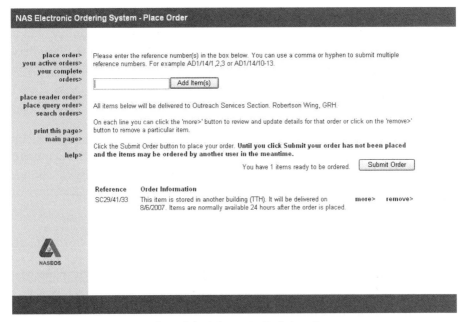

Screenshot of the Electronic Ordering System.

maximum of three documents at one time, but if your research requires you to see more than three at any one time, please ask the search room staff. You may order up to twelve items per day if they are stored in Thomas Thomson House. You may order items in advance of your visit by contacting the search rooms, as the EOS is not available online. Library items may still be ordered using paper order slips, one per item.

7.10 The catalogues of most record groups contain an introduction to the background and content of the collection, along with a more detailed contents list. If there is no contents list, see if the Summary Catalogue supplies this defect. Modern catalogues are compiled to a common form, with the reference numbers in the left-hand margin.

7.11 Surnames beginning with 'Mc' or 'Mac' may be indexed as if 'Mc' (or 'Mac') was a separate letter of the alphabet or may be combined with the letter 'M' in the English fashion. On very rare occasions, they may be indexed by the letter following the 'Mc', i.e. 'Macdonald' would be found under the letter 'D' (e.g. in LC9/3/1).

7.12 'Mc' means 'son of' and in the Highlands and Islands until the eighteenth century its appearance in a name might mean just that. Duncan Dow

McEan VcEwen was the son of Ean (John) and grandson of Ewen (Dow being a nickname meaning 'black'). Duncan's son would probably bear the name 'McDonachie' or a variant thereof. Similarly, in the Northern Isles, particularly Shetland, Andrew Davidson could be the son of David Manson, who was the son of Magnus. It is difficult to specify a date when such 'patronymics' stuck as modern surnames.

7.13   In Scotland, a woman does not in a legal sense 'change her name' on marriage. Thus, married women are usually described in documents and indexed under their maiden name or, more recently, with alternative surnames (eg Mary Stewart, wife of William Sim; Mary Stewart or Sim).

7.14   In the older catalogues and indexes, two types of numerals may be used: roman numbers (i, ii, iii, iv etc) and our conventional arabic numbers (1, 2, 3, 4 etc). If these numbers are part of a reference or call number, convert a roman number into an arabic number, when ordering out or referring to a document.

7.15   Some older catalogues give surnames and place-names as they are spelled in the document. Current practice is to provide the original form of the name, with the modern form in brackets, but formerly this was done vice versa. Some indexes modernise names, some do not. Look under all possible variants of the surname you are seeking, because the catalogue cannot do this for you.

7.16   Most catalogues and indexes give not only the forename(s) and surname of each individual but also his 'designation'. This designation may include his occupation, where he lives, or a relationship, usually the name and designation of his father: eg John Fulton, bonnet-maker in Kilmarnock, George Duncan, son of John D., portioner of Auchtermuchty ('portioner' means he owned part of these lands).

7.17   Some of the more important records are public registers, which may consist not only of volumes, but also of 'warrants'. A warrant is the authority for certain information to be put into the register. Sometimes the warrant is an original document, sometimes signed, that has been copied into a volume of the register.

7.18   You will soon become accustomed to variant and eccentric spellings in the documents you read. Newcomers to research in Scottish documents will encounter two other particular problems. The first is that documents before the eighteenth century were written in unfamiliar scripts, with many letterforms different from those we use today. Learning to read these older scripts is not difficult, but does take practice. Online tuition is readily available through an NAS website *www.scottishhandwriting.com*. Useful books are *Scottish Handwriting 1150–1650* by Grant G Simpson (Tuckwell Press, 1998) and *Scottish Handwriting 1500–1700: a self-help pack* by Alison Rosie (Scottish Record Office and Scottish Records Association, 1994). If you live in or near Edinburgh, you might like to attend an evening class on Scottish Handwriting held in General Register House each winter under the auspices of Edinburgh University.

7.19 The second problem is the language in which documents are written. Until recently, many Scottish documents were written in Scots, a form of English with its own vocabulary and phraseology. This is where a dictionary becomes invaluable. More awkwardly, until well into the nineteenth century important legal documents were written in Latin. However, a very small knowledge of Latin and some practice in recognising the salient parts of such documents can help considerably. In post-medieval Latin documents, surnames and place-names are mostly in Scots and English. An indispensable guide to the form of Scottish documents is Peter Gouldesbrough's *Formulary of Old Scots Legal Documents* (Stair Society, 1985)

7.20 In subsequent chapters, advice is given on how to search relevant groups of records. There is one group of records that appears in most chapters and therefore it is convenient to describe it here. That group consists of records known as Gifts and Deposits (GD), which are the records of private individuals, families, organisations and business concerns, which have been gifted or are on loan to the NAS. They contain an enormous variety of records and information, and they often supplement other groups of records. Look at the online catalogue or at the paper index to the Summary Catalogue in the Search Rooms, to see if the GDs include a collection of papers in which you are interested, and if there is a catalogue of that particular collection. A few of the GDs are also summarised in two published volumes, *List of Gifts and Deposits in the Scottish Record Office* (1971, 1976). Smaller GDs are referenced as GD1. Larger GDs each have their own reference number, eg the Earl of Airlie's records are GD16. Other collections of family and business papers may be found in local archives (see Appendix A).

7.21 Of the GD collections, the most useful for you are probably those of the big landowning families, as the names of those who lived on their estates may appear among their estate papers. If you know the area where your ancestor lived, you may want to find out who were the landowners in that area. The parish reports printed in the *Old* and *New Statistical Accounts of Scotland* usually provide this information for the end of the eighteenth century and around 1840 respectively. These are also available online at *http://edina.ac.uk/stat-acc-scot/*. Another useful guide is *A Directory of landownership in Scotland c1770* edited by Loretta R. Timperley (Scottish Record Society, 1976).

7.22 There is also a series of private records referenced RH15. The titles of these collections are indexed both in the Summary Catalogue and in a separate RH15 index. RH is the reference number for a varied series of records of mixed and sometimes uncertain origin. They include transcripts and photocopies (RH2) and microfilms (RH4) of various records held elsewhere.

7.23 Copies of most documents may be bought, provided the format and condition of the records is suitable and there are no copyright or preservation restrictions. Searchroom staff can provide advice on all aspects of copying.

7.24 A small number of the records are closed to public access. These are a few GD collections which the owner has placed under restriction, collections which have not yet been catalogued, collections containing sensitive personal data, the disclosure of which would be likely to cause substantial damage or distress, and some recent government records.

7.25 In the past, closure periods on government records ranged from 30 to 100 years. The traditional system of closure periods ceased to operate when the 2002 Freedom of Information (Scotland) Act came into effect on 1 January 2005. From that date, all information held by bodies covered under the Act – including all government information – is assumed to be open unless it falls under one of the exemptions from FOI listed in the Act. It is possible to request access to those records which were held under the old closures, although some may still be exempt from the provisions of FOI. NAS search room staff will be able to advise you about the request procedures.

West Register House.

7.26 The National Register of Archives for Scotland (NRAS) is the branch of the NAS which surveys historical records held in private hands in Scotland. Copies of its surveys are available in our searchrooms or through the NRAS online Register *www.nas.gov.uk/nras*. If you want to consult documents mentioned in a survey you should contact the Registrar for further information. However, papers that are still in private hands are often not available for genealogical research.

⨽8⨼
Births, Baptisms, Marriages and Burials

8.1 If you are searching before statutory registration began in 1855, and cannot find a record of birth, marriage or death in the Old Parish Registers in New Register House, then you should look at the records in the NAS. Remember that Old Parish Registers were compiled by ministers of the Church of Scotland. Your ancestor may have been a member of one of the many other Presbyterian churches in Scotland, or an Episcopalian or Roman Catholic. It therefore helps considerably if you know the religious denomination of your ancestor, as well as the essential information of the approximate place of residence. *The Old Statistical Account* is a useful source of information as to which denominations were active in particular parishes at the end of the eighteenth century. The books listed in **19.1** record the locations of most of the Presbyterian (sometimes also called 'non-conformist') congregations which have existed in Scotland.

8.2 *If your ancestor was Protestant*, go to the catalogue labelled CH. The non-conformist records are numbered CH3 and CH10–16, of which the bulkiest are CH3, the records of the former free churches which have become re-united with the Church of Scotland. Other churches covered by these series are:

- Society of Friends or Quakers (CH10)
- Methodist (CH11)
- Episcopal (CH12)
- United Free Church (CH13)
- Congregational (CH14)
- Unitarian (CH15)
- Free Church (CH16)

For information on the complicated history of the various Presbyterian denominations in Scotland, look at Andrew Drummond and James

Bulloch's two books *The Scottish Church 1688-1843* and *The Church in Victorian Scotland, 1843-1874* (St Andrew Press).

By no means all of the congregations of these churches have deposited their records in the National Archives of Scotland, and it is worth checking whether records are held in local archives. The NAS has microfilm copies of a few Episcopal Church registers (CH12/50).

8.3   Search the online catalogue or look at the index of churches in the CH catalogues for the name of the likely congregation or name of the town and its congregation. This index will provide you with the reference number of the congregation's records, eg Milnathort Antiburgher church is CH3/542. Within the list of records of that congregation, you will be looking for records of baptisms or marriages or burials, either as separate volumes or in the same volumes as kirk session minutes: eg Lethendy Associate Congregation Session minute book (CH3/214/1) includes baptisms, 1803-1840. The catalogue will say if there is such a record: normally, minutes do not include such information. Remember that many Free Church congregations did not exist until 1843, when the Free Church was formed by the Disruption from the established Church of Scotland.

8.4   For most records up to 1901 you will only be able to see digital images in the 'Virtual Volumes' resource in the Search Rooms. You look up each volume by using the three-part reference, eg CH3/214/1. The second number is the number of the congregation and the third the volume number. When ordering out original post-1901 records you use the same three-number system.

8.5   Some of these church records have been transferred to local archives, but you can see digital images of the records up to 1901 in NAS.

8.6   If the records of the congregation you want are not in the NAS, look in the Scottish Archive Network website, *www.scan.org.uk*. Next, consult the surveys produced by the National Register of Archives for Scotland (NRAS). Failing that, you should contact the headquarters of that particular church. The addresses of some will be found in *The Church of Scotland Year-Book*, or look online.

8.7   *If your ancestor was Roman Catholic*, search the catalogue of RH21, which lists photocopies of the surviving records kept by Roman Catholic parish

Receipt for baptism entry, North Leith parish, 1839 (CH2/716/52).

priests of baptisms, marriages and deaths. These are arranged by diocese. The earliest date is 1703, but most registers do not start until the nineteenth century. Many registers will be available through ScotlandsPeople from autumn 2009. There is also a microfilm of the baptismal register of the Catholic Apostolic Church, Edinburgh, 1833–1949 (RH4/174).

8.8 We have to emphasise the incompleteness of all these church records, their existence having depended on the dedication of the clergymen and session clerks, and accidents of survival. They are also inconsistent in the details supplied.

8.9 Records of baptisms will usually give the names of the child and of the father, sometimes that of the mother, and in the case of the Roman Catholic records, sometimes those of the godparents, who may be relatives. If the clergyman included it, there may occasionally be additional information, eg '4th Sept Margaret Riccalton Dickson daughter of Walter Dickson (above 70 years of age) and his wife Eve Riccalton' (1833 – CH3/667/1).

8.10 Records of marriages will generally give only the name of the marrying couple, but some RC registers invaluably give the parishes in Ireland from where the couple came.

8.11 There are very few death records among the CH3 records and these usually only give the name of the deceased, sometimes the age. Because the Roman Catholic priest needed to give the last sacrament to a dying person, the RC records of deaths are fuller, usually giving the name, age, marital status and cause of death, eg 'John Carley, a married man, was suddenly suffocated in an old coal pit at Campsie by Damp Air' (1815 June 27th – RH21/62/10, p.251).

8.12 There are further records which provide evidence of the birth, marriage and decease of individuals.

Fornication

8.13 The records of both the Church of Scotland and the free churches report the appearance before the kirk session of couples whose extra-marital fornication had resulted in the birth of a child. Access to the records of the kirk sessions of the Church of Scotland (CH2) is similar to those of the free churches already described (**7.3**). Search the online catalogue or look at the index of churches in the CH2 catalogues. Each parish has a reference number. Look up the volumes listed under that number: each volume has its own number. Note the relevant volume of the kirk session minutes by its reference number, eg CH2/842/2, and look it up in 'Virtual Volumes' in the Search Rooms. When ordering out original post-1901 records you use the same three-number system. Fornication by unmarried couples (whether or not a child was the result) seems to have been the main concern of many kirk sessions before 1900, and their minute books may contain little else. The name of the child will not be given, but you will find proof of the birth of a child to a named mother and, with luck, father and the approximate date of birth. An occasional problem arises when the name of the father given by the mother appears to be false. Such entries sometimes demonstrate that the unmarried mother had recently arrived from another parish.

8.14 Cases involving fornication or adultery could be brought by the church before the civil courts. The High Court of Justiciary (see Chapter 15) may record such cases until the early eighteenth century, and the authorities had long memories. In Dumfries in 1709, we discover that James Rig

Hugh Anderson mo̅d̅. (101)

1711) May 6th. 711.

The Coll: for ỹ Poor was 1·03·6

May 13th

William Winster (red haird) who long since broke
the acts anent ỹ ware; did this day make his pub:
:lick profession of repentance for ỹ scandal, and pro:
:mising in all time coming to walk orderly was ab:
:solved from the same.   *Winster Waver abset.*

The Coll: for ỹ Poor was 1·06·6

May 20th.

Mr Alexander Anderson Minr att Duffus preach:
:ed in the forenoon; & our Minr in the afternoon.

After Sermon, the Minr told the people, ỹ our
last School Master, had some time agoe demitted his
office, & now had left ỹ place; & that we endeavour: *paply school mr.*
:ed, with consent of Sr Robert Gordon, timeously
to provide one fit for ỹ post; that so there might be
no vacancy: and ỹ now he was come and entred nt
the School: and that they might send their Children
to him, and give him all suiteable encouragement,
and ỹ it was much their own advantage to do so.

This day Samuel Paply School-mr did precent.

The Coll: for ỹ Poor was 1·57·10

May 27th.

No Sermon; our minister preaching at Alvis, by
the Presbitries appointment.

June 3d.

The Seamen were publickly admonished, to attend   *Sea-men admonish'd.*
better in ỹ Afternoon; or that else some oyr course
would be taken to obledge them thereto.

This day the Sossion did meet; & after Prayer,
acted as follows:

The Coll: for ỹ Poor was 1·11·4   *Ro'son & marishal related.*
Alexander Falconer in Cuisea complained upon
Margaret Robertson & Janet Marshal there, for cur:
:sing him: we enjoyned him the next day to give in
his Bill of complaint (with 40 sh.) and told him, we
should yr examine ỹ matter; appointing ỹ officier
to cite to ỹt diet what wittnosses he pleased.

Also William Hesbin, Elder, complained of Wm
Innos in Stotfold, for frequent cursing and striking   *& Innes for cursing*
his wife: they, wt what wittnosses ỹ S: William should
name, were appointed to be summoned to our next
diet.

Also complaint was given in against John   *cloggie & Kintre.*
Cloggie & Isabel Kintre, both in Kinneddar, that
they were suspected guilty of fornicat'n; they are
appointed to be summoned to our next diet.

The Minr represented to ỹ Elders, that, Samuel

Samuel Paply Sess. Clk.

Fornication: the entry at the foot of the page summons to the Kirk Session a couple
accused of fornication, 1711 (CH2/384/2).

of Cairgen was indicted for adultery, 'committed by him about thirty years ago' (JC12/1, p.73). Further evidence of illegitimate births may be found in actions before a sheriff court to order the father to contribute to the maintenance of the child. The record of these actions for aliment will usually provide the names of the mother and father and the date of birth and sex, but not the name, of the child. See **14.39-46** for further explanation of these sheriff court records, which are only partly indexed.

Adoption

8.15 Adoption was not recognised in the law of Scotland until 1930. Adoptions obviously did occur before 1930 but they were informal arrangements and rarely recorded. From 1855, a few may be noted in the Statutory Register of Births when a registrar added that information to the record of birth of a child. The General Register Office for Scotland (see **5.1**) maintains an Adopted Children Register, which is open to public inspection, as is the original birth entry of an adopted person. However, by law the information connecting the two entries cannot be seen, except by court order, by anyone other than an adopted person who has reached the age of 17 and to whom the information relates, or a local authority or approved adoption agency which is providing counselling. NAS holds records of adoption in the Court of Session records (CS312) and Sheriff Court records, but they are closed for 100 years. Information may only be supplied from these records to the adopted child having reached the age of 17, or by order of the Court of Session or the Sheriff Court concerned. For details of how to get access to the adoption records see the guidance on the NAS and GROS websites.

Legitimation

8.16 The disciplinary procedures of the kirk sessions show that many children were born illegitimate. Some were legitimated by the subsequent marriage of the parents. Others might be legitimated by the Crown or as a consequence of a court declaration.

8.17 Legitimations by the Crown are contained, along with other business, in the records of the Privy Seal (PS). A catalogue of these records has been published for the years 1488-1584 in eight volumes, *The Register of the Privy Seal of Scotland*. Each of these volumes has an index of persons, which will lead you to an entry in the catalogue. At the end of the entry, there is a roman numeral and an arabic numeral, representing respectively the volume and folio number of the original entry in the Privy Seal record. To see the original, which will be in Latin, you order by the reference number PS1 and the volume number, converting it into an arabic numeral (eg PS1/11). For the period between 1585 and 1660, there is no index and you have to use the Privy Seal minute books (PS6/3 and 4), which are written in chronological order. These give only the surname of the person concerned (and what he has been granted, such as legitimation) but provide the volume and folio number in the register (PS1). For the period since 1660, look at the 2-volume index to the Privy Seal 'English record' (ie written in English) held in the NAS. The first volume, up to 1782, indexes persons without distinguishing legitimations, but the second volume does specify them. If you wish to see the original entry in the Privy Seal register, order by PS3 and the volume number. Remember that legitimations might be granted at any age.

Legal records on Marriage and Divorce

8.18 Legitimation can be proved in court by proving the marriage of the parents. Irregular marriages could be recognised by a court of law. Divorce has been possible in Scotland since 1560. From the Reformation until 1830, the court which was responsible for cases involving legitimation and the constitution and dissolution of marriage was the Commissary Court of Edinburgh (CC8). From 1830 until 1984, the responsible court was the Court of Session, though between 1831 and 1835 some cases were still dealt with by the Commissary Court. The Court of Session has adopted a simplified divorce procedure from 1983, which forms a separate series (see **14.22**). However, since 1984 almost all divorces have been heard by the sheriff courts, and the outcome is recorded by the General Register Office for Scotland in the Register of Divorces (see Chapter 5).

8.19 The divorce and other consistorial cases heard by the Commissary Court of Edinburgh cover all aspects of marriage, separation, divorce and legitimacy, yielding a profusion of detail about marital and domestic circumstances. Although most cases involve well-off people, many lesser folk such as tradesmen can be found raising actions. A small proportion even had their case paid for by the parish poors' fund. All the processes have been individually re-numbered and re-catalogued in detail. The catalogue therefore supersedes the arrangement which was partly published in the *The Commissariot of Edinburgh — Consistorial Processes* *and Decreets, 1658-1800* ed. Francis J Grant (Scottish Record Society, 1909). A case may be ordered by the reference number CC8/6 and the individual process number.

8.20 Cases are searchable by name, date and type of action. For example we find a process of divorce, 14 October 1767, raised by Elizabeth Paterson, late mantua maker in Edinburgh, thereafter in Dundee, spouse of George Ramsay, staymaker in Canongate, against the said George Ramsay, son of the deceased George Ramsay, stabler in the Canongate, who were married October 1765 (CC8/6/435). Further information may be found in the decisions of the court known as decreets or decrees (CC8/5), for the years 1684 to 1832. In this example the catalogue tells us that the decree begins at CC8/5/11/775, ie volume 11, folio 775. Bear in mind that not all processes resulted in decree.

8.21 For lawsuits regarding marriage, divorce and legitimacy heard by the Court of Session since 1810, you must go to the records of that Court (see **14.3–20**).

Proclamation of Banns of Marriage

8.22 Before a regular marriage took place, the intention to marry had to be publicised by a proclamation in church. As the parties had to pay a fee, kirk session account and cash books sometimes give the names of couples about to marry, in such terms as 'To cash received from James Kirk in Auchterderran when contracted with Catherine Haxton in this Parish' (Kinglassie, 1783 June 6, CH2/406/7). Unfortunately, many of these account book entries simply state 'Proclamation' and the amount paid, omitting the names of the parties. If you wish to follow this line of inquiry, the relevant records are listed in the CH2 catalogue, described in **8.13**.

Marriage Contracts

8.23 Until recently, it was the practice, when members of propertied families got married, for a marriage contract to be drawn up, whereby the families made financial provision for the couple, particularly for the future financial security of the wife and children. These contracts could be drawn up either before or after the marriage ceremony. You would expect to find in a marriage contract the names of the couple and their fathers and possibly other relatives. The date of the contract would usually but not necessarily be close to the date of the marriage. As these were private documents, there is no guarantee that the one you are seeking has survived, but the following groups of records should be consulted.

8.24 Registers of Deeds (RD, SC, etc) – see **13.2-17**. One difficulty in searching for marriage contracts in this source is that a marriage contract might be registered years after the date of the marriage, perhaps after the death of the husband. There was no compulsion to register a marriage contract.

8.25 Register of Sasines (RS). As many marriage contracts included provisions for a liferent income from land, the subsequent instrument of sasine should be recorded in a Register of Sasines – see **11.3-18**.

8.26 Gifts and Deposits (GD). If either of the parties was a member of a family whose records have been gifted to or deposited in the National Archives of Scotland, then their marriage contract may be among these records – see **7.20-21**.

8.27 Miscellaneous papers – Marriage Contracts (RH9/7). This is a collection of 306 miscellaneous marriage contracts. They are arranged and listed in two series, the first chronological from 1591 to 1846 and the second rather haphazardly arranged but dated between 1605 and 1811. They are not indexed but are clearly catalogued in the RH9 catalogue.

8.28 One should bear in mind that occasionally a marriage contract was not followed by a marriage (see **14.58**).

Irregular Marriages

8.29 Until 1940, irregular marriages, in the form of a declaration by the parties before witnesses, but not before an established clergyman, were perfectly legal. However, such marriages were frowned upon. The parties might be rebuked by their kirk session and they and their witnesses were liable to be fined. Thus evidence of such marriages may be found in kirk session minutes described in **8.13** and in JP and burgh court records (see **14.49-51**). They are further explained in the introduction to *Calendar of Irregular Marriages in the South Leith Kirk Session Records* 1697-1818 (Scottish Record Society). The Ewart Library in Dumfries is the best source of information about irregular marriages at Gretna Green. The NAS has copies of registers of similar marriages at Lamberton Toll, Berwickshire, 1833–1849 (RH2/8/84).

Inhibitions

8.30 Evidence of marriage might also appear when a husband stopped his liability for his wife's debts (see **14.59-61**).

Fatal Accidents

8.31 The Fatal Accidents Inquiry (Scotland) Act, 1895, provided for public inquiries by sheriff and jury into fatal accidents occurring in industrial employment or occupations. If you are looking for information about a fatal accident at work from 1895 onwards, you can search the catalogue for the person's name, as most FAIs have been catalogued. You should find the name of the widow, the employment and employers of the deceased, and the date and cause of death. If you cannot find a relevant entry, it could be because the records are not yet in NAS, or are incomplete, for there are gaps in the records for many courts for parts of the twentieth century. It is worth checking the sheriff court's jury trial record, or the acts and decrees, in which records some courts entered FAI proceedings (see the list of sheriff courts in **14.39**). These records are not indexed. Bear in mind that local press reports were often detailed, and sometimes provide more information than the official record.

Mortcloth and Burial Records

8.32 It used to be common for the kirk session of the parish church to hire out a mortcloth to cover a dead body during the funeral service. The kirk session accounts, by recording a payment for a mortcloth, give the approximate date of death of the deceased. Records of mortcloth payments may appear in the kirk session minutes or account books (CH2 – see **8.13**) or in the accounts kept by the heritors (HR – see **11.41**). Such accounts may also include payments for coffins or digging the grave of named persons.

8.33 A few of the CH2 kirk session records include records of burials, specified in the list of records of that kirk session. Among the burgh records in NAS there are cemetery records for Dunbar, 1879-1902 (B18/18/24), and Tranent, 1885-1949 (B77/5/2-4). However, cemetery records are mostly held by the local authority in whose area the cemetery lies, so enquiries should be made in the first instance to the department which manages cemeteries in the appropriate council The examples mentioned here may be transferred to local custody in future. The NAS holds very few district council records and the only burial records therein are those of Prestonpans – look up DC2/5/23-28 in the catalogue. Such burial records may be more concerned with the purchaser of a place of burial than with who is actually buried there.

8.34   The Edinburgh Cemetery Company administered seven cemeteries in the city. Its records, formerly held by the NAS, are now in Edinburgh City Archives.

8.35   The inscriptions on gravestones are usually of great genealogical value. The microfilm series (RH4) includes copies of monumental inscriptions noted by S Cramer in burial grounds in various parts of Scotland (RH4/16 and 41). Look at Appendix 13 in the RH4 catalogue for the full list of these burial grounds.

8.36   A survey of monumental inscriptions (known as MIs) throughout Scotland was begun by the Scottish Genealogy Society some years ago. These are arranged in volumes by county or part-county, in which the arrangement is by alphabetical order of churchyard with an index of surnames for each churchyard. A similar series of monumental inscriptions in North Ayrshire has been compiled by the local council. Copies of all these volumes are in the NAS library, and are usually available in local libraries.

Anatomy

8.37   Not all bodies go directly to their grave. Some are supplied to schools of anatomy for the benefit of the students. Since 1842, the Inspector of Anatomy for Scotland has kept registers that are preserved in the NAS as part of the records of the Ministry of Health. Look for the registers listed under the reference MH1. There were schools of anatomy at Aberdeen, Dundee, Edinburgh, Glasgow and St Andrews. There is a 50-year closure period on this record. The registers are arranged chronologically and give the name, age, sex, last place of abode (typically the Royal Infirmary or Charity Workhouse), and date, place and cause of death, of each deceased. The registers are not indexed.

⋘9⋙
Inheritance: Wills and Executries

9.1 Apart from the records of births, marriages and deaths, the most useful records for genealogical research are those which deal with inheritance and the disposal of the property of a deceased person. Searching for wills and testaments and related records up to 1901 has been transformed by the creation of digital images, and a unified index which has superseded all the previous finding aids, both published and unpublished. The digital images can be seen in the NAS search rooms as 'Virtual Volumes' and are also available in the ScotlandsPeople Centre. The index can be searched online on the ScotlandsPeople website at *www.scotlandspeople. gov.uk* and copies ordered. The following sections therefore offer a supplementary guide to searching the testamentary records for the period to 1901, and more detailed guidance for the period since 1902.

9.2 In legal terms, property may be either heritable or moveable. Heritable property consists of land, minerals in the ground, and buildings. Moveable property is property that can be moved, such as money, furniture, animals, machinery and implements. Only from 1868 onwards could heritable property be bequeathed, and until 1964, the rules of inheritance in Scotland were different in respect of heritable and moveable property. Because of this distinction, the information about inheritance in heritable and moveable property is, by and large, kept in different records and therefore is best considered separately. In this chapter, we shall consider the records that concern the disposal of moveable property of a person who has died, especially registers of testaments in commissary and sheriff courts. You should bear in mind, however, that from the early nineteenth century onwards it is not uncommon to find records relating to heritable property, such as trust dispositions and settlements, recorded in commissary court registers.

9.3 When a person dies, an executor should be appointed to administer the moveable estate of the deceased. If the deceased has left a will, then the executor will usually be appointed by the will, though this appointment

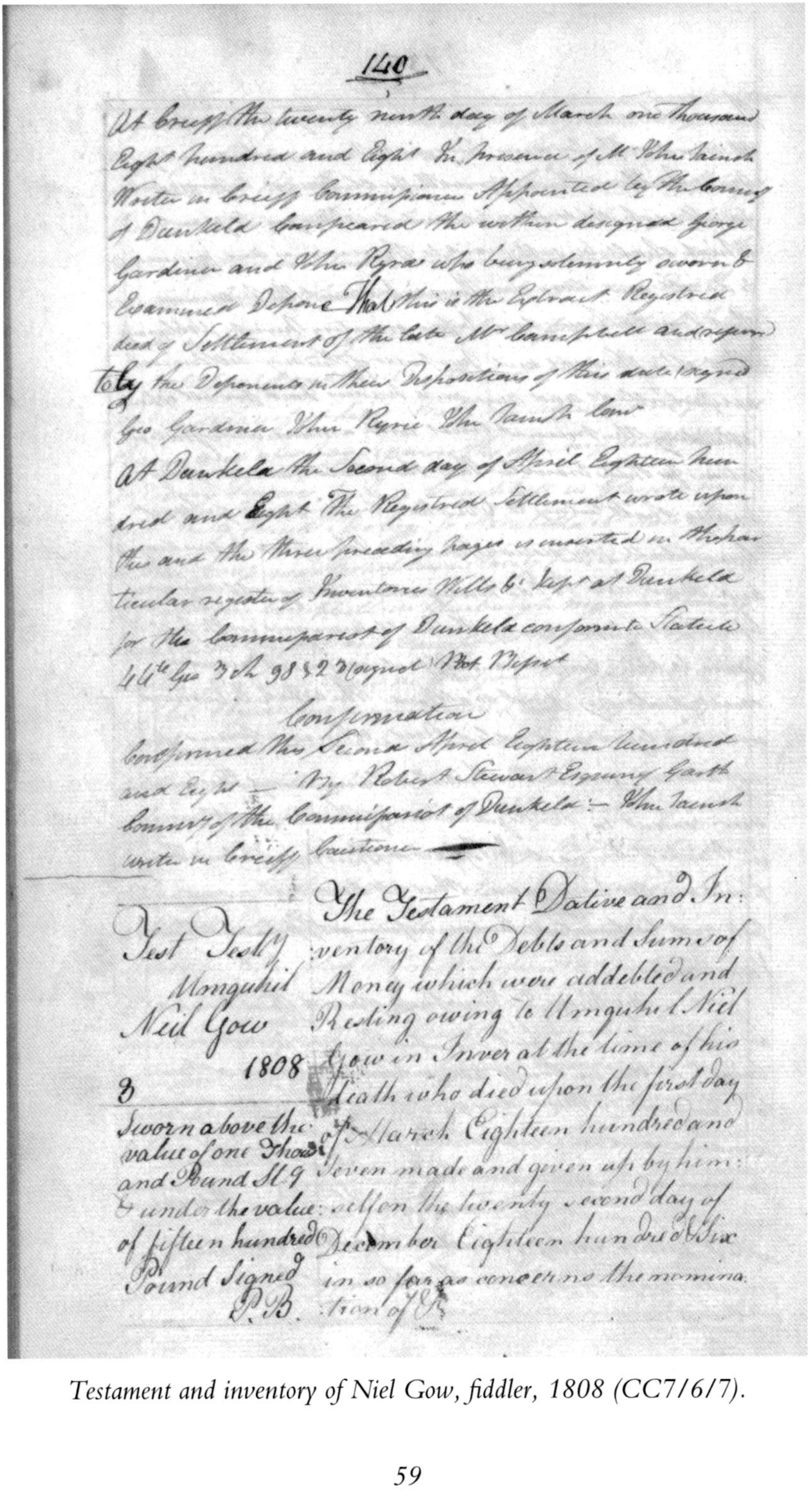

Testament and inventory of Niel Gow, fiddler, 1808 (CC7/6/7).

will require confirmation by the relevant court. If the deceased has died intestate (i.e. has not left a will), then the executor will be appointed and confirmed by the court. Thus the records which concern us are the records of the confirmation of executors, whether or not there is a will. These records are known as testaments, a testament-testamentar if there is a will, a testament-dative if there is none. Each testament will give the name and designation of the deceased, usually the date of death, the confirmation of the executor, an inventory of the moveable estate of the deceased (which may include household furniture, implements of trade, and debts owed to and by the deceased), and the will, if there is one.

9.4   The relevant court was a commissary court (CC) until the 1820s and thereafter a sheriff court (SC). Obviously, before you search for the will or executry of an ancestor, it helps to know the approximate year of death and where in Scotland he or she lived.

9.5   Before investigating the relevant records, you should be aware of certain snags.

a. Not only did very few people leave wills, but, in the majority of cases, the family of a deceased person did not bother with the formality of confirming an executry. 'We keepit siller in the crap o' the wa', jist stappit in. We had nae lawyers, a' body just fechted it oot amang themselves.' *(Innes Review,* vol. VII, no.2 (1956)).

b. Some records have not survived because of the depredations of fire and other accidents.

c. As an eldest son inherited the whole of the heritable property of his deceased father, he did not receive any of the moveable property in intestacy and therefore the eldest son's name may be omitted from his father's testament.

d. If the deceased had died in debt, his nearest of kin might not wish to take on his executry (and therefore liability to his creditors). Thus sometimes a creditor is named as executor. In such a case, the testament is unlikely to contain genealogical information.

e. Testaments are usually confirmed within a year of death, but this is not always so, eg Captain James Carmichael died at Nairn on 17 May 1813 but his executry was not confirmed until 30 October 1827 (SC26/39/1, p. 326).

Executries before 1824

9.6 If your ancestor died before 1824, then the relevant court is a commissary court. There are records for 22 such courts covering different parts of Scotland. The commissary courts acquired the jurisdiction of the pre-Reformation church courts and the areas they administered (known as commissariots) were based on the areas of these church courts, which are different from any modern administrative areas.

9.7 Thanks to the modern index available in NAS search rooms (and the version available through ScotlandsPeople), it is unnecessary to discover which commissary court or courts cover the area in which your ancestor lived in order to find a will. However, it can be useful to do so for exploring other commissary court records (see **8.18–20**). A useful series of maps published by the Institute of Heraldic and Genealogical Studies, Northgate, Canterbury, Kent, gives the boundaries of the commissariots and the parishes which lay within them: a set of these maps is kept in the Historical Search Room. Other guides to which parishes were in which commissariots are mentioned in **2.4**. However, changes in parish boundaries and the irregularity of the bounds of the commissariots mean that it may be easier for you to use the following table which simply shows modern counties and their equivalent commissariots. It is worth remembering that you may find an executry in the commissary court of Edinburgh rather than the local commissary court because, while Edinburgh dealt mainly with the executries of people who lived within the commissariot of Edinburgh, it could also confirm the executors of people who lived elsewhere and particularly those who died furth of Scotland.

County	Commissariot	Reference Numbers
Aberdeen	Aberdeen	CC1
	Moray	CC16
Angus (Forfar)	Brechin	CC3
	Dunkeld	CC7
	St Andrews	CC20
Argyll	Argyll	CC2
	The Isles	CC12
Ayr	Glasgow	CC9
Banff	Aberdeen	CC1
	Moray	CC16
Berwick	Lauder	CC15

County	Commissariot	Reference Numbers
Bute	The Isles	CC12
Caithness	Caithness	CC4
Clackmannan	Dunblane	CC6
	Stirling	CC21
Dumfries	Dumfries	CC5
Dunbarton	Glasgow	CC9
	Hamilton and Campsie	CC10
East Lothian		
(Haddington)	Edinburgh	CC8
	Dunkeld	CC7
Edinburgh City	Edinburgh	CC8
Fife	Dunkeld	CC7
	St Andrews	CC20
	Stirling	CC21
Glasgow City	Glasgow	CC9
	Hamilton and Campsie	CC10
Inverness	Argyll	CC11
	Inverness	CC11
	The Isles	CC12
Kincardine	Brechin	CC3
	St Andrews	CC20
Kinross	St Andrews	CC20
	Stirling	CC21
Kirkcudbright	Dumfries	CC5
	Kirkcudbright	CC13
	Wigtown	CC22
Lanark	Glasgow	CC9
	Hamilton and Campsie	CC10
	Lanark	CC14
Midlothian (Edinburgh)	Edinburgh	CC8
Moray (Elgin)	Moray	CC16
Nairn	Moray	CC16
Orkney	Orkney and Shetland	CC17
Peebles	Peebles	CC18
Perth	Dunblane	CC6
	Dunkeld	CC7
	St Andrews	CC20
Renfrew	Glasgow	CC9
	Hamilton and Campsie	CC10

County	Commissariot	Reference Numbers
Ross and Cromarty	The Isles	CC12
	Ross	CC19
Roxburgh	Peebles	CC18
Selkirk	Peebles	CC18
Shetland	Orkney and Shetland	CC17
Stirling	Glasgow	CC9
	Hamilton and Campsie	CC10
	Stirling	CC21
Sutherland	Caithness	CC4
West Lothian		
(Linlithgow)	Edinburgh	CC8
	Dunkeld	CC7
Wigtown	Wigtown	CC22

9.8 The printed indexes to the 'Commissariot Records', published by the Scottish Record Society (1897-1904), and the NAS typescript indexes covering 1801-1824, have been completely superseded by the online search facilities in the NAS and ScotlandsPeople. However, some of the same principles apply to searching the information. Married women are indexed under their maiden name, but can also be searched for under their married name. Other forms of electronic searching include searching by surname, forename, occupations or designation, date, commissary or sheriff court, and places. Variant spellings can be used, and there are other useful search tools to help you get the most from the index.

9.9 The original registers of testaments are no longer available for general consultation, and you should either use the electronic versions of the registers in the NAS or available through ScotlandsPeople.

9.10 In the NAS search rooms, having found the person you are looking for in the index, you are linked directly to the digital image of their testament. The name of the deceased is usually placed clearly in the margin, sometimes with the date of confirmation, or the date of confirmation should appear in the last or second last paragraph of the testament. The testaments usually provide the name of the spouse and children, and other relations who were beneficiaries or executors. In the NAS you can browse the images of the registers electronically. As most volumes are arranged chronologically by dates of confirmation, it is normally simple to locate the correct part of the volume. There is often no gap between one testament and the next, so look for the words 'The Testament' ('Dative' or 'Testamentar') which starts each testament.

9.11 Sometimes, a volume of a register of testaments has not survived, but related documents called 'warrants' (see **7.17**) have done so. Many of the warrants which act as a substitute for a lost register have been digitally imaged and can be searched like other testaments. The following commissariots have been covered in this way: Aberdeen, Brechin, Kirkcudbright, St Andrews, Stirling and Wigtown. For other commissary courts the warrants have not been digitally imaged. The printed indexes should indicate warrants with a letter 'T' or 'W', and they can also be identified in the indexes in ScotlandsPeople. Consult the CC catalogue for the reference number of the warrants of testaments, which are arranged by box or bundle.

9.12 The Register of Testaments and most other records of Aberdeen Commissary Court were destroyed by fire in 1722. Afterwards, copies of some earlier testaments and other writs were collected into a series now referenced CC1/15. These are not indexed but are listed in a minute book (CC1/11/9). The testaments date back into the seventeenth century.

9.13 Where a series of testaments or warrants is lacking, other papers in the commissary records, for example edicts, may provide details such as the names of executors. For example, supplementary documents in the Argyll commissary court records (CC2) have been described in detail in a catalogue of records which complement the register of testaments: *Argyll Commissary Court: A Calendar of testaments, inventories, commissary processes and other records, 1700-1825.* This was compiled by Mr F W Bigwood, Flat B, The Lodge, 2 East Road, North Berwick, EH39 4HN, from whom copies may be purchased; the index may also be consulted in the Historical Search Room.

Executries between the 1820s and 1875

9.14 By the Commissary Courts (Scotland) Act, 1823, the commissary courts ceased to exist on 1 January 1824 and their jurisdiction in executry matters was transferred to the sheriff courts, which now became responsible for confirming executors. An important exception to the transition was that Edinburgh, Haddington and Linlithgow remained part of the commissariot of Edinburgh until 1830. Elsewhere the transfer was not made precisely and there is considerable overlap between the testamentary records of the commissary courts and those of the sheriff courts, both before and after January 1824. The overlapping records have been imaged, so that in these cases the reader can choose between different versions of the same testamentary records. Generally the version taking up more pages (indicated in the index) will be clearer because the writing will be less cramped. The following table of counties shows the end dates of the commissary court records and the start dates of the sheriff court records.

County	Commissariot	Sheriff Court
Aberdeen	1823	1824 (SC1)
Angus (Forfar)	1823	1824 (SC47)
Argyll	1823	1815 (SC51)
Ayr	1823	1824 (SC6)
Banff	1827	1824 (SC2)
Berwick	1823	1823 (SC60)
Bute	1823	1824 (SC8)
Caithness	1827	1824 (SC14)
Clackmannan	1825	1824 (SC64)
Dumfries	1823	1827 (SC15)
Dunbarton	1823	1824 (SC65)
East Lothian (Haddington)	1829	1808 (SC70)
Edinburgh City	1829	1808 (SC70)
Fife	1823	1824 (SC20)
Glasgow	1823	1824 (SC36)
Inverness	1824	1825 (SC29)
Kincardine	1823	1824 (SC5)
Kinross	1825	1824 (SC64)
Kirkcudbright	1824	1824 (SC16)
Lanark	1823	1824 (SC36)
Midlothian (Edinburgh)	1829	1808 (SC70)
Moray (Elgin)	1827	1824 (SC26)
Nairn	1827	1824 (SC26)
Orkney	1832	1824 (SC11)
Peebles	1827	1814 (SC42)
Perth	1825	1824 (SC44 & 49)
Renfrew	1823	1824 (SC58)
Ross and Cromarty	1824	1824 (SC25 & 33)
Roxburgh	1827	1827 (SC62)
Selkirk	1827	1824 (SC63)
Shetland	1826	1827 (SC12)

County	Commissariot	Sheriff Court
Stirling	1823	1809 (SC67)
Sutherland	1827	1799 (SC9)
West Lothian (Linlithgow)	1829	1808 (SC70)
Wigtown	1826	1826 (SC19)

9.15 Each sheriff court had its own way of organising its executry (or commissary) records, so the records are not arranged consistently. Sometimes there are three separate series of commissary records, all of which you may wish to examine, but sometimes two or all three series may be combined. Though the names they were given also vary (eg 'commissary record books'), the basic three are records of confirmations (of executries), wills ('settlements', 'testamentary deeds'), and inventories (of the moveable estate of the deceased). Remember that if your ancestor died intestate, then there will be no will, although there may be an inventory of moveable estate.

9.16 Wills were normally recorded in the sheriff court for the county in which the person lived. When a person lived outwith Scotland, but died leaving moveable property within Scotland, then confirmation of the executry was the responsibility of the commissary office of the sheriff court of Edinburgh (SC70). The following table shows each modern county and the equivalent sheriff court which dealt with commissary business between the 1820s and 1875.

County	Sheriff Court	Reference Number
Aberdeen	Aberdeen	SC1
Angus (Forfar)	Dundee (from 1832)	SC45
	Forfar	SC47
Argyll	Dunoon	SC51
Ayr	Ayr	SC6
Banff	Banff	SC2
Berwick	Duns	SC60
Bute	Rothesay	SC8
Caithness	Wick	SC14
Clackmannan	Alloa	SC64
Dumfries	Dumfries	SC15
Dunbarton	Dumbarton	SC65
East Lothian (Haddington)	Haddington (from 1830)	SC40

County	Sheriff Court	Reference Number
Edinburgh City	Edinburgh	SC70
Fife	Cupar	SC20
Glasgow City	Glasgow	SC36
Inverness	Inverness	SC29
Kincardine	Stonehaven	SC5
Kinross	Alloa (to 1847)	SC64
	Kinross (from 1847)	SC22
Kirkcudbright	Kirkcudbright	SC16
Lanark	Glasgow	SC36
Midlothian (Edinburgh)	Edinburgh	SC70
Moray (Elgin)	Elgin	SC26
Nairn	Elgin (to 1838)	SC26
	Nairn (from 1839)	SC31
Orkney	Kirkwall	[In Kirkwall]
Peebles	Peebles	SC42
Perth	Dunblane	SC44
	Perth	SC49
Renfrew	Paisley	SC58
Ross	Dingwall	SC25
	Stornoway (to 1850)	SC33
Roxburgh	Jedburgh	SC62
Selkirk	Selkirk	SC63
Shetland	Lerwick	[In Lerwick]
Stirling	Stirling	SC67
Sutherland	Dornoch	SC9
West Lothian (Linlithgow)	Linlithgow (from 1830)	SC41
Wigtown	Wigtown	SC19

9.17   If your ancestor lived within the jurisdiction of a sheriff court in Scotland and died between 1846 and 1867, or between 1827 and 1865 in the case of Edinburgh, Haddington and Linlithgow, you may wish to look at a series of printed indexes in the Historical Search Room entitled *Index to Personal Estates of Defuncts*. Although they have been almost entirely superseded by the electronic index, the printed entries contain two useful details which are not in the NAS index: the date of death, and a code letter telling you whether the person died testate or intestate. Each volume contains a group of counties, within which the deceased are indexed in alphabetical order. Within each surname, the men are listed before the women.

9.18   In many instances the inventory states that a will was registered in the 'Sheriff Court Books' of the county. These sheriff court books are the Register of Deeds of the particular sheriff court (see further in **13.13**) and you should find another copy of the will recorded in a volume of the Register of Deeds.

9.19   As mentioned above, if your ancestor lived outside Scotland, but owned property in Scotland, then the sheriff court of Edinburgh (SC70) was responsible for his executry. If his executry was confirmed before 1858 or you simply want to see the inventory of his Scottish property, then you search as if he had died in Edinburgh. If the executry was confirmed between 1858 and 1900 and he lived in England or Ireland, there will be a copy of the English or Irish probate in the Probates Resealed series (SC70/6). The whole series up to 1900 has been digitised along with the registers of testaments.

Executries from 1876 to 1901

9.20   For the period from 1876 to 1901 the wills have been digitally imaged and fully indexed. The index provides the full references of the records, and it has largely superseded the annual printed volumes of the *Calendar of Confirmations*.

Each index entry gives the name and designation of the deceased, the date and place of death, whether testate or intestate, and where and when confirmation was granted.
A typical entry reads:

> 13 November 1891
> STEVENSON, James
> Mason, residing at New Cross, Beith, who died 24
> July 1891, at Beith, testate

9.21   The details which you can find in the *Calendar* which have been excluded from the ScotlandsPeople index are the dates when the will was made and recorded, the name of the executor and the value of the estate. The Historical Search Room holds a full set from 1875 to 1901. Several of the larger Scottish libraries and some archives also hold copies of the *Calendar*.

Executries from 1902

9.22 For 1902 to 1984 you will be consulting original records, and may need to order them in advance. You should note that the wills from 1902 onwards are being digitised, and the (unindexed) images gradually made available in 'Virtual Volumes' in the search rooms. From 1902 to 1959, there is a series of annual printed volumes called the *Calendar of Confirmations and Inventories*, as noted above. The Historical Search Room has a set; thereafter the series may be consulted on microfiche in the Legal Search Room. Several of the larger Scottish libraries and some archives also hold copies of the printed *Calendar*.

9.23 This *Calendar* indexes all those persons whose executry has been confirmed in Scotland in that particular year, regardless of where they lived. The index is in strict alphabetical order, except that some entries may appear in addenda at the end of the volume. Married women are indexed only under their married name. If you do not find the entry you want in the year of death, check the subsequent years.

9.24 Each entry gives the name and designation of the deceased, the date and place of death, whether testate or intestate, where and when confirmation was granted, the name and designation of the executor and the value of the estate. If the deceased was testate, you are given the date of the will and the court books in which it has been recorded and when. Additional inventories ('eiks') are usually noted by hand. Note down the name of the sheriff court where confirmation was granted (which is in heavier type), the date of confirmation, and if there is a will, in which court, and when, it was recorded.

9.25 For example, if you look up 'HARDIE, James Keir, M.P.' in the *Calendar of Confirmations and Inventories for 1915*, you find that confirmation to his wife and daughter as executors was granted at AYR on 28 December and that his will was recorded in the court books of the commissariot of Ayr on 27 December. You therefore look at the catalogue for Ayr Sheriff Court (SC6). You find that the confirmation of his executors is in the volume referenced SC61/48/56, but you are more likely to want to see his inventory and will. The Register of Inventories is SC6/44 and the volume which covers December 1915 is SC6/44/77, while the Register of Testamentary Writings is SC6/46 and the volume including December 1915 is SC6/46/42. Both of these volumes are arranged chronologically and you will find the inventory and will each recorded under the date 27 December 1915, i.e. they had to be recorded before confirmation was granted the next day, 28 December.

9.26 From 1960 until 1984 the Calendar of Confirmations took the form of index cards for each year, which are only available on microfiche in the Legal Search Room. Each index card contains the name of the deceased, whether they were testate or intestate, the sheriff court, and the date of confirmation of the executors. Using the date provided you then need to consult the relevant sheriff court catalogue as above to identify the reference(s) of the volume(s) covering the confirmation date. If the confirmations are in a separate series, you will first need to order out the confirmation in order to establish the date on which the testament and inventory and any eiks (additional inventories) were recorded, usually several days or weeks earlier.

9.27 After 1985 testaments, inventories and confirmations from all the sheriff courts were microfilmed by the Commissary Office in Edinburgh. A copy of the microfilm (SC70/17) and the electronic index are available in NAS after 10 years. Enquiries for testamentary records up to 10 years old should be directed to the Sheriff Clerk's Office, Commissary Section, Sheriff Court House, 27 Chambers Street, Edinburgh EH1 1LB (Tel. 0131 225 2525, Fax 0131 225 4422, E-mail: *cru@scotcourts.gov*).

9.28 The wills of persons dying furth of Scotland between 1858 and 1901 may be seen as 'Virtual Volumes' or via ScotlandsPeople (see **9.1**). The index supersedes the typed index to the 'Probates Resealed', and, for deaths after 1876, the *Calendar of Confirmations* in the NAS. These probates do not include the inventory of goods belonging to the deceased in Scotland. That information is in the Edinburgh Register of Inventories (SC70/1). Letters of administration (SC70/6-7) give only the total value of the estate of people dying abroad.

Wills Elsewhere

9.29 If you have been unable to find a record of your ancestor's executry in the Commissary Court and Sheriff Court commissary records, there are other sources you can try.

9.30 RH9/8 is a collection of miscellaneous executry papers, 1481-1882. The catalogue is based on and effectively supersedes the index published by the Scottish Record Society in 1904.

9.31   If your ancestor was a member of a family whose records have been gifted to or deposited in the NAS, then a copy of a testament may survive among the records of that GD (see **7.20**).

9.32   Mention has been made above of wills recorded in the 'Sheriff Court Books'. Many wills are registered in various other registers of deeds, which are described in Chapter 11. As explained there, not all of these are indexed and therefore easy to search. What is loosely termed as a 'will' may appear under different names, 'Latter Will and Testament', 'Deed of Settlement', 'Trust Disposition and Settlement', 'Mutual Disposition and Settlement', etc. Dispositions and settlements were often used to get round the rule that heritable property could not be bequeathed. Wills thus registered are likely to be those of better-off folk and of course none should be registered till after the death of the testator.

9.33   Separate series of wills of servicemen exist for the twentieth century, mainly for the First and Second World Wars (SC70/8-10). See **18.10-12** for further details.

9.34   *Calendars of Probate and Letters of Administration* for England and Wales can be searched online. A printed set covering the years 1858-1970 was provided for the use of the Commissary Office in Edinburgh, and is held by the NAS (SC70/13).

9.35   The NAS occasionally receives claims by people seeking to trace money supposedly left by ancestors who died intestate, and whose money has allegedly been 'left in Chancery'. These bequests are almost invariably mythical. In rare cases where the beneficiary of a will could not be traced, the property concerned had to be reported to the Queen's (or King's) Lord Treasurer's Remembrancer. In cases of an intestate person with no known heirs, their property fell to the Crown as *ultimus haeres* (the last heir). See **10.31-38** for further information.

Death Duties

9.36   Connected with the records of executries are estate duty records (IRS5-14). These may not give any genealogical information other than what you can obtain from the commissary and sheriff court records, which you should investigate first.

9.37   The estate duty records are part of the records of the Inland Revenue in

Scotland and begin in 1804. Look first at the catalogue under IRS for a detailed explanation of 'Estate Duty Office Registers'. There are various series of books and registers, relating to the various taxes which have been levied on the estates of deceased persons. There is a 75-year closure on these records. The categories of estate duty register and the useful non-financial information you might find in them are as follows. The indexes usually give only the relevant folio, and the relevant volume has to be discovered by searching the catalogue for the IRS series, eg IRS5.

- **IRS5** Personal Legacy Registers, 1804-1829. These state the relationship of the legatees to the deceased, though not always very specifically, eg 'Mrs Amelia Farquharson, descend' of Brother of mother' (IRS5/3).

- **IRS6** Return Ledgers for Inventory Duty, 1831-1892, which account for repayments when there has been over-payments. Date of death. May give name of lawyer.

- **IRS7** Residue Duty Account Books, 1819-1838, account for payments of inventory duty. Name of executor. Indexes, 1808-1850 and 1885-1897, which are indexes to the inventories which are numbered.

- **IRS8** Legacy Receipt Books, 1796-1865. Relationship of legatees.

- **IRS9** Register of Inventories received from Commissary offices, 1824- 1876. Indexes, 1863-1884.

- **IRS10** Testate Register and Indexes, 1828-1879. Date of death. Executor. Relationship of legatees.

- **IRS11** Intestate Register and Indexes, 1829-1879. Executor. Persons beneficially entitled and their relationship. Solicitors.

- **IRS12** Succession Duty Register and Indexes, 1853-1868. Date of death. This record relates to succession in heritable subjects (i.e. land and houses mainly) which could not be transferred by an ordinary will until 1868. The entries explain why the named successor is succeeding to the heritable property, whether by a legal document or in right of a relationship.

- **IRS13** General Registers, 1880-1906. Date of death. Relationship of beneficiaries.

- **IRS14** Indexes, 1870-1907, to IRS10, 11, 12 and 13. Date of death. Closed for only 30 years.

❧10❧
Inheriting Houses and Land in Scotland

10.1 This chapter is concerned with the records of inheritance of heritable property (houses and land). Clearly, this will matter to you only if your ancestor was likely to have owned his own house or land. Most Scots did not.

10.2 Historically, the system of land-holding in Scotland was a feudal one. In theory, land belonged to the Crown, but the Crown granted land to subjects, who could then make grants to others, while retaining certain rights. Before 1868, heirs had to prove their entitlement as heritable property could not be bequeathed. The requirement for an heir to prove his right to inherit created records which are useful to the genealogist. However, the death of a landowner did not inevitably or immediately result in such a record. Often, the heir simply occupied the lands and did not go through the correct procedures for years. A landowner might grant lands to his eldest son, reserving rights to himself during his lifetime. After 1868, heritable property could be bequeathed. However an heir acquired a property, any such transfer of ownership after 1617 should eventually be recorded in the Register of Sasines (see **11.3** onwards).

10.3 Where there had been no grant or bequest by a deceased property owner, until 1964 the law of primogeniture applied. By this the eldest son inherited all the heritable property, excluding his siblings. If there were no sons but there were daughters, all the daughters inherited equally.

Retours (Services of Heirs)

10.4 The most accessible record of the transfer of heritable property is the record of Retours, which is part of the Chancery records (C). When a subject of the Crown died, his heir had to prove his right to inherit his ancestor's lands by the procedure of an inquest and 'retour' (= return) to Chancery. Retours could also be used by less exalted folk to provide evidence of their right to the heritable property of an ancestor. Retours which specified the lands were called special retours. General retours did not name any lands. These special and general retours, which are also known as services of heirs, will tell you the names of the heir and the ancestor, their relationship and sometimes the date of death of the ancestor.

10.5   The retour procedure was also used to appoint a tutor to administer the affairs of a fatherless child (a 'pupil', under 14 if a boy, 12 if a girl). The tutor was usually the nearest adult male relative of the father.

10.6   The retours date from 1530 and are in Latin until 1847 (excepting the years 1652-1659). They are indexed throughout but the style of indexes changes dramatically after 1700. The year 1700 is covered in both series of indexes.

Retours before 1700

10.7   A summary of the retours up to 1700 was published in 2 volumes in 1811 and an index thereto in a third volume in 1816. The 3 volumes are entitled *Inquisitionum ad Capellam Regis Retornatarum Abbreviatio*. The title on the spines of the volumes in the Historical Search Room is shortened to *Inquisitionum Retornatarum Abbreviatio*. The Scottish Genealogy Society has also produced a CD-ROM for the years 1544-1699. The summaries and indexes of the special retours are arranged separately within counties. Look in volume 3 under the county in which your ancestor owned land. Under each county, there is an index of names ('Index Nominum') and an index of places ('Index Locorum'). Also look under the headings 'Inquisitiones Generales' and 'Inquisitiones de Tutela' at the 'Index Nominum' of each. Heir, ancestor, tutor and pupil are all indexed.

10.8   An awkwardness in using these indexes is that names are printed as they appear in the original document, the forenames in their Latin form, and the surnames in variant spellings (eg 'Garden' may appear as 'Gairdin') and therefore not in the form or order you might expect.

10.9   In each index, each name is followed by a number. This number is the running number of the summaries. You then go to volume 1 or 2 and look up that number under the particular county within the 'Inquisitiones Speciales', or under the 'Inquisitiones Generales' or under the

'Inquisitiones de Tutela', depending on the index in which you have found the number. If the entries in a county within the 'Inquisitiones Speciales' seem not to go up to the number you have, then look at the supplementary pages in volume 2 which follow the entries for Wigton.

10.10 Most summaries are in Latin. Each summary is headed by its date, then you get the name of the heir, the name of the ancestor, and the relationship, and, in the 'Inquisitiones Speciales', the lands. The date of death is not given, though it may appear in the original record of special retours. In the 'Inquisitiones de Tutela', the first name is that of the tutor, followed by his relationship to his 'pupil' (the child), whose name follows. At the end of each summary, you will find a roman number (= the volume number) and an arabic number (= the folio number) or you will find a letter of the alphabet followed by an arabic number. If you want to see the full document in the Chancery records, you order by the reference C22 and the volume number, converting that number into an arabic one. The letter references A to I represent volumes now numbered C22/177-185 (look at the C catalogue for the details). Thus, if the reference is G.172, you order out C22/183 and, having obtained that volume, look up folio 172.

10.11 If you have failed to find your ancestor in the *Inquisitionum Retornatarum Abbreviatio*, then look at the very end of the Historical Search Room copy of volume 11, where you will find four inserted pages, printed in 1900, containing abridgements, in the same format but arranged alphabetically by name of heir, of a few retours from 1303 to 1622 omitted from the official register, but rescued by a Mr Alexander Macdonald. To read the full text of these retours, you order out C39/4 (a volume of transcripts). The number at the end of each abridgement is the folio number in that volume.

10.12 As there was no time limit for recording retours, some pre-1700 retours were recorded after 1700, occasionally well after.

Retours from 1700

10.13 Starting in 1700 and up to the present day, there is a series of printed 'Indexes to the Services of Heirs in Scotland', decennial up to 1859, annual thereafter, with the title 'Services of Heirs' on the spine. There is more than one decennial or annual index in each volume. These are indexes to the general and special retours, but they do not index the appointments of tutors. Before using these indexes for the first time, you should read the 'explanations' which introduce the volume for 1700-1749. The Scottish Genealogy Society has made a CD-Rom version for 1700-1859.

10.14 These indexes index by name of the heir ('the Person Served') not the ancestor, but at the end of each volume or ten-year period there is a supplement, which lists alphabetically the names of ancestors ('Persons Served to') whose heirs do not have the same surname, cross-referring to the names of the heirs. In the index, after the name of the heir, you will find 'distinguishing particulars', i.e. the heir's designation, the relationship and name of the ancestor, sometimes the latter's date of death, what type of heir, the lands if he is heir special, and the date of the retour. There follows the date of recording and a monthly number: note both of these if you are to proceed further.

10.15 To obtain the call number of the service of heir itself, you must look in the C catalogue under C22 up to 15 November 1847 and after that date under C28. Choose the volume which includes the date of recording you have found in the index. In that volume, look for the date of recording and the monthly running number, both of which will appear in the margin of the text.

10.16 For example, say you are interested in James Duncan, son of John Duncan, minister in Zetland [Shetland], who in 1736 was served heir to his uncle Henry Robertson, apothecary in Edinburgh. The index tells you that the date of recording was 1736 November 24 and the monthly number is 14. The volume for that date is C22/64. The entries in the volume are in chronological order and you read in the margin 'no 14 of novr. 1736' beside the copy of the retour, which explains in detail the relationship between the deceased and his heir.

10.17 The date of death of the ancestor is sometimes stated, but more often is not. In the simpler entries of sons succeeding fathers, there may be no more information in the text (in Latin until 1847) than there is in the index (in English).

10.18 If you are looking for a service of heir between 1700 and 1796 and cannot find it in the 'Services of Heirs' in its proper place, try the one-page 'List of Unrecorded Retours' which is placed in Volume 5 of the 'Services of Heirs' between 1905 and 1906. Those listed which start with the letters A–J will be found by ordering out C25/10 and with letters L–Y in C25/11.

10.19 If you are looking for a service of heir between 1792 and 1846 and cannot find it in the 'Services of Heirs', try the 'Index of Retours of General Service', which were dated before 1847 but recorded after 1859. This index is also placed in Volume 5 of the 'Services of Heirs' between 1905 and 1906. You will find these retours either in C22/175 or 176, depending on the date of recording.

10.20 If you are looking for the retour of the appointment of a tutor to administer the affairs of a child, there is a typed index covering the period 1701-1886 (which index also covers the appointment of curators to administer the affairs of insane persons until 1897). The index is by name of the child and gives the volume and folio numbers of the record. Order by the reference C22 and the volume number. There are no such retours after 1886, as this method of administering the affairs of a child had fallen into disuse, having gradually been replaced by an alternative method, that of the appointment of a factor loco tutoris by the Court of Session (see **14.25**), or, after 1880, by a sheriff court if the estate was small (see **14.39–46**).

Inquests

10.21 The decision that someone was indeed the heir of a deceased person or the right person to be tutor to a fatherless child was made locally by an inquest. The decision of the inquest was then 'retoured' to Chancery. At the beginning of every retour, we are told in which sheriff or burgh court the inquest was held. Sometimes, but only sometimes, the sheriff court preserved the records of the inquest and these records may provide further family details (and are in English). For example, in the Register of Retours we are told simply that, in 1844, Thomas Crocket, plasterer in Dumfries, was served heir to his great-grandfather, Andrew Thomson, slater in Dumfries (C22/166). The equivalent sheriff court records provide the names of Thomas's parents, grandparents and a great-aunt (SC15/64/2). To find if the required sheriff court records have survived, look in the contents list of the relevant SC catalogue for 'Services of Heirs' or 'Record of Services' or similar headings.

10.22 Those of Jedburgh sheriff court have been published in *Services of Heirs, Roxburghshire* (Scottish Record Society, 1934). Inquests held in a burgh court may be recorded in the burgh court book (see **14.51**). Unless the inquest decision was not retoured, this source is unlikely to provide additional details to those in the retours, but will be in English.

Clare Constat

10.23 The heir of a crown vassal had to have a special retour before he could inherit his ancestor's lands. An heir, whose deceased ancestor was the feudal vassal of a subject-superior, might obtain a document called a precept of clare constat from that superior before he could legally own his ancestor's lands. In this document (usually in Latin), the superior acknowledged that it clearly appeared to him that the heir was the heir of a deceased vassal in specified lands. A precept of clare constat will tell you who the heir and ancestor were, and their relationship. There is no register of such documents, but some survive in private collections (GDs, see 6.19-20), while the instruments of sasine, which followed both them and special retours and repeated the information therein, may be found both in GD collections and in the Register of Sasines (RS – see **11.3** onwards).

Tailzies

10.24 In the Services of Heirs, you may have noticed that an heir may be served as 'Heir of Taillie'. 'Taillie' or 'tailzie' is the Scots form of the word 'entail'. By an Act of the Scottish Parliament 1685, c.22, a landowner was allowed to decide who would succeed to his estate for generations to come by means of a deed of tailzie or entail. An estate was entailed to prevent it going out of the family, either through sale or by marriage. Such a deed had to be recorded in the Register of Tailzies (RT1) and, in the naming of a series of substitute heirs, may include detailed information about the family at that time. For example, in the deed of entail by Major Charles Hamilton of Fairholm, recorded in 1777 (RT1/19, f.265), he names as his heirs, in order, his natural son, a cousin german (first cousin on father's side), another cousin german, his natural daughter, and then six other cousins. Remember that an heir of tailzie usually had to take the surname of the entailer along with the lands, and therefore might have to change his name.

10.25 There is an index to the Register of Tailzies between 1688, when the Register starts, and 1833. This index is a mixture of print and manuscript and lists the granters of the deeds, arranged chronologically under each surname letter. You order by the reference RT1 and the volume number given in the index; which also gives the folio number. The names of the heirs often appear well into a rather lengthy document.

10.26 A digest of the Register of Tailzies between 1688 and 1810, in the Historical Search Room, is of little use to the family historian as it omits the names of the heirs.

10.27 If you are looking for an entry in the Register of Tailzies after 1833, you should go to the Legal Search Room to consult a two-volume manuscript index, referenced RT3/1/1-2 and titled 'Register of Entails'. This indexes the period 1688-1938. Again, the arrangement is alphabetical by first letter of the surname only, then chronological. At the end of each entry, there is a volume and folio number: eg if the entry concludes '114-275', then you order RT1/114 and look up folio 275 therein. Since 1914, the Register contains only disentails.

Beneficium Inventarii

10.28 Until 1847, an heir who took over an ancestor's heritable property could be liable for all the ancestor's debts. However, by an Act of 1695, c.24, an heir who entered by the procedure 'cum beneficio inventarii' was liable only to the extent of the value of the heritable property, provided it was done within a year and a day of the ancestor's death. This procedure is recorded in the Register of Inventories of Heirs Entering Cum Beneficio Inventarii (RD20), which dates from 1696 to 1850. This register is not indexed. A list of the volumes in the Register and the dates they cover is in the RD catalogue. The name of a party is put in the margin at the start of each entry, but this may be the name of either the heir or of the ancestor. You will find in each 'inventory' the names of the heir and his deceased ancestor, sometimes the date of death, and an inventory of the heritable property and the income therefrom.

10.29 The lack of an index limits the usefulness of this record, but there is information in it. Heirs may be cousins. The heirs are not necessarily well-to-do. In 1826, James Davidson, labourer in the parish of Ardclach, was heir to his brother David Davidson, vintner in Nairn (RD20/14, f.153). The next entry in the same volume illustrates how far Scotsmen travelled – Robert Walkinshaw, 'at present in Mexico', was heir to his brother William Walkinshaw, captain in the service of the Honourable East India Company, who died at Ghazapore in the East Indies (RD20/14, f.156).

10.30 Another record which contains information about heirs who were liable for their ancestor's debts is the Register of Adjudications (see **14.62–64**).

Ultimus Haeres

10.31 Perhaps you are seeking an ancestor who was believed to have died without a known heir. In such a case, the Crown would be the ultimus haeres (last heir) and the heritable and moveable property of the deceased would have been paid into the Exchequer, any lands being sold or granted to a new owner. Fortune hunters should be warned that almost all ultimus haeres estates comprise small amounts of money and that such estates are usually distributed to people who have a moral claim, though not a legal one, such as a relative by marriage who cared for the deceased in his old age. Such claimants would petition for a share of the estate.

10.32 Obviously, you must know the name of the deceased and the approximate date of death.

10.33 Because of legal limitations in the past on those who might succeed on intestacy, the Ultimus Haeres records contain more genealogical information than you might expect. Such limitations were:

a. If a man died childless and intestate, but left a widow, she could claim only part of the estate.

b. An illegitimate person could be succeeded in both heritable and moveable property only by the offspring of his own body. Until 1836, if an illegitimate person had no children, he could not bequeath any property to anyone, unless he had received letters of legitimation from the Crown.

c. There was no succession to or through the mother in either heritable or moveable property, i.e. if a person died intestate and childless, with no relations on his father's side, but with relations on his mother's side including half brothers or sisters, they were excluded and all his property went to the Crown as ultimus haeres. (Since 1855 there has been gradual reform in this legal area.) Thus, many of the petitioners for a gift of an ultimus haeres estate were maternal relations of the deceased and their petitions contain much information about their families.

10.34 Ultimus Haeres records change dramatically in 1834.

Ultimus Haeres before 1834

10.35 Records before 1834 relate almost entirely to the granting of ultimus haeres property to petitioners. Such grants of moveable property were made under the Privy Seal (see **8.17**). Those up to 1584 will be found in the printed volumes of the *Register of the Privy Seal*, in which both the deceased and the recipient are indexed. Between 1585 and 1660, you must use the minute books (PS6) to search for such a grant. The originals are ordered by PS1 and the volume number. From 1660, there are two indexes, but only the index from 1782 identifies the gifts of ultimus haeres, indexing both the recipients and estates. Order by the reference PS3 and the volume number. The record of grants of heritable property exists only for the periods 1750-1761 and from 1831 and is unindexed: see the catalogue for C14.

10.36 Petitions for grants of ultimus haeres are preserved among the Exchequer records (E303). The accompanying papers usually include a report advising whether or not a grant should be made. These records are incomplete and unindexed. If you wish to investigate them, look at the list of E303 in the Exchequer catalogue. Some do give detailed family information, eg the papers in the case in 1797 of Lt Col John Rose, who died in Corsica, demonstrate his relationship to a number of people in

Relations of Lt Col John Rose, 1797 (E303/6).

the Nairn area, including a minister and a bailie, as well as a bricklayer in Glasgow and a book-keeper in Jamaica (E303/6).

Ultimus Haeres from 1834

10.37 The present procedure for dealing with ultimus haeres cases dates from 1834 and from then there are consistent records. These are in various series, which are explained in the catalogue (E851–870). There is no overall index, but each individual volume is indexed by name of the deceased person, giving the surname and forename only.

10.38 To search, firstly you want to check if the estate of someone you are researching did fall to the Crown. Look at the indexes in the Procedure Books (E851), which give a summary of proceedings relating to every case. Some of these books have two indexes (a separate one for illegitimates). Alternatively, from 1886 you can look at annual alphabetical lists (E869). Once you have established that there was an ultimus haeres case of interest to you, you can look it up in a relevant volume or file of the other series. Particularly useful are the Treasury Reports (E853) that repeat the claims of the petitioners and often include detailed family relationships and histories.

11

Owners of Land and Houses

11.1 The previous chapter concerned the transfer of heritable property when the owner died. The ownership, and transfer of ownership, of land and houses is of such importance that records of this are among the earliest to survive. The system of land-holding in Scotland was historically a feudal one. In a feudal system, all land is held of the Crown, either directly or through a subject-superior.

11.2 A grant of land was usually made in a charter by the Crown or subject-superior, but used to require a series of legal documents. You will find examples of the more important ones, which were often in Latin, in Peter Gouldesbrough's *Formulary of Old Scots Legal Documents* (Stair Society, 1985). The most important was the instrument of sasine, which until 1858 finalised all grants of land (including Crown ones) and was essential evidence that change of ownership had taken place. From 1617, such instruments were copied into the Register of Sasines, which is the primary source of information of ownership of property.

Register of Sasines

11.3 Whenever heritable property changed hands or was used as security for a loan, then the document narrating the legal transaction should have been copied ('recorded') into the Register of Sasines. The Register was founded in 1617, though there had been a trial run between 1599 and 1609 called the Secretary's Register, and continues to the present day, when it is being replaced by Registration of Title in a separate register. The Secretary's Register is now treated as part of the Register of Sasines and therefore will not be dealt with separately.

11.4 We talk of the Register of Sasines, but in fact there are several registers of sasines. The Secretary's Register was kept in various divisions of the country, 1599-1609. Between 1617 and 1868, there was a General Register of Sasines, in which could be recorded documents relating to property in any part of Scotland, and Particular Registers of Sasines (PRS), each for a particular area of the country. Since then, there has been a separate division of the Register for each county. There were separate registers for property in the royal burghs (see **11.16-18**).

11.5 The Register of Sasines is particularly useful to genealogists, both because fathers often made gifts of land to their children, and because a document narrating the sale or mortgage of lands may tell you the designation of the granter when he acquired the lands. Therefore you can trace in the Register the development both of families and individuals. Documents therein often refer back to earlier transactions and thus may name persons who died prior to the date of the document.

11.6 From 1781, the Register of Sasines is indexed and easy to search. A growing number of the original registers can be seen instantly on 'Virtual Volumes' in the search rooms. Before 1781 the Register is only partly indexed, but much has been imaged and is on 'Virtual Volumes'.

Register of Sasines 1617-1780

11.7 First, you should know in which part of Scotland your ancestor may have owned land. Unless the property lies within a royal burgh, you should search the relevant Particular Register. The following table gives the modern county and the equivalent Particular Register and says whether a pre-1781 index exists. The indexes marked with an asterisk have been published and should be available through a library. They will be made searchable electronically in 2010.

County	Particular Register of Sasines	Indexes
Aberdeen	Aberdeen till 1660 (RS4–5)	1599–1660★
	Aberdeen and Kincardine from 1661 (RS8)	
Angus (Forfar)	Forfar (RS33–35)	1620–1700★
		1701–1780
Argyll	Argyll etc (RS9–10)	1617–1780★
Ayr	Ayr etc (RS11–14)	1599–1660★
Banff	Banff (RS15–17)	1600–1780★
Berwick	Berwick etc (RS18–19)	1617–1780★
Bute	Argyll etc (RS9–10)	1617–1780★
Caithness	Inverness till 1644 (RS36–37)	1606–1780★
	Caithness from 1646 (RS20–21)	

Clackmannan	Stirling etc (RS58-59)	None
Dumfries	Dumfries etc (RS22-23)	1617-1780★
Dunbarton	Argyll etc (RS9-10)	1617-1780★
East Lothian		
(Haddington)	Edinburgh etc (RS24-27)	1599-1700★
		1741-1780
Edinburgh City	Edinburgh etc (RS24-27)	1599-1700★
		1741-1780
Fife	Fife and Kinross till 1685	1603-1660★
	Fife from 1685 (RS30-32)	
Glasgow City	Renfrew and Glasgow (RS53-54)	None
Inverness	Inverness etc (RS36-38)	1606-1780★
Kincardine	Kincardine till 1657	1600-1657★
	Aberdeen and Kincardine	
	from 1661 (RS6-8)	
Kinross	Fife and Kinross till 1685	1603-1660★
	Kinross from 1688 (RS30-31, 39)	
Kirkcudbright	Dumfries etc (RS22-23)	1617-1780★
Lanark	Lanark (RS40-42)	1618-1780★
Midlothian		
(Edinburgh)	Edinburgh etc (RS24-27)	1599-1700★
		1741-1780
Moray		
(Elgin)	Elgin and Nairn (RS28-29)	1617-1780★
Nairn	Elgin and Nairn (RS28-29)	1617-1780★
Orkney	Orkney and Shetland (RS43-47)	1617-1660
Peebles	Roxburgh etc (RS55-57)	None
Perth	Perth (RS48-52)	1601-1609
	Stirling etc (RS58-59)	None
Renfrew	Renfrew and Glasgow (RS53-54)	None
Ross and		
Cromarty	Inverness etc (RS36-38)	1606-1780★
Roxburgh	Roxburgh etc (RS55-57)	None
Selkirk	Roxburgh etc (RS55-57)	None
Shetland	Orkney and Shetland (RS43-47)	1617-1660
Stirling	Stirling etc (RS58-59)	None
Sutherland	Inverness etc (RS36-38)	1606-1780★
West Lothian		
(Linlithgow)	Edinburgh etc (RS24-27)	1599-1700★
		1700-1780
Wigtown	Wigtown (RS60-61)	None

11.8   Determine which Particular Register is the one likely to include your ancestor, and look up the relevant index. The indexes vary in style, but will give the volume and initial folio for each document in which your ancestor appears. All parties who are mentioned as having or having had a heritable right (i.e. not tenants) in the property should be indexed, not just the main parties in the transaction. In some indexes, the volume will be expressed in roman numerals and you will have to convert that into its arabic form. You order by the RS reference number and the volume number, eg RS29/7. Because most of the indexes were compiled before the reference number system was introduced, the RS reference number will not be in the index, but it is usually noted at the start. If in doubt check the RS catalogue.

11.9   If there is no index for that Particular Register or period, then look at the RS catalogue for the minute books of that Register. The starting dates of these minute books vary considerably. If there is a minute book for the relevant period, order it out by its call number like any other document. The contents of the books are arranged chronologically by the date of recording. Each minute also states the names of the main parties and lands, and the relevant folios in the volume of the Register. The volume number may not be apparent and should be ascertained, along with its call number, by its dates, from the catalogue.

11.10   If there is no minute book or index, you have to browse through the volumes of the Register itself, which can be a formidable task.

11.11   As the majority of documents in the Register are instruments of sasine, you should familiarise yourself with the structure of this type of deed. Gouldesbrough's *Formulary* contains examples in Latin with English translations. If you are lucky, the copy in the Register will start with an introduction which will tell you to whom the lands were granted, or his name will appear in the margin. In the instrument itself, the first name to be mentioned should be either the grantee or his legal agent. The granter may also have a legal agent (called a 'bailie'). In other words, you must read the document carefully to disentangle who is doing what. In genealogical terms, an added advantage is that witnesses were often relations of the parties. There are two lists of witnesses in an instrument of sasine, one near the end and one about two-thirds through the document at the end of what was known as the precept of sasine.

11.12   As well as searching for your ancestor in the Particular Register for the area in which he owned land, you should also look in the General Register of Sasines, which is indexed up to 1735. From 1736 to 1780 you have to use the minute books, which you will find listed in the catalogue under the reference RS62.

Register of Sasines after 1780

11.13 Go to a Historical Search Room computer and click on the 'RAC' search tool icon. This tool allows searching of the digitised Sasine indexes and the related Abridgements and their indexes. The Abridgements contain summaries of all the documents recorded in the Register of Sasines from 1781, chronologically within counties. They are indexed by persons from 1781 to the present and by places from 1781 to 1830 and from 1872 to the present. The original paper Abridgements were replaced by the electronic version in 2007, and are not on open access.

11.14 From the drop-down list select a year, and the county in which your ancestor may have owned land. It is possible to extend the year range by +5 or +10 years, but this may make the search slower. Next fill in the surname and forename text boxes, and then click on the 'Search Index of People' button. The system will display a list of any entries it finds. The numbers shown are the year/s and running numbers of the summaries in the Abridgements. You can either view the Abridgement summary, or view an image of the original Abridgement. The summary will be headed by a date and then will tell you, among other things, the names and designations of the new and previous owners and a description of the property. All parties are indexed. If your ancestor's name is a common one and you know the name of the property he owned, you might wish to search by place as well as by person to see if any of the summary numbers coincide.

11.15 The Abridgement summary may give you enough information, but if you wish to study the full text of the document in the Register of Sasines, note the numbers at the end of the summary. A list of the call numbers from the RS catalogue is displayed in the search rooms. To order the original Sasine use the Electronic Ordering System (EOS), or view digital images in Virtual Volumes. The volumes of the General Register and of the Particular Registers of Sasines for all counties, 1781-1869, are due for completion in 2009. Edinburgh is mostly covered from 1781 to date. Many other counties have been digitised for the years 1869-1934 and 1973-1989, and all counties from April 1989 onwards.

	on Trust Estate of, North College Street, Elgin, 22/48)		✓	✓		
☐	1877-06-21, (No.), 297, BENTON, John, BENTON John, College Street, Elgin, 22/50)		✓	✓		
☐	1877-06-21, (No.), 297, BENTON, John, BENTON John, Collie Street, Elgin, 22/50)		✓	✓		
☐	1877-06-21, (No.), 297, BENTON, John, BENTON John, Elgin College of, 22/50)		✓	✓		
☐	1877-06-21, (No.), 297, BENTON, John, BENTON John, Moy Manse, 22/50)		✓	✓		
☐	1877-06-21, (No.), 297, McKAY, James Thompson, McKAY James Thompson, College Street, Elgin, 22/50)		✓	✓		
	1877-06-21, (No.), 297, McKAY, James Thompson, McKAY James Thompson, Collie Street, Elgin.		✓	✓		

(297)   Jun. 21. 1877.

Disp. by JOHN BENTON, Farmer, Sheriffhaugh, Banffshire, to James Thompson Mackay, Jeweller in Elgin,—of Piece of ground, with Dwelling House thereon, partly converted into a Shop, bounded on the north by COLLEGE STREET and on the west by and extending 56 Feet along COLLIE STREET, being part of the Manse called the MOY MANSE, with Houses, &c. thereof, in the COLLEGE of ELGIN and Regality of Spynie. Dated May 23, 1877; with Warrant of Registration thereon, on behalf of said Grantee.   22. 50.

(298)   Jun. 22. 1877.

Bond for £130, and *Disp.* in security, by DAVID HISLOP, Mason, residing at Pilmuir near Forres, to Felix Calvert Mackenzie, Solicitor in Forres,—of Piece of ground (1 Rood 5 perches and 16½ yards), marked as No. 26 on Plan, bounded on the south by the Public or Commutation Road from Forres to Balnageith, on the north by a proposed new Street and on the east by a proposed new Road, forming part of the land of PILMUIR, in Parish of Forres, particularly described in Extract Decr. of Sp. Serv. in favor of Robert Donald Grant, recorded in this Register 14th Apr. 1871. Dated Nov. 18, 1876; with Warrant of Registration thereon, on behalf of said Felix Calvert Mackenzie.   22. 51.

RAC Search Tool screen and related Sasine Abridgement for Elgin and Forres, 1877 (see **10.13–15**).

Work is progressing on other years. If the number at the top or end of the summary is preceded by the letters GR, then the document will be in the General Register of Sasines (RS3); if by the letters PR, then it will be in the Particular Register of Sasines which includes that county; and if it is preceded by no letters, then it will be in one of the post-1868 county divisions of the Register. As usual the first number is the volume number, and the second number the folio number, and you order by the RS number and the volume number. For example, a Clackmannan abridgement dated 'Dec. 28, 1802' ends 'PR.37.333'. The Particular Register of Sasines for Stirling and Clackmannan is RS59 and you order out RS59/37. An Elgin and Forres abridgement in 1877 (see illustration) ends with the reference '22.50'. You find from the list in the RS catalogue that the county call number is RS109 and order out RS109/22.

Burgh Registers of Sasines

11.16 Each royal burgh was entitled to have its own burgh register of sasines. If your ancestor owned property in a royal burgh, then the record of that ownership will probably not be in the General or a Particular Register of Sasines, though it is wise to check them as well as the burgh register. Remember that many of these burghs lay within much smaller boundaries than they do today. The National Archives of Scotland holds the registers of sasines of the burghs of Aberdeen#, Annan*, Anstruther Wester*, Arbroath*, Auchtermuchty*, Ayr#, Banff*, Brechin*, Burntisland*, Crail*, Cullen*, Culross*, Cupar*, Dingwall*, Dornoch, Dumbarton*, Dumfries, Dunbar#, Dundee#, Dunfermline#, Dysart*, Earlsferry*, Edinburgh*#, Elgin*, Falkland#, Forfar*#, Forres*, Fortrose*, Haddington*, Hawick, Inverbervie*#, Inverkeithing*, Inverness#, Inverurie*, Irvine#, Jedburgh#, Kinghorn*, Kintore*, Kirkcaldy*, Kirkcudbright, Kirkwall*, Lanark*, Lauder*, Linlithgow*, Lochmaben*#, Montrose*, Nairn*#, Newburgh*, New Galloway, North Berwick*, Paisley*, Peebles*, Perth*, Pittenweem*, Queensferry*#, Renfrew*, Rothesay*, Rutherglen*#, St Andrews*, Sanquhar*, Selkirk*, Stirling, Stranraer*, Tain*, Whithorn*, Wigtown*. The Glasgow burgh register and the Aberdeen and Dundee pre-1809 registers are kept by Glasgow City Archives, Aberdeen City Archives and City of Dundee Archive and Record Centre respectively (addresses in Appendix A).

11.17 The start dates of the Burgh Registers of Sasines held by the NAS vary tremendously from 1602 (Dysart) to 1881 (Forres). They were discontinued at various dates between 1926 and 1963, and thereafter all properties appear in the General Register of Sasines.

The burgh registers marked with an asterisk in **11.16** have typescript indexes, but no index starts before 1809 (except Rutherglen, which covers 1631-1777), and they index only those who are being granted ownership. If your ancestor lived in one of the asterisked burghs after 1809, look up the relevant index. Each index entry gives a volume and folio number, but to find the call number, you have to consult the catalogue (B), eg in the index to the Burgh Register of Sasines of Whithorn, there is an entry for Peter Houl, soldier in 7th Hussars, in 1815. The volume is 1, the folio 100, and you order out B71/2/1 and look up folio 100. As Whithorn, like most burghs, has more than one series of its Register of Sasines, you must make certain by checking the date that you are ordering the volume from the correct series.

The burgh registers marked # are covered by a separate series of indexes in NAS (GD1/1409). Overall they cover the years 1870-1946, but the years vary between burghs. The catalogue mentions the relevant index volumes. The indexes were created by the long-established record search company, Messrs Millar & Bryce.

11.18 To search an unindexed Burgh Register of Sasines look up the introduction to the Burgh catalogue (B), find the number that relates to that particular burgh (eg Culross is B12), and look up the pages under that number to find the dates of that Burgh Register. Check to see if there is an index or minute book, which you may consult. If there is not, you will have to go directly to a volume of the Burgh Register of Sasines, some of which have a contents list or index in the volume.

Notarial Protocol Books

11.19 If you are seeking an ancestor who owned heritable property before the setting up of the Register of Sasines in 1617 or before the start of the burgh registers of sasines, or if you cannot find an entry in the Register of Sasines before 1660, you might investigate the Notarial Protocol books. These were record books kept by notaries, who were lawyers officially authorised to draw up certain legal documents, including instruments of sasine. Their books contain copies or notes of the documents they compiled. Not all these books were kept to the standard one might expect in a public register.

11.20 If your ancestor owned property in a royal burgh (see **11.16**), look up the B catalogue at the list of records under the name of that burgh to see if they include any protocol books (not all do). There you will find the reference number and covering dates of each protocol book. A handful are indexed, but most are not, and therefore you must simply order out the book which covers the approximate date and browse through it.

11.21 If your ancestor owned property anywhere else, go to the catalogue of Notarial records (NP). This includes a topographical guide, mainly under the names of counties, which will provide you with the reference numbers of the books of notaries who worked in different parts of Scotland: eg if you look up Shetland, you will find only one notary who operated there between 1576 and 1615, the reference number of his protocol book being NP1/36. None of these books is indexed, but the catalogue notes those that have been printed by the Scottish Record Society and those for which there are abstracts. These abstracts are referenced RH2/1/16-26. You may find the abstracts and printed versions, both of which are translated into English, easier to read than the originals, and the printed books are indexed.

Crown Grants of Land

11.22 If you think your ancestor was granted lands by a Crown charter, there are three other records you should examine – those of the Great Seal, Privy Seal and Signatures. The copies of charters in the Register of the Privy Seal and the Signatures were, in effect, drafts of those in the Great Seal Register. The Signatures have the advantage that they are in English while the Great and Privy Seal records are in Latin. We suggest that you search first in the Great Seal Register, and then search in the Privy Seal Register or Signatures if the charter is not in the Great Seal Register or you require the English version in the Signatures.

Great Seal

11.23 The record of the charters issued under the Great Seal dates from 1314 and is published up to 1668 in the eleven volumes of the *Register of the Great Seal of Scotland* (or *Registrum Magni Sigilli Regum Scotorum,* or RMS for short). As volume 1 of the RMS was compiled from a variety of sources and few people are likely to trace their ancestry back to the fourteenth century, the following comments relate to the record from 1424, when volume 2 of the RMS starts.

11.24 Each volume of the RMS is indexed. The charters (in summary form) and indexes are in Latin until 1651. If you are looking for a Crown charter to your ancestor up to 1668, look up the 'Index Nominum' in the volume of the RMS which covers the likely date. In these indexes up to 1651, forenames are in Latin or are abbreviated and designations are in Latin. Each entry in the index is followed by a number – this is the running number of the summaries in the volume. These summaries are quite detailed, but if you want to see the original, take note of the numbers at the end of the summary, the roman number being the volume number and the arabic the running number (not the folio number) of the charters in the original record.

11.25 If the roman number is preceded by the letters 'PR' (which stands for 'Paper Register') order out by the reference C3 and the volume number (converted into arabic). Otherwise, the call reference is C2 and the volume number, but, as many of the volumes are in two bulky parts, you should look at the Chancery catalogue under C2 to check which part you should order. For example, in the RMS, volume 4, you have found an entry concerning a family named Leslie, and at the end of the entry you read 'xxxiv.582'. If you look in the catalogue, you find that volume 34 is in two parts and no.582 is in the second part. If you order out C2/34 you may receive both parts.

11.26 If you are seeking your ancestor in this record from 1668, look at the several typed indexes to the various series of Great Seal records. The indexes which deal with grants of lands are a 4-volume index to the Register of the Great Seal itself, 1668-1919, an index to the Paper Register, 1668-1852, and an index to the Principality Register, 1716-1913. The introductory notes to these indexes explain the differences between the records. Each index gives the name and designation of the grantee, the lands granted, the date, and the volume and either folio or running number of the charter in that volume. If the charter is in the Great Seal Register, order by C2, the volume number and the part number if the volume is in two parts (the catalogue will tell you). If it is in the Paper Register, order by C3 and the volume number. If it is in the Principality Register, check the introduction to the index to find out the call number (mostly C16) and order by that and the volume number. The Paper Register continues after 1852 but contains no further grants of land.

Privy Seal

11.27 How to search the Privy Seal has been described in **7.17**. Use the printed and indexed *Register of the Privy Seal of Scotland* up to 1584, and the minute books thereafter. The call number up to 1660 is PS1 and the volume number. After 1660, the call number of the 'Latin Register' in which grants of land are recorded is PS2 and the volume number. The only indexes to PS2 are a rather variable set of manuscript indexes between 1660 and 1705, which you order out by PS7/2.

Signatures

11.28 The surviving Signatures date from 1607 to 1847. There is a 2-volume index which tells you the name of the grantee, the lands, the date, and the box and running number or volume and folio number of the signatures. Order by SIG1 and the box and running number or SIG2 and the volume number.

Original Charters and Other Writs

11.29 If you have been unable to find a grant of land to your ancestor in the Crown records or registers of sasines or protocol books, you should investigate original documents, particularly before 1660. After that date, the Register of Sasines is complete enough to be reliable.

11.30 The main source for original legal documents in the NAS is the Gifts and Deposits series (see **7.20-21**). Check the catalogues of GDs which concern likely families or relevant parts of Scotland. A few GDs include cartularies, which list grants given by subject-superiors.

11.31 Other series of original documents may be found in the inventories of the RH class of records. Particularly useful are RH9/15, which contains miscellaneous writs of lands in Orkney and Shetland, arranged by place-names, and RH6-8, which contain miscellaneous charters and other writs.

11.32 The writs in RH6 date between 1142 and 1600. They are calendared in 15 volumes ('Calendar of Charters', on the open shelves) and indexed in 8 volumes. All parties, including witnesses, are indexed. The index gives each personal name and designation and the running number in the calendar. RH6 has one running number throughout. The entry in the calendar may be enough for you and it is in English, but if you wish to see the original, order by RH6 and the running number.

11.33 The writs in RH7 date from 1601 to 1830. As they are not individually listed, there is no easy way of identifying the persons involved in them, but, as they are arranged in strict chronological order, if you are looking for a writ of a particular date, you can order out the box which includes writs for that year by the reference RH7 and the box number you find in the catalogue.

11.34 The writs in RH8 are dated between 1700 and 1800 and are arranged by name of the grantee. There is a two-volume inventory. If you wish to see a document, order by RH8 and the running number in the margin of the inventory.

Valuation Rolls

11.35 Information about the ownership and sometimes tenancy of land and houses was often gathered because of taxes on the value of such properties. From 1855, the Valuation Rolls (VR) themselves supply this information consistently for the whole of Scotland. Before that date, records of such information for tax purposes are occasional.

Valuation Rolls before 1855

11.36 Valuation rolls before 1855 are sporadic and inconsistent. As the purpose of such a record was to record the value of lands, in some instances that is all that is given and the names of proprietors and occupiers are simply omitted. Still, however imperfect for your purposes these records are, you may wish to take pot luck with them. If you do find the name of a proprietor you are seeking, you may be led on to search a more productive record, such as the Register of Sasines or a GD collection.

11.37 Firstly, look in the catalogue of Exchequer records (E) for E106. Here are listed valuation rolls, arranged by counties and dated variously between 1643 and 1835. Published versions are noted. If you order out a roll, you will discover that it is arranged by parishes. Sometimes no personal names are given; sometimes only the biggest landowners are named, eg 'Robert Arbuthnot of Katerlane for himselff and remnant heritors' (E106/1/2); but occasionally tenants are named in the description of lands, eg 'That part of Old Mains posest by Jas Forsyth' (E106/14/2). *A Directory of Land Ownership in Scotland c.1770* by Lorretta R Timperley (Scottish Record Society) is largely based on these valuation rolls for 1771 and is indexed.

11.38 Next, if you are interested in early nineteenth century valuation rolls, look at the Inland Revenue catalogue (IRS). It lists land tax or valuation rolls for the following counties and dates before 1855. Within counties, the arrangement is by parishes.

> Aberdeen, 1847-57 (IRS4/1)
>
> Ayr, c1837-1839 (IRS4/2)
>
> Banff, 1836-1837 (IRS4/3)
>
> Dumfries, 1827 (IRS4/S)
>
> Fife, 1837 (IRS4/7)
>
> Lanark, 1837-41 (IRS3/11) and 1846-60 (IRS4/8)
>
> Midlothian and Edinburgh City, 1814, 1837-71 (IRS4/9)
>
> Roxburgh, 1842 (IRS4/12)
>
> Stirling, 1831 (IRS4/14)

Again, the information supplied varies. You will probably be given the names of the proprietors or most of them. They may be listed alphabetically, showing the parishes in which they owned land. If you are lucky, you may find the names not only of proprietors, but also of tenants who paid land tax. Watch out for later annotations, of unspecified date, which may confuse the information.

11.39 There are some valuation rolls among the Gifts and Deposits. Many can be located using the NAS's electronic catalogue. The few GD collections not yet on this system will require more hunting.

11.40 If your ancestor owned property in a royal burgh, then these valuation rolls will not be useful. A separate collection of land tax was made within each royal burgh from the inhabitants thereof. Of the royal burgh records at present within the NAS, only Dunbar, Inverkeithing, Jedburgh, Linlithgow, North Berwick and Peebles include cess or stent rolls which list the inhabitants liable to pay tax, before 1855. These records sometimes state the trade of the inhabitant, but rarely the property owned. Look them up in the B catalogue to find the dates covered and the reference number.

11.41 Similar valuations were made of each parish by the heritors and some survive in the Heritors Records (HR). The heritors were the landowners in each parish who until 1925 were responsible for the maintenance of church, manse, school and (until 1845) the poor of the parish. The money to pay for these outlays was raised from the landowners themselves by assessment on the value of their lands. Records of such assessments survive for a minority of parishes and are mainly nineteenth century. The heritors are always named in them, their lands not always. If you know the name of the parish in which your ancestor may have owned land, look it up in the index of parishes, which is part of the HR catalogue. The index will supply the reference number of the parish, eg Dunbar is HR69. You then look in the catalogue at the list of records under that reference number for any assessment rolls or book or lists. (For example, Dunbar has assessment rolls between 1773 and 1904 – HR69/10/4). As landowners could reclaim from their tenants half of the sum they paid towards poor relief, these assessment rolls very occasionally include the names of tenants with or without the names of their farms. Lands in a royal burgh were usually assessed and paid in a block, without naming the property owners.

11.42 The names of property owners may also be found in the tax records referenced E326 and 327, discussed in **16.5-11**. If your ancestor owned or occupied a property in Midlothian, including Edinburgh, between 1803 and 1812, you should find him in the Property Tax records (E327/78-121) or Small House or Cottage Tax records (E327/122-127).

Valuation Rolls since 1855

11.43 The Lands Valuation (Scotland) Act 1854 established a uniform valuation of lands and houses throughout Scotland. Separate valuation rolls were to be compiled annually for every burgh and county, listing every house or piece of ground, along with the names of the proprietor, tenant and occupier, and its value. Occupations are frequently, but not always, included. A more important proviso is that the occupiers of property which was let at less than £4 per year did not need to be named. With that exception, if your ancestor owned or occupied property in Scotland since 1855, their name should appear in the Valuation Rolls although only the heads of households would be named. Each roll runs from Whitsunday of one year (15 May) to Whitsunday of the next, effectively a financial year, so that the first roll is for 1855-56.

11.44 The National Archives of Scotland (NAS) holds the most complete set of Valuation Rolls (VRs) for Scotland. All of the rolls from 1855-56 to 1915-16 have been digitised and are available on Virtual Volumes in the search rooms of the NAS. Digital images of VRs for 1916-17 to 1957-58 are due to become available during 2009-2010.

11.45 An electronic index is now available in the NAS search rooms for the VRs for the inter-census years, i.e. 1855-56, 1865-66, 1875-76, 1885-86, 1895-96, 1905-06 and 1915-16. This index can be searched one year at a time according to person, group or place. The index entry gives you the description and situation of a property, and the names of its proprietor(s), tenant(s) and occupier(s). The information on each person, where given, will include title, first name and surname. No occupations are shown in the index but this information may be included in the record. A group search allows you to search for companies, organisations, authorities and groups of individuals such as trustees or representatives. A place search allows you to search across whole rolls for a city or burgh; particular streets; settlements large and small, which do not have burgh status; and property types such as farms, flats, churches, coffee houses or factories.

For VRs which have not been included in the index, use the NAS online catalogue to find the list of VRs for the burgh or county in which you think your ancestor owned or occupied property. The VRs are arranged alphabetically by burgh and then by the counties and cities, so Airdrie Burgh is VR1 and Wigtown County is VR123. The catalogue will tell you if the volume you want to consult has been digitised or not. Some rolls contain indexes of streets and place-names – these are noted in the catalogue. Within the annual volume for a county, the arrangement may be alphabetical by parishes. Ayr County is divided into Carrick, Cunningham and Kyle, but a list of parishes in each of these districts is placed at the start of the list of Ayr County rolls. Lanark County is divided into Upper, Middle and Lower wards.

11.47 Searching for a particular person, even if you know the likely address, can be painstaking. A good starting point is to check the electronic index for the nearest inter-census year, as you may find key information on parishes, wards or streets which you can then apply to the unindexed but digitised volume. If you are searching in a well-populated part of the country, there may be several volumes for each year through which you have to search. The arrangement within volumes may not always seem logical and is not necessarily consistent year-by-year. The entries for one street will often be dispersed. It is not uncommon for street numbers or names to have been changed over the years.

11.48 Edinburgh and Glasgow VRs are particularly awkward to search. Glasgow, up to 1909, is divided into the civil parishes of Glasgow, Govan and Barony. An index of streets in 1875-6 is available in the Historical Search Room. As it shows the parish each street is in, it can be used for other years to identify the volume you should order out. Edinburgh is divided by parishes up to 1895, and thereafter by wards. A preliminary study of nineteenth century large-scale Ordnance Survey maps and city directories is recommended, perhaps in combination with a visit to the Edinburgh Room in the Edinburgh Central Library. The Edinburgh Valuation Rolls since 1912 have street indexes which are available in the NAS Legal Search Room. The annual Post Office Directories for Edinburgh and Glasgow often included a note of the ward number in their streets index. You may wish to consult local copies before visiting NAS, or use the NAS library copies.

11.49 The Local Government Finance Act 1988 introduced the Community Charge for domestic ratepayers. The new tax replaced the system described in paragraphs **11.43–11.48** and the Valuation Rolls that continue after 1 April 1989 list only those premises which are liable for non-domestic rates. They are therefore of little or no use to family historians.

Community Charge Registers 1989 to 1993

11.50 The Community Charge for domestic ratepayers was introduced into Scotland on 1 April 1989. It was a tax on individuals rather than on property, which is why it was soon nicknamed the 'Poll Tax'. All adults aged 18 or over had to pay unless they were exempt (eg because they were in prison).

11.51 NAS holds microfiche copies of all the Community Charge Registers for Scotland, but these are closed for 30 years. The registers are arranged by region, and within that by district, then ward, then street. If your ancestor was eligible to pay the Community Charge, he will be listed at the address where he was registered, together with his date of birth. Full-time students living away from home were registered at their study address rather than at their parents' address. The registers occasionally give alternative correspondence addresses for individuals, and sometimes specify whether someone was the property's owner or a tenant.

11.52 The Community Charge lasted until 1993, when the Local Government Finance Act 1992 replaced it with a tax based on property value: the Council Tax. NAS holds microfiche copies of the Council Tax valuation lists, but these are not useful for family history because they do not list residents or owners of the properties – just addresses and Council Tax valuation bands.

Electors

11.53 As, until 1918, ownership of heritable property above a certain value was a qualification for the right to vote in a parliamentary election, your land-owning ancestor may appear in the records described in **30.2-6**.

Insured property owners

11.54 From 1720 property owners in the liberties of Edinburgh were able to benefit from a mutual fire insurance scheme, which in 1728 formally became the Edinburgh Friendly Fire Insurance Company. Those who paid premiums effectively had rights to dividends on the profits of the company, which could be transferred to successive owners and, if personal circumstances changed, resigned in the company's favour.

11.55 The bonds of resignation, and also some bonds by which owners undertook to pay their premiums, were recorded in the company's registers, 1728-1840 (B22/18/1-10). For each insured property the bond mentions the names of the owners, who may or may not have been related. For example, a discharge and renunciation dated 1769, refers to a policy on a tenement on the High Street taken out in 1727 by Barbara Brown, relict of William Johnston, skinner burgess of Edinburgh, from which we learn the names of her sons John, also a skinner, and Thomas, a shipmaster in Rotterdam, Thomas's son William, and two later owners (B22/18/7, f.117). The insured property is also described, usually in relation to adjacent properties, whose owners and tenants may also be mentioned. The insurance records themselves are not indexed, but the index of names published in James Gilhooley, *The Edinburgh Recorder 1720-1840* (privately printed, 1990), provides the dates of the renunciations, which can then be found in chronological order in the relevant register in B22/18.

⚭12⚭
Tenants and Crofters

12.1 The chances are that your ancestors were tenants rather than owners of where they stayed. Since 1855, the Valuation Rolls, described in 11.35 onwards, record most, though not all, tenants in Scotland and you will look for your more recent ancestors in that record. Unfortunately, before 1855, no consistent record was kept of tenancies. Also, records that were kept and that have survived are largely of tenancies of farms. Records of ownership of property, described in Chapter 11, often contain incidental references to tenancies, sometimes identifying a piece of land by the name of its tenant. Between 1832 and 1918, registers of voters state if the voter was a tenant and of what property (see Chapter 30). This chapter will deal with other records which you might examine if your ancestor was a tenant, especially a tenant-farmer. Remember that many people, such as farm workers, would be neither tenant nor owner of where they stayed.

Rentals and Tacks

12.2 A tenancy was agreed by a document known as a tack (lease), but there was no register of tacks, and, after a tenancy had run its course, no legal necessity to preserve the tack. However, some have survived in private papers, as have rentals, in which many landlords, particularly big landowners, listed their tenanted properties. Rentals, like the older valuation rolls, may sometimes just name the lands and not the occupiers, and, though they generally name tenants, these will only be the heads of household and will commonly omit any designation.

12.3 Rentals and tacks are records of private individuals. You need to know which family owned the property of which your ancestor may have been a tenant, and then to find out if the records of that family have survived. This leads us again to the GDs, described in **7.20-21**. In most of the larger GDs, there will be a separate section for estate papers, which should include any records of tenancies. The Breadalbane papers (GD112) have a particularly good series of rentals and tacks for north Perthshire and part of Argyll dating from the sixteenth century.

12.4 If the GDs fail you, you might wish to check for rentals in certain public records.

12.5 The Commissioners of Crown Estates (CR) also held records of Glenlivet and Fochabers. These two estates belonged to the Duke of Gordon, but fell to the Crown in lieu of death duties in 1937. Look in the CR catalogue under CR6 and CR8. There are rentals between 1770 and 1890. As the Duke of Gordon's own papers are also in the NAS (GD44), you have a fair chance of finding a reference to an ancestor who was a Gordon tenant.

12.6 Estates forfeited because of their owners' support for the Jacobite cause in 1745 were administered by the Barons of Exchequer and records of that administration are preserved in the Exchequer records. To see if these estates include one relevant to your research, look at the catalogue of the Forfeited Estates papers (E700-788), at the contents list under 'Particular Management' or the location list under county and parish. There are rentals of all the estates (with contents lists by name of the forfeited owners) for the period 1747-76 under the reference E707 and rentals of particular estates under the reference number for that estate. These rentals include some 'judicial rentals' which are records of statements by tenants about their tenancies and which supply slightly more information than an ordinary rental. There is also a published list of tenants of farms on some of these estates in 1755 in *Statistics of the Annexed Estates.*

12.7 There are also some rentals in the RH series. Look in the catalogue for RH9, which lists most of these miscellaneous rentals, and for RH11, which lists a few rentals among local court records.

12.8 Rentals provide an example of how similar records can be found in a variety of record groups. For instance, say your ancestors were tenants on the estate of Callendar near Falkirk in the eighteenth century. You will find rentals dated 1717 in the RH series (RH11/10/1), dated 1748 in the Forfeited Estates paper (E761/1/3), and dated 1785-91 in the Forbes of Callendar muniments (GD171/2100), now transferred to Falkirk Council Archives (address in Appendix A).

12.9   Estate records often include plans of the estate, on which the names of tenant might be annotated on their piece of land. Such plans in the NAS are in the Register House Plans series (RHP), described in **23.3**. Search the electronic catalogue for the name of the farm itself, or for the parish in which the relevant estate, farm or other property lay.

12.10   Tenants at the end of the eighteenth century may be found in the tax record discussed in **16.5-9**, including a useful record of tenant-farmers in the record of taxes on work-horses (E326/10).

Tenants in Trouble

12.11   Records of some tenants have survived because they failed to pay their rent or refused to leave at the end of their tenancy when the landlord wished to re-acquire the property. The landlord might then pursue the tenant in a court of law. Until 1747, this would be most likely a local court (see Chapter 14) which might well be the landlord's own court. After 1747, the court would be a sheriff or burgh court (see **14.39-46** and **14.51**). The records of such cases are generally intermingled with those of other court cases, are not indexed and therefore may require a lot of searching. Separate records of such cases in the sheriff courts exist only from the later nineteenth century, when information about tenancies is more easily obtained from the Valuation Rolls. However, you may wish to investigate these records.

12.12   Look in the contents list of the catalogue of the relevant sheriff court for 'Register of Sequestrations for Rent'. If there is no such entry, look up 'Register of Sequestrations', as that may include sequestrations for rent. These records most commonly start in 1867, but some start later, while Cupar (SC20/11) starts in 1839. As a separate entity, records of cases of removal of tenants only occur in the twentieth century – look for 'Summary Removing Court Books' in the catalogue – except for the Dundee court where they start in 1885 (SC45/10).

Crofters

12.13   Crofters are a class of agricultural tenant, for the most part in the Highlands and Islands. Records about crofters postdate the Valuation Rolls, but may provide a record of low-rent tenants omitted from the Valuation Rolls. References to people who lived or worked on the land might appear in the files of the Department of Agriculture and Fisheries

```
                          Police  Station,
                   BARRA.  18th July, 1908.


Sir,
              SQUATTERS   ON   VATERSAY.
           ───────────────────────────

           I beg to report that after visiting the Island of
Sandray, as separately reported, I proceeded from there
on this date to Vatersay Island, and found in all 32
Squatter's huts, situated as follows:-

      22 around head of Vatersay bay, immediately below
Vatersay house occupied by Mr Macdonald, Farmer; 4 at
Eorisdale; 3 at Aoidh; and 3 at Caolis.

           Accompanied by P.C. Macdonald, I visited each of
these and found them occupied as follows:-

    1.         Mary Campbell or Campbell, wife of Duncan Campbell,
           from Kentangaval, Barra- now undergoing sentence
           of 2 months imprisonment for Breach of Interdict,
           and their three sons, Neil, 19 years; Alexander,
           18 years; and Michael, 12 years.

               She told me her husband went there in the Autumn
           of 1906, erected the wooden hut in which I found her,
           and cultivated following spring about an acre of land
           on which he planted potatoes.   This piece of land is
           now under corn, and about another acre cultivated last
           spring and now under potatoes.   She also told me she
           has a pet lamb and 2 cows now grazing on Vatersay.

    2.         Mary Ann Campbell or Sinclair, wife of John
           Sinclair, fisherman, from Mingulay- now undergoing
           sentence of 2 months imprisonment for Breach of
           Interdict, and their 4 children, Andrew, 5 years;
           Peter, 4 years; Allan Joseph, 2 years; and Mary,
           11 months.
```

Report on Vatersay land raiders, 1908 (AF67/137).

and it may be worth investigating the AF files if your ancestor fell into this category.

12.14 The records of the Royal Commission on the Highlands and Islands (the Napier Commission), 1883, are an important source of information about crofters. Look up the catalogue of the Department of Agriculture and Fisheries (AF) for AF50. There are two sets of relevant returns, AF50/7 and AF50/8. AF50/7 consists of returns, bound by counties, of crofters. Within the county volume, the arrangement is alphabetical by estate. The information given includes the name of the township and/or croft, the name of each tenant, the number of families on the croft and the number of persons habitually residing in the croft. AF50/8 consists of unbound returns of cottars, who are tenants of cottages without land attached. These returns are by estate, and, as well as giving the name of each cottar, specify their occupation or means of subsistence, eg 'supported by a son at sea – a Sailor' (AF50/8/2). The Commission's report was published in 1884.

Land Court

12.15 If your ancestor was a crofter after 1886 or a small agricultural tenant anywhere in Scotland after 1912, you might want to look at the records of the Scottish Land Court (LC) which has jurisdiction in certain matters relating to these landholdings. First read the introduction to the LC catalogue. Most of the Land Court records are arranged by county. The records of each county include landholders books and court rolls. Particularly before 1912, the cases are predominantly for valuation of fair rent. Both the landholders books and the court rolls are indexed by the name of the applicant, i.e. the tenant or crofter. This gives this record a searching advantage over the Valuation Rolls in respect of tenants who applied to the Land Court. The applications are closed for 75 years.

∽13∽
Other Legal Transactions

13.1   During his lifetime, your ancestor may have been engaged in a variety of legal transactions, which required documents which bear his name – bonds, contracts of sale, contracts of partnership, and so forth. While there was generally no public compulsion to preserve such records of private enterprise, many such documents have survived. Your problem is to find any which relate to your ancestor.

13.2   Fortunately, there was and is a type of record which was created for the purpose of preserving such legal documents (or 'deeds'), though only if the parties wished. In the sixteenth century, it became the practice for most courts of law to have a register of deeds, in which such documents were copied, either simply to ensure their preservation or to facilitate a legal action grounded on the deed. The original document was also often kept by the court. Up to 1809, any court had power to register deeds. After that date, only the Court of Session, sheriff courts and royal burgh courts had the power. If you are looking for a deed which you hope will have been copied into a register of deeds, you will need to look at both the register compiled in the Court of Session and the registers of any courts which had jurisdiction where your ancestor lived or was engaged in business. Any legal document might be copied into these registers. Deeds are arranged therein by date of registration, not the date of the deed. Some deeds have been registered years after the date of the deed. Thus, in seeking a deed which you hope has been registered, you may have to search several records and a longish date period, often without the aid of indexes.

Books of Council and Session

13.3   The register attached to the Court of Session is known both as the 'Books of Council and Session' and, simply, 'The Register of Deeds' (RD). Indexing of this huge Register is patchy. We will consider its accessibility before and after 1660.

The Register of Deeds before 1660

13.4   While the Register of Deeds is officially regarded as starting in 1554, it was not a tidy start. Deeds had been previously registered in other Court of Session court books and some continued to be so. There are calendars available of deeds in the Acta Dominorum Concilii 1501-1514 (CS5), Acta Dominorum Concilii et Sessionis 1532-1559 (CS6) and Acts and Decreets 1542-1581 (indexed, CS7). Order by the CS reference and volume number.

13.5   There is a Calendar of Deeds in the Register of Deeds itself for the period between 1554 and 1595, in a series of volumes with a lot of date overlap. These are partly indexed in separate volumes. Order the Register volume containing the deed by RD1 and the volume number.

13.6   Between 1596 and 1660, there are no calendars or indexes, and thus, to search the Register of Deeds, you will have to use its minute books. Before 1660, there are five series of minute books, partly concurrent. Look up the Register of Deeds catalogue under the reference RD6. Each of the five series appears under a name: 'Scott', 'Gibson', 'Hay', 'Dounie', and 'Brown', the names of the clerks' offices which compiled the Register. Order out the minute books which cover the date period you are searching. Each minute book is arranged by date of registration and gives that date, an abbreviation of the type of document, and the surnames only of the principal parties, expressed as if parties in a legal dispute. If you find a promising entry, order out the RD1 volume that covers the date and which, according to the catalogue, bears the same office name as the minute book. For example, when you are looking for an ancestor named Kincaid, you find in a Hay minute book under the date 'undecimo decemb: 1639' (undecimo being Latin for eleven) an entry 'Gray qr Kincaid – disch' ('qr' is short for 'contra'). Therefore you order out RD1/524, which, the catalogue tells you, is the Hay volume covering November 1639 to July 1640. In this volume, the dates of registration are placed prominently and the names of the parties are placed in the margins, and therefore the entry is easy to find. The deed is a discharge by Jean Kincaid, relict of umquhile Mr Thomas Gray, advocate, of payment in terms of their marriage contract.

The Register of Deeds from 1661

13.7   From 1661 to 1811, the Register of Deeds was compiled in three separate but concurrent series, known as 'DAL', 'DUR', and 'MACK', which

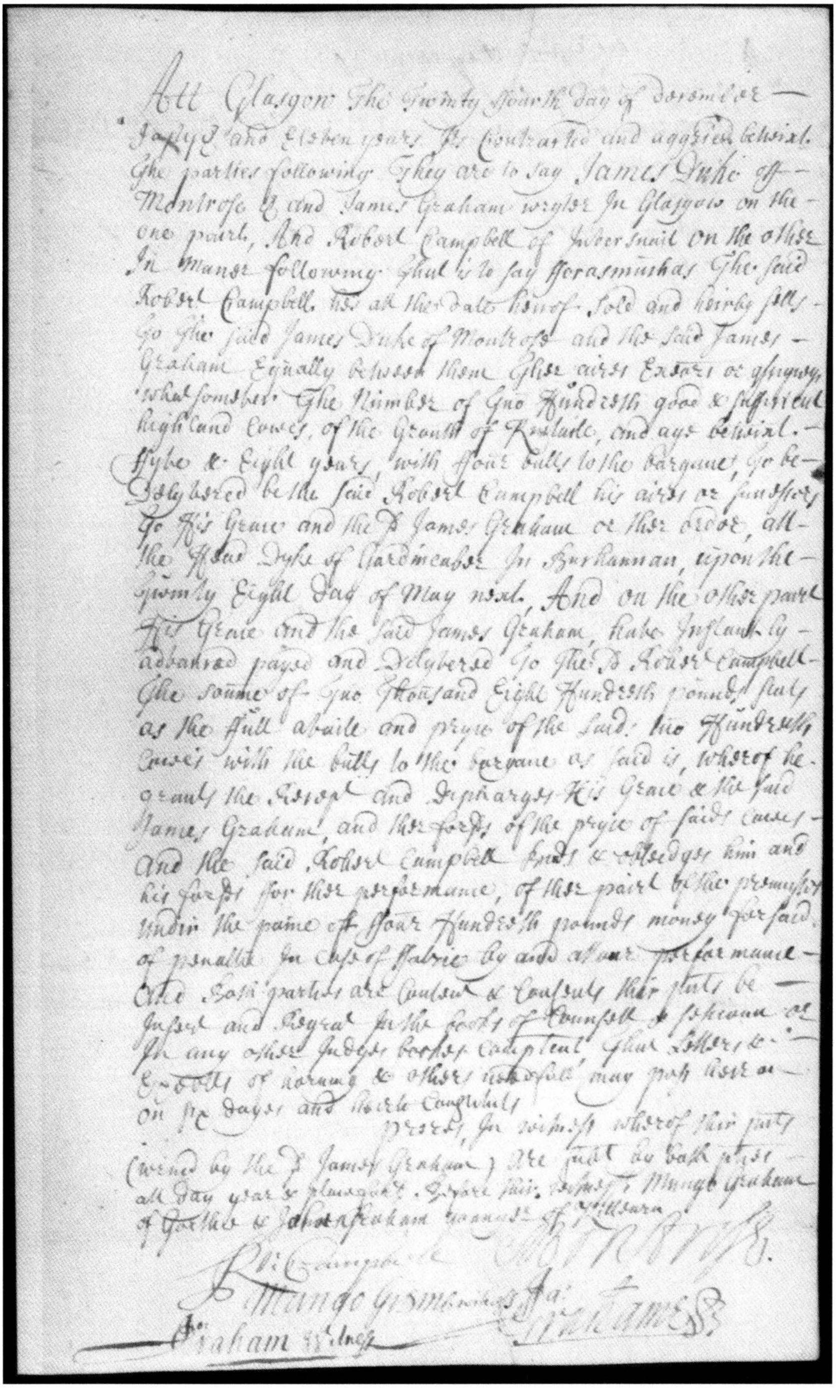

Rob Roy's contract with the Duke of Montrose, 1712 (RD14/52).

are abbreviated forms of the names of the three clerks' offices which compiled the Register, i.e. Dalrymple, Durie and Mackenzie. As there is no content distinction between the three offices, any deed might be registered by any of them and you have to search all three. Fortunately, the indexes are to all three series in one.

13.8 From 1661-1696, there are printed annual indexes, and typescript indexes for the years 1697-1702, 1705-7 and 1714-15. Copies may be obtainable through your local library. The style of these indexes varies, but all provide the name and designation of each party, and the volume and folio number of the deed. All principal parties are indexed. To order out a volume of the Register, if the volume number in the index is preceded by DAL, order by RD2 and the volume number; if DUR, order by RD3 and the volume number; if MACK, order by RD4 and the volume number. Occasionally, a deed has been omitted from the volume of the Register but has survived among the original documents kept as 'warrants' of the Register. If the index says 'warrant' instead of a volume number, order by RD12 (for DAL), RD13 (for DUR), or RD14 (for MACK), a number for the year (1 for 1661, 2 for 1662 and so on up to 151 for 1811), and the warrant number, eg RD13/33/ no.547. For warrants after 1811, you order by RD15, the year number, which is 1 for 1812, 2 for 1813 and so on, and the warrant number, if you know it. If you want to order an original deed, but do not know its warrant number, you can order by the RD number, the year number (as before), the month and day of registration, and the names of the parties.

13.9 A regular series of indexes starts again in 1770. Up to that date there are modern indexes for 1750-52 and a manuscript index for 1765. More than half of the eighteenth-century Register of Deeds remains unindexed.

13.10 To search for a deed registered in the unindexed years, you have again to use minute books, of which there are three concurrent series to search: DAL (RD7/1), DUR (RD7/2) and MACK (RD7/3). Look at the catalogue for the reference numbers of minute books covering specific dates. Again, you have to browse through the minute books, all three sets, each arranged chronologically by date of registration, to find an entry which may seem to be relevant. The later minute books state the forenames as well as surnames of parties, which helps. For example: you will find in a DAL minute book (RD7/1/5) on 30 March 1714, an entry 'Cont of Mar Arnot & Spalden', which leads you to the volume of the Register referenced RD2/103/2, in which you will find the date of registration at the top of each page and the names of parties at the head of each deed; and thus you find the contract of marriage, dated in 1694, between Archibald Arnott, chirurgeon apothecary in Dundee, and Catherine Spalding, daughter of Mr John Spalding, minister in Dundee. In a MACK minute book (RD7/3/10) on 3 July 1750, you find 'Latter Will George Brodie to Katherine Brodie'. The will, which is in RD4/176/2, does not appear to be in the Commissary Court records, and is the will of a soldier, signed at Breda in 1748, bequeathing his property to his four sisters.

13.11 Annual indexes have been compiled to the Register of Deeds since 1770 – there is a complete set from 1770 to date in the Historical Search Room. Their main disadvantage is that they index granters only. Alongside the name and brief designation of the granter, there is the name of the grantee, the type of deed, dates of deed and registration and the volume and folio number. In the RD2, 3 and 4 series, often one volume number is allocated to one calendar year, while the amount of deeds in that year requires two volumes, parts 1 and 2. Thus when, in the volume column of the index, you find (eg) an entry '2/240' with 'Dur' in an adjacent column, you order out RD3/240/2. From 1812 on, you will be glad to hear, there are no longer the three separate offices, and the Register of Deeds exists in one series: order by RD5, year of recording and volume number, e.g. for a deed recorded 20 Dec 1898 in vol. 2917, p.157, you would order out RD5/1898/2917 and look for the start of the deed on page 157.

13.12 A common entry in the minute book is 'pro' for 'protest', a particular step in some actions for debt and often entered in registers of deeds. Protests are not included in the post-1770 indexes, and therefore to search for them, you will need to continue to use the minute books. From 1812, there is a separate Register of Protests (RD17) that you search by means of its minute books (RD18).

Sheriff Court Registers of Deeds

13.13 Extending your search for a deed to the registers of deeds kept by lesser courts may not be simple. There are a variety of courts and hardly any indexes. The next most important registers of deeds are those of the sheriff courts. Not all sheriff courts kept a register of deeds, but there is at least one for each sheriffdom. As usual, look first in the catalogue of the records of a relevant sheriff court to see if it has a register of deeds. These registers of deeds vary tremendously in their earliest date and in how well they have survived. The earliest surviving is Perth (SC49), which starts in 1570. The majority of sheriff courts have, as well as the registers of deeds themselves, minute books and warrants thereof, but not necessarily all three concurrently. For example, the Wigtown sheriff court (SC19) has minute books from 1636, warrants from 1690, but no register until 1809. More commonly, minute books post-date their register and its warrants. From 1809, these registers were kept in a consistent form and such indexes as exist mainly date from then, but this type of record is largely unindexed. Check first to see whether there is an index for your sheriff court and date, or a relevant volume of the register has an internal contents list, or there is a contemporary minute book. Otherwise, you will have to sift through a register or box of original warrants of relevant date. The sheriff courts also have separate registers of protests from 1809 (some earlier), which are unindexed. Deeds registered in Cupar sheriff court, 1715-1809 (SC20/33), are indexed online by the Fife Family History Society at *www.fifefhs.org/*. An index in the Historical Search Room covers deeds registered 1809-1900 (SC20/34).

Burgh Registers of Deeds

13.14 The NAS holds registers of deeds for a number of the royal burghs. Look in the B catalogue at the contents list of the records of the burgh where your ancestor was to see if there is a register of deeds. The dates of these vary considerably, starting with Edinburgh in 1561 (B22/8). They continue into the twentieth century. Very few have minute books. If you are lucky, the appropriate volume may include an index or contents list. If not, look for the names of the parties in the margin beside or at the head of each entry in the register. For the Fife burghs of Burntisland, Culross, Dunfermline, Dysart, Inverkeithing, and Kirkcaldy, whose records are in NAS, a typescript index to the principal persons mentioned in the deeds, 1673-1896, is available in the Historical Search Room. It also covers burghs in north and east Fife, whose records are held at St Andrews University Archives and elsewhere. It was created for the Fife Family History Society. A few burghs kept not only a register of deeds but also concurrently a register of probative writs, which was a class of deed. If so, that should also be consulted.

Commissary Courts Registers of Deeds

13.15 If you are searching for a deed before 1809, you might look at the Commissary Court registers of deeds. Between them, they cover the whole of Scotland, except that the Wigtown court has no register of deeds, while for Aberdeen and the Isles only warrants survive. Look at **9.7** to find out which commissary court(s) served the county in which your ancestor lived. Then look at its (or their) contents list(s) in the CC catalogue. Look carefully: there may be a separate register of probative writs; there may or may not be minute books. Many of these registers have gaps; if so, look also at the warrants of these registers. A few of the volumes may have contents lists, and there is an index to deeds in Moray Commissary Court, 1785-1823 (CC16/9/7-12). In terms of contents, there is no difference between these registers of deeds and those of other courts. You have to wade through many documents relating to debt to find the occasional marriage contract or will.

Local Courts Registers of Deeds

13.16 If you are looking for a deed dated earlier than 1748, then you might also search the RH11 catalogue, to see if the records of a relevant 'local court' include a register of deeds. The paper catalogue includes an index of courts by their place-name. The lists of court records note not only registers of deeds, but also the existence of deeds in other court books. For example, the regality of Kilwinning (RH11/45) has a register of deeds for 1620-51 and 1664-96, part of the gap being filled with deeds entered in a court book. There are no indexes, but contents lists are noted when they occur.

13.17 Many deeds are scattered throughout the Gifts and Deposits and similar collections (see **7.20-21**).

∽14∽
Litigants

14.1 Compiling registers of deeds was only a subsidiary part of the work of a court and the records of the main business of courts of law may contain information valuable to the ancestor-hunter. If your ancestor ran into debt or was of a disputatious nature and sufficiently prosperous, he probably got himself involved in litigation, and you will want to look for him in the records of those courts which dealt with legal disputes between private parties.

14.2 Your initial problem is – which court? There are courts that heard cases arising from any part of Scotland – the Court of Session, the Privy Council, the Admiralty Court, the Court of Exchequer. There were courts with a jurisdiction which was restricted to a particular administrative area – sheriff courts, commissary courts, burgh courts, Justice of the Peace courts, the 'franchise' courts. As most cases could be raised in more than one court and there were often appeals from a lower to a higher court, you may have to pursue your search in the records of several courts. It is difficult to give general advice on which court to start on. Maritime cases were heard by the Admiralty Court, cases involving marriage were heard by the Commissary Court of Edinburgh until 1830 (see **8.18–21**), thereafter by the Court of Session; but apart from those, if the matter in dispute was minor, such as a small debt, you are best to start with a local court and, if the dispute was more significant, with the Court of Session.

Court of Session

14.3 Let us start with the highest civil court in Scotland, the Court of Session. It has a vast bulk of records, which are undersupplied with straightforward guides and are arranged in a complicated manner because that is the way the Court worked. Until 1821, the records of the Court were created within different offices, usually three concurrently. The cases were divided into two categories, those cases of which the final decree is 'extracted' and those of which it is not. If a decree was extracted, then it was copied into the Register of Acts and Decreets and the papers in the case preserved as 'extracted processes'. The records of all other cases, whether they reached decree or not, were preserved as 'unextracted processes'. There is no difference in legal validity between an extracted or an unextracted process. An extracted process is one which has completed its passage through the legal system i.e. one of the parties has had an extract of the court's determination made to enforce the court's decision. An unextracted process may have been abandoned at any previous stage. Even if the case reached a conclusion, the absence of an extract simply shows neither party felt the need to obtain an extract to enforce the court's judgement.

14.4 There is no distinction in content between extracted and unextracted cases or between the various offices. Consequently, you may have to examine several sets of records. To complicate matters further, at various times there have been divisions and separate departments of the Court of Session, with their own records. It is therefore difficult to explain simply how to gain access to the Court of Session records. However, we shall try, though you may still have to refer to the staff for further advice.

14.5 You had best start by looking at the guides to the Court of Session on the NAS website, and the chapter on the Court of Session in *Guide to the National Archives of Scotland* (Stationery Office/Stair Society, 1996). These serve as an introduction to the Court's different functions, summarise the records briefly and are crucial in navigating your way around Court finding aids and records. Bear in mind that descriptions of individual cases in some Court series are gradually being added to the catalogue.

14.6 Your first task is to find out if there was a case before the Court of Session in which your ancestor was a party. Though there are some modern indexes, you will mostly have to look at the Court minute books and other imperfect guides. There are various problems. Often the cases will be described only by the surnames of the parties; indexes are usually of pursuers only, which is awkward if your ancestor was the defender; cases often change their names as they progress; cases often took several years to progress. Thus, Campbell v Macdonald, 1676, may later appear as Macdonald v Campbell, 1681.Though you may find short cuts, you will usually have to start by searching a minute book to ascertain if a case was heard by the Court, and persevere from there.

Court of Session before 1660

14.7   There are general minute books which note all the cases before the Court of Session, and particular minute books which note the cases dealt with by a particular office. Before 1650, the offices are called Scott, Gibson and Hay; between then and 1659, Brown and Durie. Because some of these minute books are damaged and therefore incomplete, you should check both general and particular ones. (If there is no surviving minute book, you just have to read through the volumes of the Acts and Decreets.) The minute books are arranged chronologically and, under each date, list each legal action by the surnames of the opposing parties. The General Minute Books also supply the name of the relevant office, while the particular minute books will also tell you what happened to the action in the court on that day.

14.8   To illustrate, in a general minute book (CS8/3) at 3 July 1579 there is an entry 'act betx Hammiltoun qr Kynneir Gibson', which means that the Court that day heard an action between parties named Hamilton and Kinnear and that the case was recorded by Gibson's office. If you look in the Gibson particular minute book for that date (CS10/1) you will find 'Hamilton qr Kynneir – decernit' which confirms that there was a case between those parties on that date and that decree was granted. You then have to look at the CS catalogue for the Gibson volume of the Register of Acts and Decreets (CS7), which includes 3 July 1579 (CS7/76). As you do not have a folio reference, you look in the volume for the date (which is expressed in Latin) and the name of the parties in the margin; and you find a decree in favour of John Hammiltoun of Drumry against a tenant David Kynneir to remove from the lands of Craigfudies; which may or may not be what you want.

Court of Session 1661–1912

14.9   To find a case, first go to the general minute books. Until 1781, these are in manuscript (CS16). From 1782, they are printed (CS17). The manuscript ones are not indexed and you have to wade through the entries until you find one that seems relevant. The printed ones, which are annual, are indexed. These indexes are to all parties, distinguishing pursuers by the letter 'p' and defenders by the letter 'd', but give the surname only, except for some common surnames. The forenames, if given, may be in an abbreviated form, eg 'Ro' for 'Robert'. In the text of these minute books, there are further abbreviations for legal terms, such as 'P' for petition and 'D' for decree. The staff will advise you further on these.

14.10 In both manuscript and printed minute books, the entries are detailed and will therefore tell you if the case is one that will interest you or not. In the margin (manuscript) or as a heading (printed) there are some initials, eg 'H.J.L.', which are the clerk's mark, which you may need to trace the case further. Then there are some details about the case, the names and designations of the parties, and finally the names of the procurator (advocate) and judge. If you want more detail, you will then look elsewhere for the record of the case, which will usually be described by the pursuer's surname v the defender's surname.

14.11 First try the indexes to the Unextracted Processes. There are four card indexes divided chronologically, so look in the one that covers the date of the case (or two if the date is near the borderline). The first three of these are arranged by surname and chronologically within surname, while the fourth is arranged by surname and forename. These cards give an old reference, eg 2P.Y.5/3, which you will have to convert into the present call number. The first number and letter will always convert into a CS number, eg 2P becomes CS247. The rest of the old reference may still be used or may have to be converted into a running number: NAS staff will advise.

14.12 If you cannot find your case in these card indexes, next try what is called the Carmichael and Elliot arrangement of processes (CS98-CS227). These are fully searchable through the electronic catalogue.

14.13 Still no success? You now want to try the Register of Acts and Decreets. How to search this depends on the date you are searching.

14.14 Up to 1810 look again at the clerk's mark which you found in the minute book. Refer to a guide to clerks' marks which will tell you whether this particular clerk was employed in the DAL, DUR or MACK offices. You now want to look at the relevant extractor's minute book. Of these, DAL is now CS19; DUR is CS23; and MACK is CS27. An entry gives simply the date and surnames of the parties. If you find a relevant entry, order out the equivalent volume of the Register of Acts and Decreets, which was kept in the three offices, again DAL (CS18), DUR (CS22), and MACK (CS26). If you want to see the warrants or papers in the case (known as 'extracted processes'), you order by CS21

(DAL), CS25 (DUR) or CS29 (MACK) plus the date and the names of the parties. These processes may not add anything to what you find in the Register, in which written pleadings are given at great length. A seventeenth-century judge described the bulk of decreets as 'nauseous'!

14.15 From 1810 to 1899 there are annual indexes to the Register of Acts and Decreets. Within each year and within each initial letter of surname, the index order is chronological. The entry tells you the type of case, the names (usually just surnames) of the parties and the date the decree was extracted. You then have to find the relevant CS number and the volume number of that CS series which includes that date. The equivalent extracted process is ordered out by the relevant CS number, date and names of parties. These processes may include information not in the Register. Cases in the Extracted Processes 3rd Series, 1810-1821 (CS31-42) and the 4th series, 1821-1829 (CS43-44), are gradually being catalogued. Use the date of the decree to order the Register of Acts and Decreets.

14.16 Let us now look at some examples.

14.17 In a General Minute Book (CS16/1/54) under the date 11th February 1721 you find an entry 'Decreet in absence Elizabeth and Helen Monteiths Daughters to umqull Alexander Monteith of Todshaugh chirurgeon in Edinburgh and their husbands contra John Fultoun chirurgeon in Douglas'. You do not find this case in the Unextracted Processes or Carmichael and Elliot indexes, but in the DAL Extractors Minute Book for that date (CS19/1/3) you find 'D [= decree] Monteiths q Fulton'. Therefore you order out the volume of the Register of Acts and Decreets, series DAL, for that date (CS18/204) and look through it to find the full report of the case, which supplies the names of the ladies' husbands and shows that the case was brought to retrieve debts owed to the deceased Alexander Monteith for 'drugs and medicaments furnished by him'. You may also order out the extracted process relevant to the case, which is CS21/1721 February 11/Monteiths v Fulton.

14.18 In a General Minute Book (CS16/1/132) under the date 27th January 1768 you find a case brought by Christian Allan, daughter to James Allan, late bailie of Hamilton, against John McNeill, schoolmaster in Hamilton. You look up the Unextracted Process card index and find 'Allan, Christian v McNiel 1767 Adams Mack A1/101'. This number converts into CS229/A1/101 which you order out and find that the action was for non-payment of rent of a house owned by the pursuer in

> *July 27. 1761.*
>
> # MEMORIAL
>
> ### FOR
>
> Poor PETER WILLIAMSON late of the Province of *Penſylvania* in *North America*, Planter, now Reſidenter in *Edinburgh*: Purſuer,
>
> ### AGAINST
>
> *Alexander Cuſhnie* late Dean-of-Guild and Procurator-Fiſcal of the Borough-Court of *Aberdeen*, and others: Defenders.
>
> With au Abſtract of the Proof.
>
> THE Purſuer was born in the pariſh of Hirnley in Aberdeenſhire, in the month of February 1730, and continued with his father, who was a reputable tenant in that country, till about the year 1740, when he was ſent to ſchool at Aberdeen, where he lived under the care and inſpection of an Aunt. At that time it was a common practice among the merchants in Aberdeen to pick up young boys from the ſtreet and in the country, whom they confined in barns and other convenient places, till ſuch time as they had got together a ſufficient number of them, when they uſed to ſend them to America, and there ſold them as ſlaves. It was the misfortune of the Purſuer to fall into the hands of one employed by Bailie William Fordyce and Company merchants in Aberdeen, to pick up
>
> A boys

Printed memorial setting out the case of Peter Williamson (CS29/103/1/1762).

the Castlewynd of Hamilton. (You may then try the Register of Sasines in the hope of finding more information.)

14.19 Having looked up the name 'Lindsay' in the index to the 1815–16 printed general minute book (CS17/1/35) you find a case heard by the First Division of the Court on 28 February 1816 'D [ecree] in ab [sence] David Freer, WS. AG [ainst] Sam [uel] Lindsay, brewer in Dunkeld'. The clerk's mark is M.H.B. You then look in the Acts and Decreets index for 1816 and find the entry 'Freer v Lindsay' with the date of extract 16 July 1816. 'M.H.B.' is the mark for volumes of the Register of Acts and Decreets referenced CS39 and extracted processes referenced CS40. You order out CS39/22 and look through this volume until you find the decree. The case is a simple one of debt.

14.20 Divorce cases were the responsibility of the Court of Session after 1830 and to find them up to 1912 you look initially at the printed minute books. You are looking for the divorce case of a couple named McKay. The index in the minute book for 1884 (CS17/1/103) leads you to an entry under the date 22nd January 1884, describing a decree of divorce in favour of Janet Rankin, or Lean, or Mckay, residing in Creetown, against James McKay, residing at Xenia, in the State of Ohio, in the United States of America. The minute also names their daughter, and his sister and mother, who live in Newton Stewart. As you want more information, you look up the index to Unextracted Processes and find a card 'McKay, Janet Rankin or Lean or, v Mckay, Divorce 1882, 2P.Mc.14/2' which number converts into CS247/4184. You order out this process and discover that the defender went to America to gain employment but has not been heard of for several years.

Court of Session since 1913

14.21 After 1912, you can find the Unextracted Processes, 1913-1994, in the online catalogue, and also the Acts and Decreets, 1900-1994. In doubtful cases the General Minute Books, which end in 1990, remain a useful guide to which actions were heard by the Court of Session. There are also annual paper indexes to the Unextracted Processes and Acts and Decreets. The indexes to Unextracted Processes are, as usual, indexes to pursuers only, giving also the nature of the action, the name of the defender and the year the case was called, which will be earlier than the year of the index.

14.22 In 1995, separate indexes of Unextracted and Extracted Processes were discontinued by the Court, and a single combined index has been produced since then (CS348). The Court also adopted a simplified divorce procedure from 1983, which forms a separate series. Both series of records are searchable through the electronic catalogue.

Bill Chamber

14.23 You may have come across cases in the minute books which you have not been able to trace or you simply wish to search further among the Court of Session records. There are some guides which we have not yet consulted. Most notably there are indexes to the Bill Chamber processes

(CS271), the Bill Chamber being a court within the Court of Session. The CS catalogue explains its functions. The index (of pursuers) covers the years 1670-1852 and is searchable on the electronic catalogue.

Jury Court

14.24 The Jury Court existed between 1815 and 1850 to hear cases referred to a jury by the Court of Session. A searchable index is available on the electronic catalogue.

Accountant of Court

14.25 The office of Accountant of Court (records from 1739) has responsibility in the supervision of estates of children and other persons unable to administer their own affairs. If you are seeking actions concerning the guardianship of infants or the appointment of factors loco tutoris, you should examine these records (CS313-317). You will remember that a tutor is appointed to administer the affairs of a fatherless child (see **10.5** onwards). If you fail to find a record of the appointment of a tutor in the record of Retours, you should try the records of the Accountant of Court. There are indexes available and CS313-314 and CS316-317 are searchable through the electronic catalogue. You may find sufficient detail in the printed minute book, however.

Sequestrations

14.26 When Scots have become bankrupt methods have had to be found to satisfy their creditors. The main legal method known as cessio bonorum was largely superseded by sequestration, which dates from 1771. Since then, there have been frequent reforms, attempting to provide justice for all parties concerned. Changes in the system mean that there is a variety of paths to follow to find a particular sequestration case. In some cases, the pursuer will be the bankrupt, in others a creditor. The *Edinburgh Gazette* is also a useful source for establishing dates and names of bankruptcies: *www.gazettes-online.co.uk*.

Bankrupts before 1839

14.27 Before 1839, to look for a bankruptcy case among the Court of Session records, you can use the procedures described above for all cases. From August 1783, you have the alternative of looking first in the printed index to the General Register of Inhibitions (see **14.59-61**), as from that date all petitions for sequestration had to be recorded in that register. It is the bankrupt who is indexed and therefore you will find out if it is worth searching the Court of Session records for the case. An additional route is to search the catalogue of a special series (CS96), containing most of the business books found in Court of Session processes. The books include sederunt books compiled by the trustees in bankruptcy. Cross references point you to the sequestration process to which the sederunt book refers. The NAS catalogue covers more such records than the version published as *List of Court of Session Productions* (List and Index Society, 1987)

Bankrupts since 1839

14.28 The sequestration records are all searchable in the catalogue, as are some other minor record sequestration series such as petitions and appeals. The processes are arranged in three series, CS280, CS319 and CS318 (the current record series). Further information is available in a Court of Session guide on the NAS website, or in an older 'Guide to Scottish Sequestrations, 1839-1913', available in the West Search Room.

14.29 Sheriff courts also dealt with bankruptcy cases. Look at the contents list of the records of the relevant sheriff court (SC) for 'Register of Seques-trations'. The Court of Session guide just mentioned will help you, as after 1840 sheriff clerks made returns to the Court of Session of seques-trations depending before their court (CS283, 331 and 332).

Privy Council

14.30 The Court of Session was, in origin, an offshoot of the Privy Council, which had judicial as well as administrative functions. The Privy Coun-cil continued to act in a judicial capacity up to 1707, issuing decrees, or making an effort 'to agree the parties', or referring a case to the Court of Session or a lower court. It tended to be the better-off complainant who took a case to the Privy Council.

14.31 The *Register of the Privy Council of Scotland* is published up to 1691, each volume being fully indexed. If you are looking for a case between 1545 and 1691, look up the name of the party in the index of the printed volume for the relevant period. The printed text is quite full, but if you want to see the original, order by PC1, up to August 1610, or PC2, after that date, and the volume number given in the PC catalogue for the date of that entry.

14.32 Between 1692 and 1695, you have no choice but to look in the original volumes of the Registers of Decreta (PC2/24-26): look for the brief description of each entry in the margin. Between 1696 and 1707, look in the minute books (PC4/2-3) which describe all the business of the Council, not just the judicial business. There you will find such entries as 'Lybell Bruce of Pitterthie agt Corstorphine of Neydie Called and remitted to the Judge ordinar' (26 January 1697), which will show if it is worthwhile examining the PC2 volumes.

Admiralty Court

14.33 The Admiralty Court had jurisdiction in all maritime and seafaring cases, both civil and criminal, until 1830, when its civil jurisdiction was transferred to the Court of Session. If your ancestor was a shipowner or shipmaster, a merchant who traded overseas, or even a crew member, then he may have been involved in, or mentioned in, an action before the Admiralty Court. The earliest record has been published, with an index of persons, places, ships etc: *Acta Curiae Admirallatus Scotiae, 6th September 1557–11th March 1561-2*, ed T C Wade (Stair Society, 1937).

14.34 The Admiralty Court records that mainly concern you are the decreets and processes (AC7, 8, 9, 10, 15), to which there are bound guides in the form of roughly chronological lists of cases. A separate guide to the records up to 1750, 'The High Court of Admiralty of Scotland 1627-1750', compiled by Sue Mowat and Eric Graham (2005), may be consulted in the West Search Room. Copies of this guide on CD-ROM may be obtained through the Early Scottish Maritime Exchange (ESME) website *www.maritime-scotland.org.uk*.

14.35 Argyll and the Isles were the responsibility of a separate Vice-Admiralty Court, whose jurisdiction ran from Dumbarton Castle to Cape Wrath, and whose records are preserved for the years 1685-1830 (AC20). A modern index to matters brought before it may also be consulted in the West Search Room. Copies may be purchased from the compiler Mr F W Bigwood, Flat B, The Lodge, 2 East Road, North Berwick, EH39 4HN.

14.36 AC7 consists of volumes of decreets, 1627-1830. For a summary of the decreets in the period 1627-1692 consult the ESME guide. For later years order out AC7/107. This lists the surnames of pursuer and defender, the date and the volume number; eg 'Mitchell Mackenzie 2 July 1725 Vol. 30'. To see that decreet, you order out AC7/30. If you are lucky, the volume will have a contents list, giving the folio number on which the decreet starts.

14.37 For summary descriptions of the processes between 1702 and 1750 (AC8, 9, 10, 15), look at the ESME guide. This gives the names of owners, masters and frequently some crew members. After 1750 look at the NAS contents lists in the Search Room. The lists give the decree or process number, the names of the pursuer and defender and the year, eg, AC10/563 Magnus Brymer v James Hutton 1779'. This case was brought by an apprentice sailmaker in Leith, who joined the navy and was then incarcerated at the instance of his master until he found someone to guarantee the completion of his apprenticeship. Most Admiralty cases concern payments, but they contain rich material on those who lived by sailing and trading, or had related businesses or crafts, such as shipbuilders, wrights and carpenters. The ESME guide also includes summaries of cases, 1654–1658 (AC2/1) and some details of other series, 1702–1750 (AC11, 13).

Court of Exchequer

14.38 Between 1708 and 1856 (when its jurisdiction was transferred to the Court of Session), the Court of Exchequer dealt with revenue cases, including debts to the Crown, seizure of smuggled goods and prosecutions for illicit brewing and distilling. Unfortunately, its records generally provide little information about individuals and there are no indexes. To investigate, look first at the minute books (E351), which will give the names but not the designations of the parties in the cases. If you find a case which seems relevant, look further at the books of orders (E352), the enrolled or original informations, which may provide designations but which are in various rather abstruse series (see the catalogue – E358-368), and the affidavits, which can be informative but many of which have not survived (E376). If your ancestor owed money to the Crown between 1711 and 1827, there may be an inventory of his property in a series referenced E371.

Sheriff Courts

14.39 Apart from the Court of Session, the court in which your ancestor would most likely be a litigant would be a sheriff court. There are the following sheriff courts, each with jurisdiction over all or part of a county. Each has its own catalogue.

County	Sheriff Courts
Aberdeen	Aberdeen (SC1); Peterhead (SC4)
Angus (Forfar)	Arbroath (SC43); Dundee (SC45); Forfar (SC47)
Argyll	Campbeltown (SC50); Dunoon (SC51); Fort William (SC52); Inverary (SC54); Oban (SC57); Tobermory (SC59)
Ayr	Ayr (SC6); Kilmarnock (SC7)
Banff	Banff (SC2)
Berwick	Duns (SC60)
Bute	Rothesay (SC8)
Caithness	Wick (SC14)
Clackmannan	Alloa (SC64)
Dumfries	Dumfries (SC15)
Dunbarton	Dumbarton (SC65)
East Lothian (Haddington)	Haddington (SC40)
Edinburgh City	Edinburgh (SC39); Leith (SC69)
Fife	Cupar (SC20); Dunfermline (SC21); Kirkcaldy (SC23)
Glasgow	Glasgow (SC36)
Inverness	Fort William (SC28); Inverness (SC29); Lochmaddy (SC30); Portree (SC32)
Kincardine	Stonehaven (SC5)
Kinross	Kinross (SC22)
Kirkcudbright	Kirkcudbright (SC16); Dumfries (SC17)
Lanark	Airdrie (SC35); Glasgow (SC36); Hamilton (SC37); Lanark (SC38)
Midlothian (Edinburgh)	Edinburgh (SC39)
Moray (Elgin)	Elgin (SC26)
Nairn	Nairn (SC31)
Orkney	Kirkwall (SC11 – in Kirkwall); Orkney and Shetland (SC10 – 17th century only)
Peebles	Peebles (SC42)
Perth	Dunblane (SC44); Perth (SC49)
Renfrew	Greenock (SC53); Paisley (SC58)
Ross and Cromarty	Cromarty (SC24); Dingwall (SC25); Stornoway (SC33); Tain (SC34)
Roxburgh	Jedburgh (SC62); Hawick (SC61)
Selkirk	Selkirk (SC63)

Shetland	Lerwick (SC12 – in Lerwick); Orkney and Shetland (SC10 – 17th century only)
Stirling	Falkirk (SC66); Stirling (SC67)
Sutherland	Dornoch (SC9)
West Lothian (Linlithgow)	Linlithgow (SC41)
Wigtown	Stranraer (SC18); Wigtown (SC19)

14.40 First, decide which sheriff court(s) had jurisdiction where your ancestor was, and then look at the relevant sheriff court catalogue. In its contents list, look at the records of the 'Ordinary Court', which are usually at the start of the catalogue.

14.41 There is little consistency among the various sheriff courts in the names they gave their series of records or in the contents thereof. Even within one series, there may be considerable variety in the sort of detail provided. The starting dates of surviving records vary greatly, and there may be unexplained gaps. Only certain categories of civil processes are preserved from 1860 onwards, but they are increasingly easy to find in the catalogue. An index to sheriff court decrees for Midlothian 1830-1900 (SC39/8) is in paper form, while another paper index to Perthshire processes, 1809-1900 (SC44/22) will become available electronically.

14.42 Depending on what categories of records have been created by each sheriff court and on what has survived, to search for a case you may have to look at minute books, act books, diet books or court books, around the appropriate date, or, from the late nineteenth century, registers of ordinary actions and of summary applications. It will be up to you to decide how to proceed. There will often also be a register of decrees and one or more series of processes.

14.43 For instance, if you are looking for a case in the Sheriff Court of Hamilton after 1770, you should look first at the minute books (SC37/4) to find the case, then at the act books (SC37/2) for details of the case, and, if the case reached decree, at the decree books (SC37/7) for more detail. You may also want to search for the process (SC37/8).

14.44 The sort of cases you may be seeking in the sheriff court records are actions for aliment, affiliation orders, registration of irregular marriages, small debt, workmen's compensation. Sometimes these cases will be found mixed among all the other cases, sometimes they will be in a

Valentine from a Sheriff Court process, produced as evidence in an action for breach of promise (SC58/22/630).

separate volume or series. For example, the Aberdeen sheriff court has a separate alimentary register 1903-24 (SC1/7/19) in the midst of the records of decrees.

14.45 Actions for registration of irregular marriages date after 1859 and are unlikely to provide information additional to that to be found in the official registers of marriages. Civil processes after 1860 are not retained in their entirety and many which were not considered worth preserving have been destroyed. There is a rolling programme to catalogue the surviving processes and many are now searchable on the electronic catalogue. The names of the parties, nature of the action and date are recorded in full.

14.46 In a sheriff court catalogue, the records of workmen's compensation cases, that is, for compensation for personal injury by accident in course of employment, are usually placed separately from those of the ordinary court. They date from 1898.

Commissary Courts

14.47 As well as dealing with executry matters, the commissary courts had a civil jurisdiction until 1823. Most of the actions heard by the courts other than the Edinburgh Commissary Court (**8.18–21**) were for debt.

14.48 Look at the table at **9.7** which shows which commissary court had jurisdiction within which modern counties. Then look in the CC catalogue for the list of records of the relevant commissariot. The records of civil actions are called act or diet books, minute books and registers of decrees, and processes. There are no indexes. All the cases should be noted in the Act or Diet Books, but often the record is brief and will probably not say what the action was about. The Registers of Decrees give a full report of the cases, but not all the cases reached decrees.

Justice of the Peace Courts

14.49 A civil case could be brought before the Justices of the Peace of the relevant county, but, apart from small debt cases (since 1795), the records of this civil jurisdiction are rather sparse, which is a pity as the JP courts sometimes heard cases of aliment.

14.50 If you want to search this record, look at the contents list of the JP catalogue for the relevant county or city and then at the court books in the records of that JP court. The records of some of these courts have been transferred to local archives.

Burgh Courts

14.51 If your ancestor resided in a royal burgh, he might have been a litigant in the burgh court. Look at the list of records of the particular burgh in the B catalogue, to see if these include court books or a register of decreets. The NAS does not hold such records for the majority of burghs, but they may be held by a local archive. These court books can vary tremendously in content, from simply stating the name of the parties to full copies of the decreets. The vast majority of the cases heard in the burgh courts were for debt. There are no indexes.

Franchise Courts

14.52 The Crown used to franchise local justice to certain landowners, who could hold courts in their own lands and administer justice over their vassals and tenants. There were four types of these courts – regality, barony, stewartry and bailiary. Most were abolished in 1747 and the rest thereafter quickly declined into insignificance.

14.53 Look at the RH11 catalogue. This has an index of courts, which directs you to the local court records in the RH11 series and also those in other classes of records. If you find a required place-name in the index and then go to the list of records of that local court, the records of litigation you require will be usually described as 'court books' or 'minutes of court'. The reports of cases in these are generally rather summary, sometimes just giving the names of the parties, but you may be lucky. The commonest actions before such courts are for payment and between landlord and tenant.

14.54 These court books are not indexed and are compiled in a variety of handwritings which make them particularly difficult to decipher. However, a few of them have been published, such as those of the regality of Melrose (Scottish History Society).

Diligence

14.55 Your ancestor's name may also appear in the records of the procedures whereby the courts tried to enforce their decrees. For this purpose, a document registered for execution in a register of deeds (see **13.2**) counts as a decree. The generic term for these procedures is diligence. The individual documents are known as 'letters of' that particular form of diligence. The commonest are letters of horning. You may be seeking such letters because you have come across a reference to them in a document or case record, or because you suspect that they may have followed on a registered deed or court decision, or just in a general trawl for your ancestors. They largely relate to debt situations.

14.56 Of the various forms of diligence which were registered, there are three consistent records: the registers of hornings, inhibitions and apprisings or adjudications. There were general registers for each, covering the whole of Scotland, and particular registers of hornings and inhibitions kept within counties and regalities. After 1781, there are indexes to the registers of inhibitions and adjudications. Otherwise, you have to search the minute books or, if there are no minute books, the record itself. Look at the Diligence (DI) catalogue to see what volumes and minute books are available.

Hornings

14.57 Letters of horning charged a debtor to pay or perform as the court instructed. They were much used and affected most classes of society. If the debtor failed to obey the letters of horning, they could be registered, opening the way for sterner measures, including imprisonment and forfeiture of goods. Registration might be either in the general register of hornings or the particular register for the county or (until 1748) regality where the parties were. As there are no indexes, you have to know the approximate date and place for your search.

14.58 However, the minute books are clear and informative about the parties, who are expressed in the creditor against the debtor format, eg in the general minute book on 1st of April 1701 (expressed in Latin) we find an entry 'Mary Haigs Eldest Laull daughter of James Haigs Gairdner at Dalkeith Agt John Mair Portioner of Pinky commonly called Greinwalls' (DI2/17). This turns out to be an untypical case, because when we get out the volume of the register for that date (DI1/345) we find that Mair is being sued for a penalty for not fulfilling a contract to marry Mary Haigs.

Inhibitions

14.59 Inhibitions were designed (a) to prevent a debtor from disposing of his heritable property to the detriment of his creditor; and (b) to stop a husband's liability for his wife's debts. From 1783, petitions for sequestration were also recorded in the general register of inhibitions. Thus, this record is only worth investigating if your ancestor was likely to have owned land or a house, or had a broken marriage, or went bankrupt. The property is not named. Again you may have to investigate three registers – the general register of inhibitions, and the particular registers for the county (until 1869) or regality (until 1748). After 1869, there is only the general register. To search these up to 1780, you have to use the minute books, which are clear and detailed. From 1781, there are indexes, separate ones for the general register (printed up to 1868, then manuscript) and for the particular registers for each county (printed).

14.60 These are indexes of the parties inhibited or sequestrated, i.e. the debtor or the wife or the bankrupt. The indexes give the name and designation of the person inhibited or sequestrated, the name of the inhibiter (plus designation if a husband), the date, the volume number (in roman numerals) and the folio number (in arabic numerals). Within each surname, companies are indexed before individuals. Women are indexed by their maiden name. Sequestrations are distinguished by the abbreviation '*Seq.*' instead of '*Inhib*'.

14.61 You order out by the DI series number, which you obtain from the catalogue, and the volume number (converted into arabic). For example, in the index to the general register of inhibitions, you find 'DICKIE, John, merchant, Dunfermline. *Seq*. Mar. 19. 1788. – cciv.931' and therefore you order out DI8/204 and look up folio 931: or in the index to the particular register for Haddington you find 'BEGBIE, Marion; *Inhib*. by James Telfer, Labourer, Haddington, her husband, Jan. 30. 1811-xxii.422.' and order out DI60/22 and look up folio 422.

Apprisings and Adjudications

14.62 If a creditor wished to attach and obtain ownership of the heritable property of a debtor in satisfaction for a debt, then he had to obtain a decree of apprising (until 1672) or adjudication (from 1672) against the debtor. From 1636, these decrees were copied into a register (DI13 and 14), the adjudications in a sensibly abbreviated form. Although these were decrees of the Court of Session, it is easier to trace apprisings and adjudications in these registers than in the records of the Court.

14.63 Until 1780, they have to be searched by means of the minute books, which are mostly nicely detailed; with the surname of the main debtor in the margin. The volume number and call number is found in the DI catalogue. From 1781, there are indexes, printed up to 1868, thereafter manuscript. These index the debtor, supplying the names and designations of both debtor and creditor, the date, and volume and folio numbers: eg 'WEIR, Andrew, late candlemaker, Edinburgh, now abroad, and Janet Kettle, his spouse; *By* Janet Swanston, in East Register Street, Edinburgh, Apr.23.1818.-clxvi.74.' The catalogue provides the reference DI14/166. The adjudication starting on folio 74 therein does not, alas, tell us why Andrew is abroad, but does give a detailed description of the lodging house adjudged from the Weirs.

14.64 These decrees and their abbreviates specify the lands to be apprised or adjudged. Obviously, you will only want to inspect this register if your ancestor owned heritable property. It is quite useful to genealogists because of the practice of pursuing the heirs of deceased debtors. In these cases, the relationship of the heir or heirs to the deceased debtor will be explained. For example, in the minute book for 21st August 1754 (DI15/15), you will find an entry labelled 'Macquaintances', which lists three members of that uncommon family who are pursued as heirs of an uncle and cousin named Forbes. The register (DI14/97) supplies no further genealogical information to that which is in the minute book.

Imprisonment

14.65 Until 1880, it was quite common for debtors who could not pay to be imprisoned at the instance of their creditors. Thus, their names may appear in prison registers along with people accused of and found guilty of crimes (see Chapter 15).

Sanctuary

14.66 Until 1880, civil debtors might avoid diligence by taking sanctuary in the palace of Holyroodhouse. There is a copy of the register of those who took this step at RH2/8/17–20. It is not indexed.

∞15∞
Criminals

15.1 It is an irony of ancestor-hunting that you are more likely to find information about an ancestor who committed a crime than one who was a respectable, law-abiding citizen. Such information may be found in records of the inquiries into the case, records of various criminal courts, and in prison records. Many of the records detailed in this chapter are available in the West Search Room of the NAS at West Register House.

15.2 The electronic catalogue entries provide access to individual criminal trial records, particularly the more serious offences heard before the High Court of Justiciary, the supreme criminal court in Scotland, and to the Crown Office precognitions. Trials in the High Court were held before a judge and jury, and are known as 'solemn' trials, as distinct from those held before a judge alone, known as 'summary' trials. In the catalogue entries for the High Court you will find the person's full name, crimes accused, where and when tried, outcome and final sentencing. In the Precognition entries you may find additional personal details such as age, designation, occupation and address. Some descriptions also contain details about the victims of crime (though only after 100 years) and where the crime took place. You are also pointed towards related papers; for example, if a precognition resulted in a trial, you will find the reference of the relevant trial papers in the catalogue entry for the precognition.

Precognitions

15.3 A precognition is the written report of the evidence of witnesses to a crime, taken before the trial to help prepare the case against the accused (whether or not he ever comes to trial). Precognitions for the more serious crimes are preserved among the Lord Advocate's or Crown Office records (AD). Hardly any survive before 1812. Up to 1900, the precognitions are referenced AD14, and, from 1901, AD15. The second number in each reference represents the year, e.g. an 1834 precognition will be

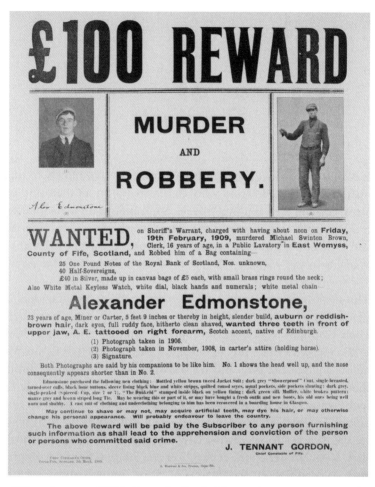

Wanted poster, 1909. From the Lord Advocate's Department records
(AD15/9/166).

numbered AD14/34. There is a 75–year closure period for precognitions. Those that are open can be found by the name of the accused. Where the information occurs in the record the catalogue will also mention the person's designation, occupation, age and address. Here you will find records of labourers, servants, hawkers and others who leave little or no trace in property records.

15.4 If you believe that your ancestor was suspected of committing a crime during the nineteenth or early twentieth centuries, search the catalogue using the name of the accused. You will find such entries as AD14/34/373 'James Robertson, alias David Smith, alias James Burns,

Cotton Spinner, Calton, Glasgow, Native of Manchester, aged 26'. He was indicted, or charged, with 'Theft by housebreaking and previous conviction'. His co-accused was 'James McMehen, alias McMicham, Painter, Main Street, Gorbals, Glasgow', charged as an accomplice with 'Theft by housebreaking'. Precognitions contain not only statements by the witnesses, but also a declaration by the accused. James Robertson's precognition contains his declaration that he had committed a theft in 1826, and been sentenced to transportation for seven years, and had returned to Glasgow in 1833. For this second offence, Robertson was sentenced to transportation for life by the High Court in Edinburgh on 14 July 1834, while McMehan was found not guilty and dismissed from the court (JC8/32, f. 89r). Crimes that led to a sentence of transportation are likely to be found among the Precognitions.

15.5   Two other of the Lord Advocate's records provide useful reports of the progress of such criminal investigations. (They are closed for 100 years.) From 1822, there are procedure books (AD9), which are arranged, first by geographical areas, and then chronologically. They record the name (but not the designation) of the accused, the crime and whether the case was to be brought to trial or not, and by what court. You will then know what court record to search for the details of the trial. Even more useful, but unfortunately dating only from 1890, is AD8, a series of ledgers which record all criminal cases reported to the Crown Agent, giving the name (not designation) of the accused, details of the crime, date and place of the trial, the plea, verdict and sentence. The arrangement is by first letter of the accused's surname and then chronological.

High Court of Justiciary

15.6   Apart from the Precognitions after 1812, the principal source to search for information about a criminal ancestor is the records of the High Court of Justiciary, the supreme criminal court in Scotland (JC). Most trial records over 75 years old are open to public inspection and are listed in the catalogue. The Court sat both in Edinburgh and on circuit in other parts of Scotland. If a crime was committed in the Edinburgh area, the case would usually be tried in Edinburgh. Otherwise, it might be tried either in Edinburgh or on circuit.

15.7   The records of the Edinburgh sittings are contained in the Books of Adjournal (JC2-5) and minute books (JC6-9). The Adjournal record usually contains a fuller record than the minute books, but does not contain anything like a transcript of the full proceedings. Many of the minute books of the High Court in Edinburgh, and of the circuit courts are available on Virtual Volumes in the NAS search rooms. All trials from 1800 onwards have been catalogued in some way. A related series of trial papers or 'sitting papers'(JC26) normally contains further useful information. It has been catalogued in some detail for the period 1822-1825 and 1828-1997. Although a description of trial records over 75 years old can be found in the online catalogue, for trials which took place less than 75 years ago you will only be able to consult the catalogue in the NAS search rooms. The records themselves are restricted for data protection reasons.

15.8   For the pre-1800 period cataloguing is ongoing, and the catalogue will be updated periodically. There are older indexes for the periods 1611-1631 and 1699-1720. Selected trials have been published in Robert Pitcairn's *Criminal Trials in Scotland,* 1498-1624 (3 volumes, Bannatyne Club, 1833), *Selected Justiciary Cases,* 1624-50, ed. Stair Gillon (3 volumes, Stair Society, 1953-1974) and *Records of the Proceedings of the Justiciary Court, Edinburgh, 1661-1678,* ed. W Scott-Moncrieff (2 volumes, Scottish History Society, 1905).

15.9   For trials not yet indexed, or in the catalogue, you should look for the name of an accused in our bound copies of manuscript lists of cases heard by the High Court in Edinburgh. These lists are inaccurately titled as 'indexes', but are effectively chronological lists of cases before the court. The accused is usually described as the 'pannel', and may be noted only on his first appearance, though the trial may continue over several days. If there are several accused in one trial, only one may be named in the list. If you find the name of an accused who interests you, look at the Books of Adjournal and/or minute books for the date given. For example, we find on 5 January 1736, the pannel is 'Barrisdale' and the crime is 'subborning witnesses'. This, incidentally, illustrates one problem of these indexes, because 'Barrisdale' is not a surname but a territorial designation; Scottish lairds and their heirs were often known by the names of their estates. This case involved a laird's eldest son Coll McDonell, younger of Barrisdale. We find the record of his trial in JC3/20 and JC7/20; it continued until 10 February, when he was acquitted.

15.10   If you suspect that your ancestor was accused of a crime and he does not appear in the High Court at Edinburgh, then it is possible that he was tried by the Court on circuit. The areas where the Court sat on circuit during the nineteenth century were Aberdeen, Inverness and Perth (the North circuit); Ayr, Dumfries and Jedburgh (the South circuit) and Glasgow, Inveraray and Stirling (the West circuit). The records of the Court on circuit are minute books (JC10-14), which exist from 1655 and fully report the trials. From 1890, there are also Circuit Books of Adjournal (JC15). To find a case during the nineteenth and early twentieth centuries, as with cases before the High Court, Edinburgh, search the catalogue under the name of the accused. Further information about circuit cases between 1830 and 1887 can be found in the AD6 volumes, which list all circuit cases for that period, giving the name of the accused, the verdict and sentence. If you find the name you seek, you can then study the account of the trial in the JC circuit minute book. If a case involved an appeal from a lower court to a circuit court after 1748, look at the Circuit Books of Appeal (JC22). The volumes are not indexed and you must just read through the record.

15.11 Cases that were appealed from the sheriff courts can be found in the High Court records (JC31). They involved lesser offences, many of them road traffic cases, but also a few cases of prostitution or keeping a brothel. (The catalogue does not always name prostitutes as such, and they must be searched for using synonymous terms, or the law they broke, e.g. contravention of the Criminal Law Amendment Act, 1885, s.13.)

15.12 An alternative source of information about nineteenth and twentieth century Justiciary Court cases may be found in the Lord Advocate's records. AD2-5 consist of bound copies of printed indictments, which give full details of each accused and crime, and list the witnesses for each trial. AD2 contains High Court indictments, 1829-91, and AD3 circuit court indictments, 1839-87, each volume including a contents list of names of accused. AD4 contains indictments relating to postal offences, 1822-74. AD5 contains miscellaneous High and circuit court indictments, 1837-43; it lacks a contents list, but is annotated with each verdict and sentence. Details from some of these entries have been added to the catalogue.

15.13 If your ancestor was transported as punishment for committing a crime, there should be a record of his trial in the JC records. Transportation ceased to be used as a punishment in 1857, but some prisoners sentenced to penal servitude were transported as late as 1867 (see **15.27**).

Privy Council

15.14 Until 1707, criminal cases might also be dealt with by the Privy Council. To find such a case, follow the advice in **14.30–32**.

Sheriff Courts

15.15 If your criminal ancestor was not tried in the High Court, the next most likely court to have judged him is the sheriff court (see list at **14.39**). The commonest crimes to be tried there were theft and assault. Assuming that you know where your ancestor was in Scotland, look in the contents list of the catalogue of the records of the relevant sheriffdom(s) for the Criminal Court records. The criminal records of the different sheriff courts bear various titles and start at widely varying dates. The main record, reporting the trials, may be called 'Criminal Court Books', 'Criminal Record', 'Criminal Register', 'Record of Criminal Trials', etc. The only indexes are within some of the volumes of the record themselves. These supply only surname and forename and only at the first appearance.

15.16 In some sheriff courts, there are separate records of trials heard by the sheriff with a jury (solemn trials) and trials for lesser offences heard by the sheriff sitting alone (summary trials). For summary trials in the general absence of case papers, a brief record of proceedings may be found in the court's Criminal and Quasi-Criminal Roll Books. If there are no criminal court records for the years you are searching, try the ordinary court records, which sometimes include both civil and criminal cases. Check also in the catalogue for criminal libels and/or indictments, as these sometimes survive from an earlier date than the court record. Indictments may include various related papers, such as a declaration by the accused. For instance, in 1828, the sheriff court of Lanark investigated a charge against one John Anderson for passing forged bank notes. His declaration shows that he was a pedlar, about 19 years of age, usually residing in Castle Douglas, born in Girvan, where his father resided, and was bred a weaver (SC38/55/1).

15.17 Minor offences were usually tried in local courts. Until 1747, such offenders might be brought before one of the 'franchise' courts, which are described in **14.52–54**. As criminal courts, they heard such cases as assault ('blood and ryot') and scandal and illegal fishing. Occasionally, such a court dealt with a serious offence, eg in 1666 James Cramond was banished from the town of Kelso for theft (RH11/42/1). In the administration of such courts, there was no practical distinction made between civil and criminal cases, which are intermingled in the court books.

15.18 A unique franchise court was the Argyll Justiciary Court which had criminal jurisdiction throughout Argyll and the Western Isles. Its formal records are preserved in four volumes dating from 1664 to 1742 (SC54/17/1/1-4), and all have been published in the *Argyll Justiciary Records* (Stair Society, 1949, 1962) in two indexed volumes. The original court processes and bonds of caution, 1664-1748, have been catalogued in detail, and are a rich source of genealogical information (SC54/17/2-3). The records include lists of rebels and others in Kintyre and Knapdale involved in the Earl of Argyll's rebellion of 1685 (SC54/17/5/2).

Burgh Courts

15.19 Minor offences within royal burghs would be tried by the burgh court. Again, the records of such trials are intermingled in the court books with the other business of the court (see **14.51**). Most offences tried by a burgh court were of the nature of a breach of a peace, but their records have a particular genealogical value in that these courts fined the participants in irregular marriages. For example, in Peebles in 1728, James Montgomery, cripple, for the present residing in Peebles, and Jean Drysdale were fined by the magistrates for their irregular marriage by the vicar of Irthington (in Cumberland) on 8th March 1726. Jean Drysdale was later banished from the burgh for another offence (B58/9/4).

Justice of the Peace Courts

15.20 See **14.49-50** for how to search the JP records. The JP courts also had a criminal jurisdiction. The records in the court books are usually brief and the offences charged vary from court to court. In country areas, the commonest crime was pursuit of game (i.e. poaching). In towns, the offences were more varied – theft, scandal, riot, breach of peace, being a prostitute. Occasionally, people were fined for irregular marriage or witnessing one. For example, in 1728, Antony Aston, comedian in Edinburgh, was fined for being witness to his son Walter's irregular marriage with Mrs Jean Kerr (JP35/4/2).

Admiralty Court

15.21 If your ancestor committed a crime on the high seas up to 1830, then the record of his trial may be among the Admiralty Court records. In the

AC catalogue, look up AC16, which lists the volumes that contain the reports of these trials. They begin in 1705. There is no index, but each volume has a contents list. There are also separate indexes to processes by the surnames of the parties. Very few such cases were in fact heard by the Admiralty Court, but for other types of case see **14.33–37**.

Witnesses

15.22 Witnesses and jurors play a crucial role in criminal trials. When a witness gave evidence, the court recorded age, marital status, occupation and abode. Their statements, also known as depositions, are mostly found in the precognitions and the High Court of Justiciary records. For example, in a precognition of 1834 we find 'John McDonald, aged fourteen, son of, and residing with, Dougal McDonald, porter at the Broomilaw, Glasgow' (AD14/34/373). In a trial record of 1736 evidence was heard from a witness, who is described as 'Evan More McAphie alias Cameron formerly in Shian in Glengarry parish of Kilnanivage and shire of Inverness now in Kilin in the shire of Perth aged 52 years or thereby married' (JC7/20). The depositions may also yield valuable information about family relationships and occupations, and sometimes even record the actual words spoken during the events being described. To find trial witnesses it is necessary to search the original records. However, occasionally the witnesses might themselves be subject to punishment, and can therefore be found in the catalogue. For example, in January 1790, Mathew Bell, carter in Paisley, was imprisoned for a month in the Edinburgh Tolbooth for prevarication upon oath during the trial of Duncan Wright, a gardener, for rape (JC3/45, p.446).

Jurors

15.23 The names and designations of jurors must be searched for in the minute books of jury (solemn) trials, because they are not included in the catalogue. However, if jurors failed to appear for a trial ('assize'), they were subject to the law, and the court's actions are recorded in the catalogue. On 4 April 1801 Robert Duff esquire, of Muirtown, Inverness, was fined 100 merks Scots for failing to appear at a circuit assize at Inverness (JC11/45, f.1v). If you are lucky the juror's explanation for his absence may be recorded, thus shedding light on personal circumstances. Look in the minute books or in the administrative papers at the end of each year in JC26. It is worth remembering that juries were originally restricted by property qualifications, and were all male until reforms in 1919.

Victims

15.24 Perhaps the most overlooked individuals among the records of criminal trials are those who were most directly affected by crime, namely the victims. Until recently they have been hidden from view because criminal records were identified by the name of the accused. The NAS catalogue now records the names of many victims in High Court and circuit cases, so it is becoming easier to trace individuals without prior knowledge of the relevant trial. For example, the sitting papers (JC26) reveal that in 1889 James Fraser of 32 Ann Street, Dundee, and Jane Lyall of 29 Rosebank Street, Dundee, were both victims of housebreaking. The perpetrator was John Garrity, who had a previous conviction for theft. In January 1890 he was found guilty at the circuit court at Dundee and sentenced to twelve months imprisonment with hard labour (JC26/1890/228). Note that not all victims' names are included in the catalogue, for example only the first few in cases involving numerous thefts of small articles. Also, for certain years the names have yet to be included, and it should be noted that information about victims is not made available from records less than 100 years old.

Prisoners

15.25 Persons accused of crimes might, before the trial, be lodged in prison, as well as finding themselves there after sentence, either for a period of imprisonment or while waiting for transportation or hanging. Until 1880, civil debtors as well as those charged with or found guilty of crimes might also be imprisoned. Personal information about prisoners may be found in those prison registers which are preserved among the Home and Health Department records (HH).

15.26 Check the catalogue for the HH21 series, or the NAS online guide to crime, to see if there is a register of prisoners in a prison in which your ancestor might have been placed. Many of the registers only cover the 1840s to the 1870s, but some continue into the twentieth century. If the register is only of criminal prisoners, this is specified in the catalogue. Most registers supply the name, age, height, marital status, places of birth and residence, occupation and religion of each prisoner, as well as his crime, the court that tried him and the sentence.

15.27 Information about prisoners who were sentenced to transportation may be found in the register of the prison which served the court where they were tried, or in the registers of prisons in Aberdeen and Edinburgh where such prisoners waited to be moved to England. The records of the Edinburgh (Calton) Prison include a separate register of convicts under sentence of transportation from 1852 (HH21/5/16). This provides the name, age, crime, place of trial, marital status and trade of each prisoner, along with comments by the chaplain.

15.28 The ships which carried convicts to Australia sailed from England, so further information about them is kept in the Home Office records in The National Archives in London. A database of transported convicts based on the TNA convict transportation registers, 1787-1870, is available online at Ancestry.com, and another at the Queensland State Library site *www.slq.qld.gov.au/info/fh/convicts*. Other specialist sites cover the convicts. NAS holds a microfilm copy of TNA's records (RH4/160). The registers are arranged by date of departure of each ship. The last reel (RH4/160/7) includes a list and an index of ships' names, with their dates and destinations. The Scottish prisoners are placed near the end of the list of convicts on each ship. The information includes the convict's name and where, when and for how many years he was sentenced. There could be a delay of several years between conviction and transportation. The last transportation ship to sail to Western Australia in 1867 carried Alex Casey, who had been sentenced to 15 years penal servitude in Edinburgh in 1858.

15.29 A small series of transportation papers can also be found in the Justiciary Court records (JC41) for the period 1653 to 1853. The early period mainly consists of certificates of transportation of convicts to America in the 1770s. The receiving authorities returned a statement that the prisoners had landed. The later papers date from 1837 to 1853 and consist of lists of convicts to be transported and extract sentences of transportation.

15.30 Apart from the HH21 series, there are two further sets of prison registers of particular interest. HH11 is the reference number of a series of Edinburgh Tolbooth Warding and Liberation Books, 1657-1816. These 39 volumes mostly have a contents list under initial letters of surnames. They deal with both civil and criminal prisoners, stating their name and designation, at whose instance they are incarcerated and sometimes which court dealt with the case. Extracts from these records, 1657-1686, were published in the *Book of the Old Edinburgh Club,* volumes 4-6, 8, 9, 11 and 12 (1911-1923). The Liberation information may occasionally be of

Prisoner in Barlinnie Prison (left), 1883 (HH21/70/97/11D) and Greenock, 1873 (HH12/56/7).

further use. For example, in October 1735, William Fowler, an Irishman, was incarcerated by a warrant of his employers, a firm of shipbuilders in Irvine, for theft. Three weeks later, he was liberated by warrant both of his employers and of the JPs 'who Indented with Mr Ferguson for the plantations' (HH11/18).

15.31 HH12 is a series of miscellaneous prison records, including records of prisoners in the condemned cell. The most valuable record in the series is a bound set of forms giving particulars of prisoners in Greenock Prison, 1872-1888 (HH12/56/7). Not only do these forms supply detailed personal information about each prisoner, but also added is a photograph of the prisoner, some apparently in their best clothes.

Suffragettes, aliens and political prisoners

15.32 Personal details of special categories of prisoners can also be found in NAS, particularly among the registers of individual Scottish prisons. They include information about those who were jailed in the early years of the twentieth century during the women's suffrage movement, those who were interned as a result of being labelled 'enemy aliens' during the First and Second World Wars, and those whose political views and activities were regarded as suspect.

15.33 Documents about the suffragettes are held mainly in government files and relate to their campaigning activities before the First World War, or the periods they spent in prison. A Register of Suffragettes received into prison in Scotland, 1909-1914 (HH12/22) records where they were tried and sentenced, and whether they went on hunger strike or were force fed while in prison.

15.34 The registers of prisoners in HH21 record men who were interned by the British Government as 'hostile' enemy aliens during both world wars. These Scots were mainly of German or Italian extraction, and were rounded up and detained under emergency powers which permitted the internment of anyone of 'hostile origin'. The internees are recorded in various prison registers, normally a few days after the declaration of war. In some cases the heads of households of entire foreign or alien communities are listed. In 1940 we find that Eduardo Paolozzi, then a sixteen year-old assistant in his father's confectionery shop in Leith, spent three months in Saughton Prison, Edinburgh, before being released (HH21/71/5). He later became one of Scotland's most famous artists and sculptors.

15.35 Internees from Scotland were housed in internment camps throughout the UK, including many on the Isle of Man. For further details of wartime internee records you should consult The National Archives at Kew.

15.36 Records concerning twentieth century political activists and prisoners can be found among trial records, particularly of the High Court or sheriff courts. Some early Scottish Office files about political activists exist in the HH series, and information can also be found in the surviving prisoners' case files (HH16), which have only been retained for notable prisoners. These include records of the activities of men such as the 'Red Clydesider' John Maclean, who was incarcerated in Peterhead prison during the First World War. A later wartime prisoner was the classical scholar and Scottish National Party member, Douglas Young, who was twice imprisoned during 1943-44 for refusing to register for military service, or as a conscientious objector. Brief details of his incarceration are recorded in the prison registers, but the series of individual prisoners' case files provides a fuller picture of his experience in prison, where he whiled away his time reading Greek (HH16/253/1-2).

Pardons and Remissions

15.37 A few criminals have the good fortune to have their crime pardoned or their sentence 'remitted'. Such remissions, often reducing a sentence of death to one of transportation, were granted by the Crown through the office of the Great Seal. If you are looking for a remission granted before 1668, use the published *Register of the Great Seal of Scotland* (see **11.23–25**) and *Register of the Privy Seal of Scotland* (see **8.17**). There is a typescript index of remissions, 1668–1906, in the West Search Room. This supplies the name, sometimes designation, place of conviction and offence of each person, with the date of remission and volume and running number (not page number) of the Great Seal Paper Register. If you find your ancestor in this index, order out as C3/ volume number, unless the volume number is preceded by a letter (eg S32), in which case refer to the introduction to the index for advice. The index includes some remissions omitted from the Great Seal Register but surviving in other records. Remissions are granted for a wide variety of crimes, adultery and drunkenness as well as murder. In 1896, William Cochrane was remitted his five-shilling fine by the Glasgow Police Court for playing football on the street (C3/47, no 64). Until 1896, these remissions are in Latin. Although they do not contain much information not in the index, for example never explaining why the remission was granted, they may be useful in leading you to the court records.

15.38 Details of remitted sentences are also recorded in the High Court Books of Adjournal and Minute Books. On 28 September 1813 Robert McLaren, a labourer from Lochee, Forfar, was tried at the circuit court at Perth for the crime of theft by housebreaking. He was found guilty and sentenced to be hanged by the public executioner. On petition, the sentence of death was remitted under the Great Seal to transportation for 7 years, which is recorded in the High Court minute book (JC8/10, f. 45v). These details can be found in the catalogue. Copies of warrants of remissions, from 1682 to 1918, may be found in the Justiciary records under JC24. English versions of remissions between 1762 and 1849 may be found in RH2/4/255-273, which contains photostat copies of the Home Office Criminal Entry Books for Scotland (originals in The National Archives in London).

∞16∞
Taxpayers

16.1 Tax records have already been mentioned in respect of death duties (**9.36–37**) and land tax (**11.36–38**), which was also known as the cess.

16.2 Various other types of taxes were levied for varying periods of years. The lists of people liable for each tax or of payments made by them may be worth examining. At least, you may find that a person of a certain name was resident in a certain parish.

Hearth Tax

16.3 In 1690 Parliament granted a tax on every hearth in the kingdom. Both landowners and tenants were liable to pay and therefore may be named in the tax records. Look at the introduction in the catalogue for E69 for more detail. The records date between 1691 and 1695, and those that have survived are arranged by counties. Within a county, look for a list of hearths or, not quite so useful, accounts of hearth money collected (these may omit personal names). Published versions of the lists for several counties exist and are mostly noted in the catalogue. All of the records have been imaged and can be seen as 'Virtual Volumes' in the search rooms. When looking at a list or account for your county, you will find it is arranged by parishes. Within parishes, there will be a list of those who had hearths in their houses, eg 'Georg Edgar tennent in Evelaw three [hearths], John Wilson coatter there one' (E69/5/1). Sometimes just the name of the hearth-owner is given, without designation. A supplementary series of hearth tax records for the same period can be found in the Leven and Melville Muniments (GD26/7/300-391). Lists of hearths in some Ross-shire parishes are in the Cromartie Muniments (GD305/1/64, nos 240-1, 243, 271-2, 277, 280-1).

Poll Tax

16.4 Poll taxes were imposed on Scotland between 1693 and 1699 on all adults except those dependent on charity. Unfortunately, the records are not complete. Look in the catalogue for E70, which consists of two series of records, each arranged by counties: the E70 series itself, and a supplementary list of poll-tax records surviving in other record groups, which also notes some of the growing number of printed versions. Having read the introduction, look at both lists under the relevant county. These describe assorted lists and accounts of pollable persons, the information, which is variable, again collected within parishes. At their most informative, these records can be genealogically useful, naming children and servants, eg 'James Rutherfurde Tennent in Sawchtan for himself, his wife, Wm, Janet and Elizat his children' (E70/8/1 – Account for parish of Crichton in Midlothian).

Post-Union Taxes

16.5 From 1748, certain assessed taxes were levied in Scotland and copies of the lists (schedules) of people assessed to pay have been preserved among the Exchequer records. Look at the E326 catalogue and read first the general introduction and the introductions to the individual tax records. The records of each tax are arranged by counties, as described in the catalogue, and within counties by parishes (not in alphabetical order), but royal burghs are listed separately – check the catalogue carefully.

16.6 Window Tax, 1748-1798 (E326/1), Commutation Tax, 1784-1798 (E326/2), Inhabited House Tax, 1778-1798 (E326/3) and Consolidated Assessed Taxes, 1798-1799 (E326/15) were all taxes on householders (owners or tenants, one per dwelling house). However, this record is not as useful as it sounds, as only the better-off were taxed. A house had to have at least seven windows or a rent of at least £5 yearly before it was liable for tax. In some rural parishes, the only persons liable for tax were the minister and a couple of lairds. The schedules for burghs and some more populous parishes are useful in listing more names, but omission of designations and of locations of the dwelling houses limits their usefulness. The schedule for the burgh of Aberdeen in 1773 lists 546 window-tax-paying inhabitants, but they include five ladies described simply as 'Mrs Forbes' (E326/1/128).

16.7 A shop tax was levied between 1785 and 1789. If you want to find if your ancestor had a shop worth a rental of more than £5 per year at that time, look at E326/4. Unfortunately, the business is not always specified.

Excerpt from Edinburgh Inhabited House Tax, 1778, giving names and occupations of householders (E326/3/40).

16.8 Taxes were levied on certain classes of servants, mainly domestic (male servants, 1777-1798, E326/5, and female, 1785-1792, E326/6). While you may want to find out how many servants your well-off ancestor employed, the schedules of these taxes are more significant in that they usually name the servants, sometimes also stating what kind of servant, and in that the record notes which masters were bachelors as they had to pay double tax. In Earlston parish in 1778, Captain Colin Falconer's footman was 'Osemin a Negro' (E326/5/1). You can see an example of taxation of male servants in Old Aberdeen etc, 1777-1778 (E326/5/1) in the Scottish Archive Network (SCAN) website: *www.scan.org.uk/researchrtools/tax.htm.*

16.9 The other assessed taxes, on carts, carriages, horses, dogs and clocks and watches, all for brief periods of years up to 1798, are, with one

146

exception, of little added use. The exception is Farm Horse Tax (1797-1798, E326/10), which is continued in the Consolidated Assessed Taxes (1798-1799, E326/15). Its value is that it helps to identify tenant farmers. In the parish of Strathdon in 1799, three persons paid window tax, five more paid house tax, but another 47 paid farm horse tax (E326/15/1). It is unfortunate that this record covers such a short period of time, as it is continued only for Midlothian up to 1812 (E327/36-54).

16.10 Income tax was first imposed in 1799 on annual incomes of £60 and over. Lists of those who made returns survive for Midlothian, 1799-1801 (E327/18-31), and for certain other counties and burghs (see the catalogue) for 1801-1802 (E326/14). One point of interest here is that abatements were made on account of children. If the number of children is not stated, it should be possible to calculate this from the sum deducted. The rules for such abatements are contained in the Duties on Income Act, 1798.

16.11 Income tax was replaced in 1803 by a property tax assessed on income from ownership and occupation of land, investments, trades and offices. The Exchequer records contain records for Midlothian only, 1803-1812 (E327/78-121). The trades and offices of taxpayers are specified, particularly in Edinburgh, where the arrangement is by street within parish. Natale Corri at the Concert Hall was assessed as making a profit in 1803 of £200 from his trade as a musician (E327/81).

∞17∞
Officials

17.1 The highest-ranking government officials are listed in the *Handbook of British Chronology* (Royal Historical Society, London). The appointments of other officials may be found in the records of the Great and Privy Seal: officials such as sheriffs and other judges, lieutenants of counties, keepers of registers of sasines, sheriff and commissary clerks. Indexes of such commissions, both of persons and of offices, are available from 1668 to 1955 (Great Seal) and from 1660 to 1898 (Privy Seal, English record). Most of these Great Seal commissions are ordered out by the reference C3 and the volume number, but not all – first check the introductory pages to the index. Privy Seal commissions are ordered out by PS3 and the volume number. For earlier commissions, you should use the printed Great and Privy Seal volumes, except for the Privy Seal record between 1585 and 1660 when you should use a list referenced PS7/1 which leads you to the entries in volumes referenced PS1. If your ancestor is unexpectedly absent from these records or you want more information about his appointment, try the records mentioned in **17.2-3.**

17.2 Lists of the holders of some of these minor offices (including HM Limner, the Historiographer Royal and Governors of Edinburgh Castle) are available in the Historical Search Room. See also a typed volume 'Civil and Judicial Establishment 1707-1830'. This is a copy of an Exchequer record (E229/10/1) that lists the holders of various offices, including the staffs of the Courts of Exchequer, Justiciary and Session. Unfortunately, this record is incomplete. Gaps may be filled by checking the appropriate Court records themselves. For example, the Lord Advocate, as crown representative and chief prosecutor in Scotland, would appoint advocates on a temporary basis to act as his representative or depute. Such appointees would present their commission of appointment at the first appropriate court sitting date. We see that on 2 April 1799, John Burnett, Esquire, advocate, was appointed as Advocate Depute to prosecute cases in the High Court for the duration of the Spring (South) circuit (JC12/23, f. 1r). Such appointments, both permanent and temporary, are recorded in the catalogue in the relevant minute book entry.

17.3   Government officials had to be paid and, as a result, post-Union bureaucracy produced several series of Exchequer records, which give information of the appointments and salaries of officials after 1707. These records overlap considerably and are not consistent throughout each series. It is not immediately apparent why information may be in one record and not another. The following are the most useful and are all in volume form. Look at the relevant catalogue for dates and call numbers of each volume. In these volumes there are indexes or contents lists of commissions and warrants, but no indexes of the persons named in the salary lists. Some also contain records of other payments, including Civil List pensions (i.e. annuities to worthy persons in need), so that you may find an ancestor who received an income from the government, even if not employed by them: but look first at the index to the Privy Seal English Record (PS3) for such pensioners.

E313   Copies of commissions and warrants for paying salaries etc, 1709-1965.

E224   Establishment entry books containing lists of salaries and pensions, 1709-1866, and warrants thereof, 1709-1834. Judges and court officials will be found throughout; later volumes include staffs of government boards and of Register House. The last list in which a person appears will often provide the date on which he died or left office.

E810   Lists of salaries, superannuations, and pensions, 1854-1930. Contain a useful range of recipients.

E811   Lists of salaries, 1869-1930. Include staffs of the Exchequer, court offices, Register House, boards and commissions.

17.4   A government employee may of course be mentioned in the records of the department in which he was employed and therefore it may be worth checking establishment or staff records in the catalogue of that department's records. For example, if your ancestor was employed in the General Register Office for Scotland between 1909 and 1920, he should appear in the files referenced GRO5/774–776. Local registrars from 1855, and GROS district examiners from 1912 onwards, are to be found in the correspondence and reports in GRO1-2. However, in most departmental records, records of staff do not start until well into the twentieth century and do not include personal files. The staff of three government organisations before 1900 are, however, well recorded – the Board of Customs, the Board of Excise, and the Post Office. Bear in mind that data protection issues may apply if you are looking for more recent staff records.

17.5 A separate Scottish Board of Customs functioned from 1707 until 1829. Look in the CE catalogue at CE3 and CE12 for establishment books. These contain quarterly lists, arranged by port, of all Customs officers, except junior clerks and the crews of the Excise vessels known as 'cutters' (commanders and mates are named). Payments of salaries to Customs officers are recorded in the Customs cash accounts (E502). The date payment stopped would be the date of death, dismissal or resignation. If your ancestor was a Customs officer in the mid-eighteenth century, look at two further records, GD1/372/1 and RH2/8/102, which list the officers in 1752 and 1755, arranged by port and supplying for each his age and character (eg, 'A tipler, Indolent, & not capable' or 'Capable & Sober. Worn out in the Service'). GD1/372/1 valuably also records the officer's birthplace, whether he has a wife and how many children.

17.6 The separate Scottish Board of Excise survived until 1830. Its records are also listed in the CE catalogue. J F Mitchell and Sheila Mitchell gathered information about the Excise officers between 1707 and 1830 from this and other sources and noted it on cards arranged alphabetically. These cards may be consulted in the NAS on microfilm (RH4/6/1-2). The information is supplied in rather succinct form, so you should first read the explanation of the arrangement of the symbols on the cards which appears at the beginning of the microfilm. Although the Mitchells searched widely, the information on the cards is not exclusive. You may find further details, or simply prefer to search first, in:

GD1/54/10, which includes a list of Excise officers in 1743

CE6/19, which lists all officers in 1794 under the initial letter of each's surname, stating his age and the number of his family, or

CE13/1-9, which is a series of volumes minuting the appointments and removals of Excise staff between 1813 and 1829. The CE13 volumes are indexed by initial letter of surnames, then by order of appearance in the book.

17.7 The Post Office records contain a series of establishment books, listing the salaried staff, from 1803 to 1911 (PO1/15-65). These books are arranged by post-towns, naming all the staff in the main post offices, including letter carriers, but do not name sub-postmasters. PO1/16, which records postal staff in 1803, notes their dates of appointment (eg Margaret MacKerchar was appointed to Aberfeldy in 1799) and also has later annotations.

∞18∞
Soldiers, Sailors and Airmen

18.1   After 1707, the Army and Navy were administered from London. Therefore, if you are seeking information about an ancestor's regular military
or naval service after 1707, or air service in the twentieth century, you
should apply to The National Archives, which holds War Office, Admiralty and Air Force records. For British Army service records for officers
and soldiers whose regular service ended between 1921 and 1997, you
should contact Army Personnel Services (Army Personnel Centre, Historical Disclosures, Mailpoint 400, Kentigern House, 65 Brown Street,
Glasgow G2 8EX). Even before the Union of 1707, references in the
NAS records to named individuals in the Scottish army, and particularly
in the navy, are sparse. Nevertheless, there are records in the NAS that
may be of use to you. In addition to those described below, it is still
worth checking the source lists of our military records, and naval and
mercantile records.

Soldiers before 1707

18.2   The main record of individuals in the Scottish army is the Muster Rolls
which are in the Exchequer records. Look at the catalogue referenced
E100. These muster rolls are arranged by regiment and, within regiment, by companies or troops. Though the earliest is dated 1641, most
are dated after 1680. They name all the officers and men in a troop or
company at a certain place and date. Ranks are stated, except for troop-
ers. Few rolls supply any other information. Your problem is that unless
you already know that your ancestor was in a particular regiment, you
may have to look through some 4,800 rolls in the hope of finding him.
It may help you that many recruits came from the estates owned by their
Colonel or his family and most regiments were known by the name of
their commanding officer (eg Lord Jedburgh's dragoons). Some of these
rolls are printed in *The Scots Army, 1661-1688* by C Dalton (republished
in 1989 by Greenhill Books), but only officers appear in the book's
index. Similar lists of those serving in particular regiments may be found

in GD collections (see **7.20-21**), where a member of that family had been granted a commission to be Colonel of a regiment.

18.3 If your ancestor was an officer, there is more likely to be a record of him than if he were a common soldier. Commissions in the army were granted by the Crown and, from 1670, some were recorded in the War-rant Books of the Secretary of Scotland, along with other government business. Look up the State Papers catalogue at SP4 to find the volume covering the relevant dates. These volumes each contain a contents list or index. The commissions supply only the name, rank, company and regi-ment of the officer, no other personal details. These SP4 commissions are noted and indexed in Dalton's *The Scots Army, 1661-1688* and thereafter in his *English Army Lists and Commission Registers, 1661-1714*. There is also a small series of commissions, 1643, 1689-1827, in RH9/9 – look up that catalogue; and commissions may occasionally be found in GD collections.

Soldiers after 1707

18.4 The only military records after the Union among public records in the NAS are those of the Militia and more recently the Territorials.

18.5 Though Militia records run from 1797 to the mid-nineteenth century, the heyday of the Militia force was the Napoleonic Wars. These records have two main points of genealogical interest: they name the young men who were balloted to serve in the Militia and they name some of their wives. Look in the catalogue of Sheriff Court (SC) or County Council (CO) records of the sheriffdom or county in which your ancestor lived. The relevant records, if they survive, will be catalogued under the head-ing of Lieutenancy and/or Militia or Miscellaneous, usually near the end of an SC catalogue. The most available guide to militia records is J Gib-son and M Medlycott's *Militia Lists and Musters 1757-1876* (Federation of Family History Societies, 1994). More useful is Arnold Morrison, *The Defence of Scotland: Militias, Fencibles and Volunteer Corps – Scottish Sources 1793–1820* (privately printed, 2000), available in the NAS Library.

18.6 As conscription was by ballot, only some men were made to serve. The militiamen had to be healthy and aged between 18 and 30, until 1802, and thereafter between 18 and 45. Certain categories were exempted, including apprentices and poor men with more than two children (see the Militia (Scotland) Act 1802 (s.38)). Despite these limitations, the Militia records name many people whose existence might not otherwise

Application by the wife of a militiaman for financial support, 1805 (SC29/72/2).

be recorded. In the Highland parish of Braemar and Crathie in 1800, 60 young men were listed (CO6/5/6). Information about individual militiamen appears in the schedules of those eligible to be balloted (some claiming exemption), in lists of men conscripted, and in minute books. The basic information supplied about a militiaman is his name, profession and place of abode, but sometimes his age is stated and, more rarely, place of birth. Thus we know that Charles Herkes aged 22, a weaver in Dunbar in 1825, was born in County Down (CO7/13/2).

18.7 When a man was serving in the Militia and his family was unable to support themselves, his wife and children under 10 years of age were eligible for an allowance. Records of claims for such allowances appear amongst Lieutenancy and Militia records. These name each wife and, usually but not invariably, her husband; say how many children, sometimes naming them; and state the parish where she lived. An additional record of such payments to wives and children in Midlothian, 1803-1815, is contained in the Exchequer records (E327/147-158).

18.8 Some militia records may be found in the GD series (see **7.20-21**). For example, the Seaforth muniments include lists of men between 15 and 60 able to bear arms in parishes in Ross-shire in 1798 (GD46/6/45).

18.9 The Ministry of Defence records in the NAS consist of Territorial and Auxiliary Forces Associations' records. These include a list of members of Dundee Volunteer Rifle Corps in 1859 (MD7/1), a muster roll of the 5th Forfarshire Volunteer Corps 1859-1886 (MD7/2), which gives the ages, occupations, and residences of the volunteers, and a list of members of the Dundee National Reserve in 1914 (MD7/3). The rest of the MD records are all post-1900 and mostly minute books. While officers are regularly named in them, other ranks are rarely named.

18.10 The wills and inventories of servicemen of all services and ranks could be recorded in the normal way, and for the period from 1876 onwards can be found in the *Calendar of Confirmations* (see **9.20-28**) A separate series contains soldiers' wills: about 300 pre-1914, 26,000 for the First World War, 4,500 for the Second World War, and a few for the inter-war years and the post-war period to 1966 (SC70/8). These records are only for soldiers up to the rank of warrant officer who were domiciled in Scotland, but they include men who were promoted from the ranks. The wills are arranged in the order in which they were administered, usually many months after the soldier's death.

18.11 All the wills can be searched for in the catalogue by name, or by other details such as regimental number, rank, unit or date of death. A separate database, which is currently only available in the search rooms, allows a more structured search using several different fields. Access to the originals is not permitted for preservation reasons, but copies can be obtained by requesting them through the search rooms. A growing number of pre-1939 wills is being made available digitally, and all wills for the Second World War and after are already imaged.

18.12 Soldiers in both world wars mostly made use of the Army's official printed forms, but occasionally they wrote their own will, sometimes in the form of a personal letter. Some wills are signed and witnessed, but the 'informal will' form in the pay book and forms used for soldiers on active service during the Second World War did not require a witness. Normally they were authenticated posthumously by an officer. The personal details which you can find in the wills include the soldier's name, War Office numbers, regimental number, rank, unit, the date and details of his bequest (usually very simple), the named beneficiary or beneficiaries and their home address, and the date and place of death.

18.13 For further details of a soldier's service records you should consult The National Archives in London.

Sailors

18.14 There are no official records of the Scottish navy, as such. A few miscellaneous naval documents survive in the Exchequer records: see list E90. The most useful of them are printed in *The Old Scots Navy, 1689-1710*, by James Grant. Those apart, information about Scottish ships and the men who sailed in them has to be gleaned from the various records of Scottish government, such as the Privy Council. The Admiralty Court records occasionally contain names, for example of the entire crew of HM ship *Lion* in 1628, to whom pay was owed (AC7/2, p.41).

18.15 Some personal details can be found of crews on the Fishery Board for Scotland's cruisers among the vessels' order and other books. For example there are registers of sailors on the *Brenda*, 1898-1954, and *Minna*, 1900-1960 (AF6/65-66). Entries are chronological by the date the sailor entered the Board's service, but unfortunately the registers are not indexed. The personal details consist of name, place and date of birth, previous post and service history in the Board, including rank(s), wages, and reason for removal from the Board's employment. Additional remarks often provide more service details. For example we find that Neil Murray, leading seaman on the *Minna* from 1907, left the Board's service on account of age and failing health in 1924 (AF6/66). The ship's articles for the *Brenda*, 1946-1949, and the *Minna*, 1933-1951 (AF6/67-68) also include crew lists with similar details, and crew members' signatures.

Merchant Seamen

18.16 Both before and after 1707, the Customs Accounts record the movement of ships in and out of ports. Usually the merchant who commissioned the voyage is named, and occasionally the captain. The Accounts do not record the names of crew or passengers. These Customs Accounts are referenced E71 (for the period up to 1640), E72 (1662-1696) and E504 (1742-1830). They are arranged by ports.

18.17 The crews of ships engaged in whale fishing between 1750 and 1825 are named in the vouchers of payments of bounties (E508/47/8-130/8). The ships, ports and owners are named in the Customs cash accounts (E502/48-130), which provide a key to the individual vouchers. Similarly, the crews of ships engaged in herring fishing between 1752 and 1796 are named in the more numerous vouchers for herring bounties (E508/49/9-96/9). Here again the cash accounts (E502) record ships, owners and ports, which should lead you to the voucher you want.

18.18 Seamen who used the port of Leith may be found in the records of Trinity House of Leith (GD226), a mutual benefit society for the support of the poor, aged and infirm mariners and their dependents. Minute and cash books date from the mid-seventeenth century and record payments by seamen as well as pensions to them and their dependents, mainly widows. Included are records of the pilots who guided ships into the harbour.

18.19 Since 1835, it has been compulsory for masters of ships to enter into agreements with any crew member before sailing. Not all records of such agreements have been kept. A small number, dating between 1867 and 1913 and relating to Scottish ships, are preserved in the NAS. Look up the catalogue referenced BT3. If this record fails you, you should try the crew lists in the Glasgow City Archives, The National Archives in London, the National Maritime Museum in London and the Memorial University, Newfoundland. These crew agreements supply the name, age and birthplace of each seaman. To search this record, you need to know the name of the ship in which your ancestor might have sailed.

18.20 Soldiers and sailors occasionally fell foul of the law and appeared in the criminal courts. Entries for High Court criminal trials may include the person's regiment and rank, or the vessel on which they served. For example we find in the catalogue that Edward Bagnet Harvey O'Keeffe, Lieutenant, 21st Regiment of Foot and Godfrey Margerey, Ensign, 3rd North British or Lanarkshire Militia were both indicted at Perth in April 1801 for murder by duelling. Having failed to appear for trial they were declared outlaws (JC11/45, f. 24v).

18.21 The Admiralty Court records can sometimes also provide the names of crew members of merchant vessels, as well as of the masters and skippers, for example in cases involving disputes over cargo or pay. The earliest crew list seems to be that of the *Bonadventure*, sailing from Lisbon to London in 1621 (AC7/2, p.53). Although most named mariners were Scots, occasionally men serving on foreign vessels are also listed. The records also occasionally contain names of fishermen, for example in a case in 1734 concerning an alleged assault on a customs officer by fisher-men and mariners from Pittenweem and Anstruther (AC8/433a).

Airmen

18.22 There are some wills of a few officers and men in the Royal Flying Corps (RFC) and Royal Air Force (RAF) who transferred from the Army during the First World War (SC70/8). There are also wills of 61 RAF officers and men, including aircrew and balloon operators, who were domiciled in Scotland and died on active service in the period 1941-1950 (SC70/10). Some of the RAF wills are contained in the airman's original Service and Pay Book, which can provide additional details of date of birth, civilian occupation, religion, marital status, terms of service, and service history.

18.23 For further details of RAF service records you should consult The National Archives in London.

Exemptions from Military Service & Conscientious Objectors

18.24 Conscientious objectors and men who sought exemption from military service, particularly during the First World War, can be found among the records of the Military Appeal Tribunals (HH30). The introduction of conscription in 1916 required all adult males aged 18-41 to regis-ter for military service unless they possessed a certificate of exemption. Applications for exemption were submitted to military tribunals by the man himself, his family or employers. They could claim exemption on the grounds that it was in the national interest for a man to continue in his current or other work, education or training, or that he was in a certified occupation. Personal reasons, such as serious hardship, ill-health or conscientious objection, were also claimed. It was certainly not the case that all applicants were unwilling to fight, because many of them were attested men, or army volunteers. Almost all appeals were refused and dismissed, after which appellants had little choice but to 'join the colours'.

18.25 The appeals are an invaluable source, and reveal details of personal, family or business circumstances. For example, in 1916 a Mrs Agnes Gillon, submitted an appeal for her only son Robert Gillon, who worked in her butcher's business in Balerno and Currie, Midlothian. She argued unsuccessfully that he was essential to the family business (HH30/2/1/42). Robert joined the army and was killed on 4 October 1917. The service careers of unsuccessful applicants can be sought in other records, for example Robert's army will is in NAS (SC70/8/905/5) – see **18.10**.

18.26 Unfortunately most Scottish tribunal records were destroyed in 1921, but 6,300 separate applications between March 1916 and October 1918 have survived for the Lothian and Peebles Military Appeal tribunal area, covering Edinburgh, the Lothians and the Borders (HH30). The applications are being catalogued and the digital images gradually being made available in the search room.

∞19∞
Clergymen and Church Members

Presbyterian Ministers

19.1   If your ancestor was a Presbyterian clergyman who had a parish or congregation, then look for him in one of the following printed sources.

Fasti Ecclesiae Scoticanae, 11 volumes (1915-2000). Originally compiled by Hew Scott, this series of volumes provides biographical, including family, details of all known ministers of the established Church of Scotland since the Reformation. Some omissions from early volumes are corrected in volume 8. As much of the information in the *Fasti* was based on record research, it may be worth following up references given in particular biographies.

History of the Congregations of the United Presbyterian Church, 1733-1900 by Robert Small (1904).

Annals and Statistics of the Original Secession Church by David Scott (1886). Unindexed.

Annals of the Free Church of Scotland, 1843-1900 by William Ewing (1914).

The Fasti of the United Free Church of Scotland, 1900-1929 J A Lamb (1956).

These last four publications contain information about the main denominations which dissented from the Church of Scotland in the eighteenth and nineteenth centuries. Additional details will be found in the records of the churches, presbyteries and synods in which these men served (see CH catalogues). Information about some dissenting ministers may be found in their Friendly Society records (CH3/515-517). CH3/515/8, a list of Relief Synod ministers, gives the dates of birth, marriage and death of them and their wives.

19.2   You may find references to students of divinity in the minutes of the presbyteries and synods (CH2 and 3) in which they were probationers. Some are mentioned briefly in the mainly nineteenth century records of theological colleges and student societies (CH3/119, CH3/273, CH3/281, CH3/305, CH3/885, CH12/).

19.3   It may be difficult to find a record of a Presbyterian clergyman who did not succeed in obtaining a church in Scotland. Some, between 1725 and 1876, may have been appointed itinerant preachers and catechists within the Highlands and Islands and, as such, appear in the records of the Royal Bounty Committee of the General Assembly of the Church of Scotland (CH1/5/51-79). These records are unindexed but include marginal tags and occasional lists of the catechists. Some missionaries and catechists had their salaries paid by the Society in Scotland for Propagating Christian Knowledge (see **20.7**) and are named in the SSPCK's scheme ledgers (GD95/7). Records of Presbyterian missionaries abroad are preserved in the National Library of Scotland.

Other Clergymen

19.4   Two useful reference works are *Scottish Episcopal Clergy, 1689–2000* by David M Bertie (Edinburgh, 2000) and *The Scottish Congregational Ministry, 1794–1993* by William D McNaughton (Congregational Union of Scotland, 1993). In the absence of published biographical details, information about non–presbyterian clergymen must be sought in the records of their churches (try the CH catalogues) or by enquiring of their present-day church headquarters.

19.5   Roman Catholic priests, 1732-1878, are listed in *The Innes Review* (Scottish Catholic Historical Association), volumes 17, 34 and 40, and after 1878 in Christine Johnson, *Scottish Catholic Secular Clergy 1879–1989* (Edinburgh, 1991). Registers of student priests at the Scots Colleges at Douai, Rome, Madrid, Valladolid and Ratisbon are printed and indexed in *Records of Scots Colleges* (New Spalding Club, 1906). The information is in Latin, but often includes the age and parentage of the student. The NAS has a photocopy of the register of the College in Rome 1602-1939 (RH2/7/14) and a microfilm copy of the registers of the College at Douai 1581-1772 (RH4/18). Further enquiries about Roman Catholic priests might be made to the Scottish Catholic Archives (address in Appendix A).

Presbyterian Church Members

19.6   Not until the mid-nineteenth century did it become common for church records to include lists of church members ('communicants') or to record the names of those who joined that church. Such information is sometimes contained in separate volumes – look in the catalogue of records of the church in question for a communion roll, list of communicants, list of parishioners, roll of male heads of families, etc. Such lists sometimes tell if a communicant came from another parish. Lists of communicants are sometimes inscribed in the kirk session minute books, particularly lists of young communicants on their joining the Kirk. The names of those who rented seats in a church may appear in account books.

List of Roman Catholics in the parish of Buittle, 1704 (CH1/2/5/3, no. 197/1).

19.7 In seventeenth and eighteenth century kirk session records, you will find the names of elders, those in receipt of poor relief, and those accused of or witness to scandalous behaviour (most commonly fornication, but it could be shoeing a horse on the Sabbath). Otherwise parishioners are not usually named, even when they move into the parish. But one cannot be categorical about this: for example, the earliest minute book of Linlithgow kirk session (CH2/740/1) records testimonials brought by incomers to the parish, 1645-1647.

Roman Catholics

19.8 Between 1700 and 1714, the names of Roman Catholics in their parishes were listed by Church of Scotland ministers and these lists of 'papists' are preserved among the records of the General Assembly of the Church of Scotland. They mainly relate to Banffshire, with a few lists for Edinburgh. Look in the catalogue for CH1/2/5 and CH1/2/29-34 for the particular reference numbers of lists of Catholics in the parishes in which your ancestors dwelt.

19.9 For more recent members of the Roman Catholic Church, check in the catalogue for RH21 whether the records of a relevant church include a register of communicants or confirmations. The earliest of these date from 1749, but the majority are nineteenth century.

Members of Other Churches

19.10 Look at the CH catalogue to see if the records of a particular church are in the NAS. Check the list of these records to see if they include a roll of members or communion roll: failing which look at minutes or other records. Among the Episcopalian records there are lists of communicants in the dioceses of Ross, Caithness and Argyll in 1762 and 1770 (CH12/1/12). The records of various denominations, such as Methodist congregations, may also be deposited in local authority and university archives. See the SCAN website (*www.scan.org.uk*) for summary details, or the NAS website (*www.nas.gov.uk*) for records formerly held in NAS.

℘20℘
Schoolteachers, Pupils and Students

20.1   The Education (Scotland) Act, 1872, was a watershed in the history of schooling in Scotland. The records which you should investigate for teachers are in the main different before and after that Act, though the ones mentioned in **20.7, 9** and **11** overlap 1872 to some extent. As there are many books about individual schools or education in particular areas, and many of the relevant records are preserved in the region or district where the school was situated, you should first investigate the sources in the local library or record office. In the NAS, the three source lists on education, although incomplete, can assist in pointing you to relevant records in GD and other collections. To trace your schoolmaster's name in the records suggested below will often involve searching unindexed minute books, some of which will have helpful marginal annotations (eg 'Ja: Turnbull schoolmaster'), some not.

20.2   The majority of schoolmasters taught in the parish or burgh school. You will find appointments of burgh schoolmasters recorded in the burgh or town council minutes (B). For example, in 1690 the council of the burgh of Dunbar nominated James Turnbull, youngest lawful son to the deceased George Turnbull, merchant burgess of that burgh, to be schoolmaster 'for learning the Childrein to read, wryt, lay compts and work arthmetick' (B18/13/2, f.34v).

20.3   Parish schoolmasters were nominated by the heritors (i.e. landowners) and minister of the parish and usually were then examined by the presbytery to ensure that they were qualified for the post. The record of the appointment of a parish schoolmaster should be in the minutes of the heritors' meetings in the Heritors Records (HR), which are arranged by parish.. If no heritors' records survive for the required parish and date, then you should search the CH2 records of that parish and the relevant presbytery. The kirk session records for the parish may contain the name of a schoolmaster, particularly as the schoolmaster often acted as session clerk. The presbytery minute books should record the presbytery's confirmation of the appointment of a schoolmaster. In the Church of Scotland, a presbytery is the court superior to the kirk session. The *Fasti Ecclesiae Scoticanae* (see **19.1**) will tell you which presbytery includes the parish in which you are interested.

20.4 The kirks of the Free Church of Scotland, which was founded in 1843, often set up their own schools. To find the record of the appointment of a teacher of a Free Church school, look up the name of the kirk in the catalogue for a list of that kirk's records (CH3). Order out the Deacons' Court minutes (rather than the session minutes), as the deacons appointed and paid the teacher.

20.5 Schoolmasters may appear in other records. The records of a parliamentary commission in 1690 include some lists of schoolmasters. Those in the counties of Angus, Berwickshire, East Lothian, Fife, Midlothian, Peebleshire, Perthshire, Roxburghshire and Stirlingshire (PA10/2) are printed in the Scottish History Society 4th series *Miscellany* X (1965). There is a list for Ayrshire among papers referenced PA10/5.

20.6 Until the nineteenth century, women teachers mainly taught practical subjects, such as sewing, spinning and knitting stockings, often as part of improving activities at a local level. Among the Forfeited Estates records we find petitions from schoolmistresses to the Commissioners of the Forfeited Estates, 1765-1780 (E777/174). Mistresses employed by the Society in Scotland for Propagating Christian Knowledge can be found in the SSPCK records (GD95), and those active between 1723 and 1872 are conveniently listed in *SSPCK: Index of Women Spinning and Weaving Mistresses*, ed. A S Cowper (1985).

20.7 Paradoxically, concern at the scarcity of schools in the Highlands and Islands led to a better recording of the schoolmasters who taught there. In the eighteenth and nineteenth centuries, the (SSPCK) erected and maintained schools in the Highlands, Islands and Remote Corners of Scotland where 'popery and ignorance' did 'much abound'. More information can be found in *SSPCK Schoolmasters, 1709–1872*, ed. A S Cowper (Scottish Record Society, 1997). To view the records of the Society, look at the GD95 catalogue. While the Society's minute books, letter books and inspectors' reports mention teachers, you will find the names of the SSPCK teachers more quickly in the register of schools, 1710-1761 (GD95/9/1); salary books, 1766-1779 (GD95/8/5); scheme ledgers, 1771-1890 (GD95/7); and abstract of school returns, 1827-1878 (GD95/9/6-7). Some of these records are arranged by presbyteries.

20.8 The SSPCK appointed its own teachers, to supplement the parish schoolmasters appointed by the heritors. There are three other records which provide further information about the parish schoolmasters in the Highlands and Islands. The Commissioners who until 1784 administered the estates forfeited after the 1745 Jacobite rising were heritors of the parishes in which these estates lay and therefore the records of their administration include the names of schoolmasters. There is a location list of the estates by county and parish at the beginning of the catalogue of their records (E700-788). Look up 'schools' in the index to the catalogue and also look at the various reports on particular estates (E729 etc), some of which are printed (and indexed) in *Reports on the Annexed Estates, 1755-1769* edited by Virginia Wills (HMSO, 1973).

20.9 By his will, a Mr James Dick set up a trust for the maintenance and assistance of the parochial (not burgh) schoolmasters in the counties of Aberdeen, Banff and Moray. If your ancestor was a teacher in these counties after 1832, look in the inventory of the Dick Bequest Trust records (GD1/4).

20.10 In terms of the Highlands Schools Act, 1838, the Treasury had to provide funds for additional schools in the Highlands. If your ancestor was a Highland schoolmaster between 1840 and 1863, look at the volumes referenced E224/32-40. The entry 'Schools, Schedule of Grants to' in the index to each volume will lead you to the list of schoolmasters who benefited from this fund.

20.11 In 1847, the Educational Institute of Scotland, a professional association for teachers, was formed. Its records, which contain the names of many teachers who joined its ranks, also include the records of earlier mutual benefit societies formed by teachers in Glasgow (1794-1836), Roxburgh (1811-1840) and Jedburgh (1824-1872). Look at the inventory of the Institute's records (GD342).

20.12 The Department of Education records include two volumes of reports by school inspectors before 1872. These are for the years 1859 (ED16/13) and 1866-1867 (ED16/14). Each volume reports on only a selection of schools, but they are indexed. Each report names the teacher and pupil-teachers of that school. Occasionally, an assistant teacher is named.

School teachers since 1872

20.13 From 1872, school boards administered education at a parish level and records of the appointment of teachers and pupil-teachers are in the minute books of these school boards. School board records are mostly preserved among the records of their county council. The county council records presently held by the NAS (but subject to change), which include school board records, are those of Midlothian (CO2/105-129), East Lothian (CO7/5/2) and Dumfries-shire (Mouswald only, CO9/2/1). The East Lothian records also include school logbooks that mention teachers (CO7/5/4). There are a few school board minutes elsewhere in the NAS – Barra (SC29/75/3), Dervaig (SC59/15/4), Kilninian and Kilmore (SC59/15/1-3), North Berwick (B56/14), Prestonkirk (B18/18/12) and Stornoway (SC33/60). For other school board records, you should enquire at the relevant local record office, archive centre or library.

20.14 The records of the Scottish Education Department include school inspection reports (ED16-18). These rarely name individuals, but can be of value in giving a general picture of the school your ancestor taught at or

Free Church Sunday School teachers annual picnic, circa 1900s (CH3/723/34).

attended. Of the reports, the most useful are referenced ED16/1–12, as, although they report on only a limited number of schools between 1896 and 1909, the reports supply the names of the teachers and pupil-teachers at these schools. Some volumes include an index of schools. ED17 and ED18 have the advantage that there is a separate file for each school, clearly stated in the ED catalogue with separate reference number, but the disadvantage that teachers are often not named or named just by their surname (eg 'Mr Cormack'). Some closure periods apply on these records.

School Pupils and Students

20.15 Records of school pupils are rare. Some happen to be noted in school log books. As mentioned above, pupil-teachers (who existed between 1846 and 1906 and had to be at least 13 years old) are named in school board records and inspection reports. Leaving certificate registers, which give particulars of every school candidate, exist from 1908 (ED36), but are closed for 75 years.

20.16 The records of George Heriot's School, Edinburgh, are held by the NAS and include admission registers of its boy pupils, 1659-1939 (GD421, section 10). The NAS also has the records of Dr Guthrie's Schools (see 32.25).

20.17 Pupils in local schools can sometimes be traced, for example in lists of girls attending the sewing schools in Muthill, Auchterarder, Crieff, Callander, and Dunblane, 1775-1783 (E777/287).

20.18 Information about students of further education is best sought from the university or college they attended. Check printed sources first, as some lists of students are published. The NAS holds records of the Drawing Academy and School of Design (later School of Art) in Edinburgh in the nineteenth century (see **24.4-5**).

Professors

20.19 Information about university staff is again best sought from that university. However, the appointments of some professors will be found in the Privy Seal records – look at the index to the Privy Seal English Record, 1660-1898 (PS3), and and also in the Exchequer records described in **17.3**.

∽21∾
Medical Professions

Doctors and Surgeons

21.1 Since 1858, all medical practitioners in the United Kingdom have had to be registered. The NAS holds the original register of doctors in Scotland (GMC1/2), which you are welcome to consult, but the information therein is more easily obtained from *The Medical Register* that is published annually and may be consulted in large public libraries. The *Register* names all registered doctors alphabetically, along with their addresses and qualifications. Remember that some doctors who registered in 1858 had been practising for many years, including William Arrott, doctor in Arbroath, whose qualifications were 'Doctor of Medicine of the University of St Andrews 1798 and Licentiate of the Royal College of Surgeons of Edinburgh 1795'. In the early entries in GMC1/2, some dates of death are later annotated. Another annual publication, which contains fuller biographical information about medical practitioners, is *The Medical Directory*. There is a separate *Medical Directory for Scotland,* 1852–1860. Scottish doctors appear in the *London and Provincial Medical Directory,* 1861–1869, and thereafter in *The Medical Directory*.

21.2 For information about physicians and surgeons who had ceased to practise by 1858, you should apply to the Royal College of Physicians of Edinburgh, the Royal College of Surgeons of Edinburgh or the Royal College of Physicians and Surgeons of Glasgow (addresses in Appendix A).

21.3 Surgeons who served at sea may occasionally be found in the Admiralty Court records, for example Ronald Arthur from Aberdeen, who sought his share of prize money while serving on the *Blessing* of Burntisland during a privateering voyage in 1626 (AC7/2, p. 87).

Other Medical Personnel

21.4   In the Home and Health Department records, there are registers of nurses, including those working in poorhouses, between 1885 and 1930 (HH2/33-37).

21.5   There are published annual registers of chemists (from 1869), dentists (from 1879), and midwives (from 1917). The NAS holds a set of the published Midwives Roll for Scotland, 1917-1940 (CMB3), but you may find it easier to consult the various published registers in a library. The register of nurses in the UK was published between 1922 and 1968. Nurses are listed by name, and you can find out their maiden surname (as appropriate), address (omitted from the 1950s onwards), and when they qualified and registered. The manuscript original of the Nurses' Register, 1921-1983, is held in the NAS (GNC12), as are registers of assistant or enrolled nurses, 1944-1983 (GNC13/1), and health visitors, 1933-1965 (GNC14/1-2). Note that records under 75 years old are subject to data protection restrictions. For further information on the profession see *www.rcn.org.uk*.

∞22∞
Lawyers

22.1 There were two principal categories of lawyers in Scotland: advocates, who alone could plead in the supreme court, the Court of Session; and solicitors, who used to be known as writers and may also be known as law agents. Law agents who plead cases in sheriff and other inferior courts may be called procurators. Since 1990 specially-qualified law agents called solicitor advocates have been permitted to plead before the Scottish supreme courts. Judges are usually appointed from the ranks of advocates. If your ancestor was a lawyer, first examine published sources.

22.2 Judges of the Court of Session up to 1832 are described in Brunton and Haig's *Senators of the College of Justice*. Advocates are listed in *The Faculty of Advocates, 1532-1943* (Scottish Record Society). Many solicitors or writers are listed in *The Register of the Society of Writers to Her Majesty's Signet* (Society of Writers to the Signet). The procurators in Aberdeen, who confusingly called themselves advocates, are listed in the *History of the Society of Advocates in Aberdeen* (New Spalding Club, 1912). Of these books the last contains the most genealogical information. The names of lawyers also appear in various published law lists or directories, notably the *Scottish Law List* which was previously called *Index Juridicus* and which dates from 1848. Many of the lawyers who practised in Edinburgh in the eighteenth century are mentioned in the notes to *Boswell's Edinburgh Journals, 1767-1786* edited by H Milne (Mercat Press, 2001).

22.3 If you have exhausted the printed sources and want to examine the records in the NAS, remember that sheriffs and other judges are appointed and paid by government and therefore you might try the records mentioned in **17.1-3**. Evidence of the professional career of judges, advocates and procurators will be found in the records of the court in which they operated. The Books of Sederunt of the Court of Session (CS1) contain copies of the appointments of the Lords of Session (i.e. the judges) and court officers and of the admission of advocates. The catalogue records petitions to the court by advocates and law agents in order to be allowed to plead, or act on behalf of others as curator bonis or judicial factor (CS258). The records of many sheriff courts include lists of procurators authorised to plead in that court, particularly since 1874, but in some courts since the end of the eighteenth century. Search for 'Register of Procurators' or 'Roll of Law Agents' or similar title, either in a special or miscellaneous series in the court's records. These rolls are sometimes indexed and will usually give you the business address of the lawyer. (Some sheriff courts also keep registers of sheriff officers, who are appointed by the sheriff to enforce court decrees, but who are not lawyers.)

22.4 Many writers/solicitors are also notaries and thereby authorised to certify certain legal documents. The NAS holds the Register of Admission of Notaries (NP2), which starts in 1563 but is not a consistent record until 1661 and, as a register, stops in 1873. The warrants of admission of notaries fill some of the early gaps (NP3) and replace the Register from 1873 (NP5). If you are looking for a notary before 1680, look first at the chronological list in NP3/1. This list covers the years 1577-1591, 1619-1623 and 1672. For other years before 1680 you will have to go straight to the Register (NP2). Between 1680 and 1792, look at the partly alphabetical chronological list NP6/1, which gives the name, designation and date of admission of each notary. Order out the NP2 volume that includes that date. Between 1792 and 1873, you have to order out the appropriate NP2 volume and look at the index in it. Notaries admitted between 1873 and 1903 are listed briefly in NP6/2.

22.5 All the entries in the Register of Notaries give the name and designation of the notary. Some of the earliest entries give his place of birth and state whether he is married or unmarried. Up to 1738, his age is usually given. After that date, the name of the notary's father is sometimes given, eg, 'Andrew Shand Writer in Thurso Son to Andrew Shand tennant at Innes in parish of Urquhart' was admitted as a notary public on 17 June 1742 (NP2/24).

22.6 The start of some lawyers' careers can be traced from the record of their apprenticeship, which may be found recorded in the register of deeds of their local sheriff court. By the late nineteenth century almost all the apprenticeships in these registers relate to legal practitioners rather than apprentices bound to masters involved in commerce or a trade.

❦23❦

Architects and Surveyors

23.1 If you are looking for an architect before 1840, first look at *A Biographical Dictionary of British Architects 1600-1840* by Howard Colvin (4th edition, Yale University Press, 2008). For architects from 1840 to 1940, consult the online Dictionary of Scottish Architects (*www.scottisharchitects.org.uk/index.php*). It contains a database of biographical information about more than 6,000 architects known to have worked in Scotland 1840–1940. A narrower range of information can be found in *Directory*

Vignette on plan showing name of surveyor, 1797 (RHP11610/1).

of British Architects 1834-1900 by Alison Felstead, Jonathan Franklin and Leslie Pinfield (London, 1993). Also still useful, for Scottish architects of any date, is *Scottish Architects' Papers: A Source Book* by Rebecca M Bailey (Rutland Press, 1996). This gives NAS references for relevant material (under our former abbreviation of 'SRO'). You may also wish to consult the Canmore resource at the Royal Commission on the Ancient and Historical Monuments of Scotland (*www.rcahms.gov.uk* or address in Appendix A); this can sometimes yield relevant references to documents in the NAS and elsewhere. In the NAS itself, there are an incomplete source list on Art and Architecture, and a separate incomplete card index of references to architects in GD collections to consult. They can sometimes be useful in supplementing the catalogue descriptions, but are no substitute for consulting the originals.

23.2 The profession of surveyor did not exist in Scotland until the mid-eighteenth century. For information about most surveyors before 1850, look at the *Dictionary of Land Surveyors and Local Map-Makers of Great Britain and Ireland, 1530-1850* by Sarah Bendall (1997) in two volumes. The entries in it are brief, but will show whether it may be worth your while to search further. As surveyors were frequently employed by landowners, their letters and reports, in addition to any plans they may have drawn, can often be found in estate papers (GD).

23.3 Information in the NAS about the plans and drawings produced by surveyors and architects is largely to be found in the Register House Plans (RHP). These plans are arranged and numbered in order of accession and there are now over 100,000 of them. The descriptions of non-architectural plans up to RHP4999 which were published in the *Descriptive List of Plans in the Scottish Record Office* volumes 1 to 4 (Scottish Record Office, 1966-1988), have been added to the online catalogue. All plans referenced RHP are included in the NAS catalogue, which you can search by place or by the name of an architect or surveyor.

∽24∽
Artists and Musicians

Artists

24.1 Early artists are listed in Michael Apted and Susan Hannabuss, *Painters in Scotland 1301–1700: A Biographical Dictionary* (Edinburgh, 1978), which usefully cites its sources, many of which can be found in NAS. Two other reference works are Peter J M McEwan, *A Dictionary of Scottish Art and Architecture* (2nd edn, 2004), and *The Dictionary of Scottish Painters: 1600 to the Present* by Julian Halsby and Paul Harris (3rd edn, 2001). Local libraries and galleries may be able to provide information on local artists, for example the Fine Art Library in Edinburgh Central Library. Information about Scottish artists is held by the National Galleries of Scotland. The Royal Scottish Academy archive holds information on its members and basic information on RSA exhibitors from 1826 onwards, with some earlier material; access is only by prior appointment. Artists' papers can be located through the online Artists' Papers Register *www. apr.ac.uk/artists/*, and also through the National Register of Archives in TNA, or the National Register of Archives for Scotland. (Addresses in Appendix A).

24.2 Originally painters and other practitioners who worked in the Scottish burghs served apprenticeships and became burgesses; they can therefore be found in the records of apprentices and burgesses (see **29.1**). Occasionally indentures of apprenticeship can be found in the registers of deeds (Chapter 13).

24.3 As the professions of artist, sculptor and engraver developed from their craft origins, training by masters became less rigid, and by the early nineteenth century the old apprentice system ceased. Formal teaching of drawing and other skills began in 1729 with the foundation of St Luke's Academy, Edinburgh. Records of students attending Scottish art schools founded from the late nineteenth century onwards are generally preserved by the schools or universities to which they are attached, but some early records are held in NAS.

24.4   Records of pupils applying to or attending the Drawing Academy in Edinburgh, run by the Board of Manufactures and Fisheries for Scotland, begin in 1818 (NG2/2/20). Petitions or applications can provide information about parentage, father's occupation, financial situation etc, especially those which include testimonials from referees outwith the family. The first register of art students lists eleven students admitted in 1828-9, including David Scott, son of Mr Robert Scott, engraver, Princes Street, Edinburgh (NG2/1/3). A fuller register exists of the hundreds of male pupils admitted during the years 1848–1856 to the Board's School of Design in Edinburgh. The details consist of the student's name, age, profession, father's name, place of residence, the name of the person who recommended him, and the dates he attended. Among those enrolled in 1849–50 we find the future Sir William Orchardson, who is described as an artist aged 17, the son of Abram Orchardson, Torphichen Street, recommended by John Sobieski Stewart Esq; he was first admitted in 1845 (NG2/1/4, p.9). The students were drawn from a wide range of disciplines, including engravers, portrait painters, architects, sculptors, carvers, upholsterers, house painters, pupil teachers, and also some pupils as young as twelve years old. A handful came from outside Edinburgh, for example George Yeats, a 26 year-old artist admitted in 1847, was the son of George Yeats, a feuar in Pitsligo, Aberdeenshire (NG2/1/4, p.21).

24.5   Similar registers of applications for admission or re-admission for the years 1852-1858 provide less personal information (NG2/1/5-7). One of them does, however, list the females attending separate classes in 1857-8. Most of the seventy students in the morning and evening class, and all fifty of the day students, are described as 'amateur'. Among the few women working for a living was Emily Gordon Smart, wood engraver, daughter of Robert Campbell Smart (NG2/1/7). An attendance register for the Board's School (now called the School of Art), lists the students' names, ages, professions and medals and other awards, 1858-1863 (NG2/1/8). As in earlier years, the students represented several arts and crafts.

24.6   Artists of all kinds can be found in many NAS collections by searching the catalogue using the appropriate term. The incomplete card index to artists in the Historical Search Room can still be useful in providing more detail than some catalogue entries. The records most likely to contain evidence of artists' work are the correspondence and accounts of their patrons in the Gifts and Deposits collections (GD), but they will not normally provide direct genealogical information. Other repositories, especially the National Library of Scotland, hold similar collections.

Musicians

24.7   The usefulness of private papers also applies to musicians, who can occasionally be traced in the GDs thanks to the patronage of the wealthier classes. In 1678 William Job, a violer and piper residing at Craiglockhart, contracted with Mr. John Clerk of Penicuik to play at his house on forty days a year (GD18/2285). During the eighteenth century the number of musicians, singers and their families grew, especially in the capital. More organised employment of professional musicians resulted from the formation in 1728 of the Edinburgh Musical Society. One treasurer's correspondence and accounts contain the names of many musicians, such as Johann Schetky, who was hired in 1772 as a violincello player with his brother, a flute player (GD113/5/210/6/3). The surviving records of the Friendly Society of Musicians in Edinburgh, 1778–1813 (CS96/1490-1492), include members' contributions, and payments of funeral charges and aliment for members and their widows. Other records may be helpful (see **16.11**). Selected musicians and composers can be traced in David Baptie, *Musical Scotland Past and Present: Being a Dictionary of Scottish Musicians from about 1400 to the Present Day* (1894).

⤳25⤳
Railwaymen

25.1 The NAS holds the surviving records of those railway companies that operated in Scotland. There used to be many railway companies which gradually amalgamated. Their records are listed, by railway company, in the BR catalogue. In the first volume of this catalogue, there is a list of the companies, giving the reference of each. For example, the records of the Glasgow and South-Western Railway Company are referenced BR/GSW. The catalogue is arranged in alphabetical order of reference letters. Within the records of each company, staff records are mostly listed in section 15. Thus, the staff records of the Highland Railway Company are referenced BR/HR/15. Some staff records may be found also in section 4 (miscellaneous records).

25.2 As a first step, if possible, look at a booklet compiled by Tom Richards, *Was Your Grandfather A Railwayman?* (Federation of Family History Societies, 2002), a directory of railway archive sources for family historians. This gives useful advice on how railway staff records were kept and lists briefly the railway staff records held by the NAS and other institutions. The Railway Ancestors Family History Society offers a useful way to discover and share information (*www.railwayancestors.org.uk*). For Scottish railway history see also *www.railbrit.co.uk*.

25.3 Staff recorded in the railway records are those who worked for the railway companies, not those who built the lines and who worked for contractors. If your ancestor was a navvy, you are very unlikely to find a record of him as such. If your ancestor worked for a railway company, you are more likely to find a record of his service if he worked in a station than if he was an engine-driver or plate-layer. You are also more likely to find him if he worked for the North British Railway Company, because more of the NB's staff records have survived.

25.4 You have to know what railway company employed your ancestor. If you know where he lived, particularly if he lived in a rural area, you

Station staff, Dreghorn, Ayrshire, circa 1907 (GD360/220).

may be able to guess which company. If he lived in Dufftown, you may presume that he worked for the Great North of Scotland Railway Company. If he lived in Glasgow, it may be impossible to guess which company. To find the routes and stations of the pre-1923 railway companies, look at *British Railways: Pre-Grouping Atlas and Gazetteer* (Ian Allan Ltd). In the NAS, the Station Handbooks (BR/RCH/S/5) also tell you which companies operated which stations.

25.5 There are various types of staff records and no great consistency in compiling them. The most useful staff registers are those which give the date of birth and show the detailed career of each railwayman, from job to job and place to place. For example, BR/CAL/15/1 shows that one John Anderson (born 15 January 1866) started work for the Caledonian Railway Company as a porter at Airth in 1881 and gradually advanced till he completed his career in 1924 as station-master at Guthrie on a salary of £260 per year. Other records will tell you who was employed in a particular station or department and why they ceased to be employed, either by a move to another station or department or by the end of their service. John Miller was employed by the Caledonian for 10 weeks in

1864 as a striker [metal-worker], before being discharged for smoking (BR/CAL/15/22). Offence books may tell you that your ancestor was drunk on duty or overslept and thereby delayed a train. Engine drivers were fined for not having steam up in time for their train's departure (eg in BR/GPK/4/1). Railway men involved in railway accidents are listed from newspaper and other sources at a special website *www.blacksheepindex.co.uk.*

25.6   Staff records are a tiny part of the BR records but your ancestor is likely to be named in other records, such as minutes or correspondence, only if he was fairly high-up in the hierarchy or involved in an accident, eg 'David Renton, Platelayer, was run over and killed by an Engine on the Line' (1854-BR/EDP/1/5). The appointment of station masters and above are usually noted in directors' minutes (section 1), though often only the surname is given. If the minute book has an index, look under the name of the station.

25.7   Some railway records have survived in private collections, of which there are some in the GD series. These may include staff records. For instance GD422/1/89 is a Glasgow and South Western Railway Company staff register, 1874-1922. The staff recorded in it include women, particularly some employed during the 1914–1918 war. One was Mary Brown Auld, whose service as a parcel clerk was dispensed with in 1919 'owing to a male being engaged'.

∽26∽
Coal Miners

26.1 Despite their historically low status, records of the names of colliers or coal miners can survive among the records of the landowner or coal company for whom they worked. In the NAS, such records are to be found among the GD collections and National Coal Board (later the British Coal Corporation) records (CB), which include records of coal companies before nationalisation. Look first at the Coal-mining source list, which will guide you to any relevant records. None will be indexed. The CB records are mainly twentieth century, but do include some eighteenth and nineteenth century records. In them, look for wages books, pay books, oncost books and output books: the names of workers appear in records of work done by them and of payments to them.

26.2 Because the colliers are usually described simply by forename and surname, care is required to ensure that you have found the right man, as is evidenced by a list of colliers at Edmonstone Colliery in 1777 (GD18/1124). The 39 colliers listed include three named Hugh Adam, three John Archibalds and other duplicated names.

26.3 Very occasionally you may find direct genealogical evidence. For example, the information 'Decr 1st 1753 Walter Simmer Son to old Thomas Simmer Entred Coliar' is noted in a Loanhead coal book in the Clerk of Penicuik muniments (GD18/990/7).

26.4 Among the Stirling Sheriff Court records, there are lists of colliers in Stirlingshire who in 1799 were in debt to the proprietors of their collieries (SC67/63/6). This is in accordance with a provision of the Colliers (Scotland) Act, 1799, which directed that debts due by colliers to their masters would cease to be valid unless they were recorded in sheriff court books within three months. There may, therefore, be such records in the records of other sheriff courts for that year.

26.5 If your ancestor met with an accident in a mine between 1861 and 1895, his name and that of the mine should be recorded in Procedure Books in the Lord Advocate's records (AD12/19–21). Mining accidents may also feature in the sheriff court fatal accident inquiries (**8.31**) and workmen's compensation series (**14.44, 46**).

∽27∽
Lighthouse Keepers

27.1 The NAS holds the historical records of the Commissioners of Northern Lighthouses, who employed the lighthouse keepers (more properly known as lightkeepers), and support and administrative staff. The Commissioners, who operate as the Northern Lighthouse Board, have had responsibility for lighthouses in Scotland since 1786, and in the Isle of Man since 1815.

27.2 The first lightkeeper, James Park, was a retired sea captain, who was employed in 1787 to operate the light at Kinnaird Head for a wage of one shilling per night plus free lodging, and pasturage for one cow. Principal lightkeepers and assistant lightkeepers were responsible for keeping the light shining throughout the night, and for cleaning and maintenance by day. At some stations they also recorded meteorological data. During the twentieth century the lighthouses were gradually automated, and the last resident lightkeepers left Fair Isle South Lighthouse in 1998. Good sources of information on Scottish lighthouses and their keepers can be found in the websites of the Northern Lighthouse Board *www.nlb.org.uk* and of the Museum of Scottish Lighthouses *www.lighthousemuseum.org.uk*.

27.3 Lightkeepers were often former mariners, and you may be fortunate to find evidence of relations also working for the Board, because the job ran in families and intermarriage between keepers' families was common. The work required self-reliant men, and both they and their families had to be willing to live in some of the most isolated parts of the country.

27.4 The main source for lighthouse keepers is the series of Registers and Lists of Lightkeepers, 1837-1980 (NLC4/1/1-7). These volumes give career histories for each keeper, noting his full name, date of birth, lighthouses worked at, promotions, demotions and date of retiral. Each volume is either indexed or arranged alphabetically according to surname and by lighthouse. For example we find that James Ducat became an assistant lightkeeper at Montroseness at the age of 22 in 1878. Three more postings followed before he became a principal lightkeeper on 17 April 1896. After three years he moved to the Flannan Isles lighthouse in July 1899. He disappeared without trace, along with his two assistants, in famously mysterious circumstances in December 1900 (NLC4/3).

27.5 At present the registers for 1837-1958 (NLC4/1/1-5) are available for consultation only on microfilm in both our West Search Room and Historical Search Room, but there are plans to digitise them. Copies of the relevant entry may be requested through the West Search Room. The register covering 1957-1970 (NLC4/1/6) has to be ordered in from TTH, while that for 1970-1980 (NLC4/1/7) is closed until 2011. The Museum of Scottish Lighthouses near Fraserburgh holds copies of some of the Lightkeepers Registers.

27.6 The Establishment Books, 1913-1957 (NLC4/2/3-4), provide details of salaried staff, who mostly worked at NLB headquarters in Edinburgh.

27.7 The Board Minutes, 1786-1984 (NLC2/1), often note the employment, dismissal, retirement of, or accidents involving, individual employees, especially in the nineteenth century. For example, we find that on 17 October 1849 the Board approved six appointments, including 'William Spink presently Principal Assistant at the Bell Rock to do duty as Principal Light Keeper at Sanna for a season'(NLC2/1/24, p.62). The Secretary's Correspondence and Reports, 1901-1987 (NLC3/1), also contain material on individual employees. Many keepers are named in the files relating to the Second World War (NLC10/3).

27.8 The General Orders, 1844-1991 (NLC5/1/1-4) detail disciplinary offences of individual keepers. For example, the General Order dated 10 Jan 1846 describes how William Budge, the principal keeper at the Calf of Man lighthouse, allowed the light to be extinguished for about fifteen minutes because he was reading in the lightroom, 'a neglect of duty which they [the Northern Lighthouse Board] view as the greatest that any Lightkeeper can commit, and which will at all times be marked by their severest censure' (NLC5/1/1). Budge was dismissed from the service.

27.9 Records which mention the Lighthouse Board's employees are closed to public inspection for 30 years from the date of the last entry in each file or volume. Note that certain records need to be ordered from our suburban repository.

⚬⚬28⚬⚬
Labourers

28.1 It is common to find a male or female ancestor described in many kinds of records as a 'labourer'. Although the term originally denoted someone involved in agricultural work, it became applied to many different kinds of occupation. It will require patience and luck to trace a labourer in one of the many manual occupations that used unskilled help, for example a mason's labourer. You may need to search various records to find more specific information.

28.2 The commonest kind of labourer in rural areas was often later described as an 'agricultural labourer'. One potential source is the records of an estate on which the labourer may have worked. Labourers do not usually appear in estate rentals (see **12.2-3**), because they did not have formal leases, and typically worked for the tenant farmers. If the labourer carried out work for a landowner on the home farm (or 'mains'), the estate wages books may record payments for labour such as manual farm work, digging ditches, building walls and estate buildings, and generally assisting in maintenance or improvements. This sort of work was carried out by day labourers, who were, as the name implies, paid by the day to carry out manual work. Estate accounts can be surprisingly detailed about an ancestor's daily activities, such as the work done by Janet Garden on a Perthshire estate in March 1821: 'taking in potatoes and gathering dung ... gathering stones and taking in hay' (GD155/681, p.44).

28.3 As manual labour was a major feature of agriculture and most industries until the recent past, it follows that labourers can be traced in records described elsewhere in this book. If you have identified a place where you think your ancestor may have lived or worked, it may be worth looking also at kirk session records (Chapter 8) and poor records (Chapter 32). Criminal and civil court cases may shed further light, or even mention your ancestors; cases frequently involved labourers of different kinds (Chapter 15). Workmen's compensation records may reveal injuries occurring at work (see **14.44, 46**). Business records of employers other than the landed estates may also help. For example, an account book records the wages of the labourers and others who built Dunkeld Bridge in 1803–5 (CS96/562).

29
Trade and Business

Burgesses, Craftsmen and Apprentices

29.1   If your ancestor was engaged in trade or business in a royal burgh, then he should appear as a burgess in the records of that burgh and possibly as a member of the guild or incorporation of his particular craft in the records of that guild or incorporation. The record of his admission as a burgess or as a member or apprentice of his craft will sometimes state a relationship. Burgesses were usually the sons or sons-in-law of burgesses. An apprenticeship commenced with an agreement (known as an indenture) between the boy's father and his master. Craftsmen admitted would usually be the sons, sons-in-law or apprentices of members of the craft.

29.2   Burghs that are served by published lists of burgesses or apprentices include: Aberdeen burgesses, 1600-1700, and Old Aberdeeen burgesses, 1605-1885, ed. Frances McDonnell (St Andrews, 1994); Ayr burgesses, 1647-1846, ed. Alistair Lindsay and Jean Kennedy (Ayr, 2002); Dumfries burgesses, 1644 to the present (Dumfriesshire & Galloway Natural History & Antiquarian Society, 1980); burgesses of Edinburgh, Canongate (Edinburgh), Glasgow and Dumbarton, and Edinburgh apprentices (Scottish Record Society, various dates); Fife burgesses, apprenticeships, ed. A J Campbell (Fife Family History Society, 1998); Perth burgesses, 1600-1699, ed. David Dobson (St Andrews, 2002). This is not an exhaustive list, so for other burghs it is worth checking the resources of local libraries and family or local history societies, or searching the Scottish Bibliographies Online catalogue at *www.nls.uk*.

29.3   Many burgh records are not kept in the NAS, but are held locally; some of the NAS records mentioned here may be transferred. For burghs whose records are in NAS, but are unindexed, check the catalogue for burgh records (B) to see whether the records of your burgh include burgess rolls or court books, which will contain the admission of burgesses. You will hope to find entries such as 'John Broun pedlar, who married Elizabeth Mure Laufull daughter of the deceast James Mure burgess of this Burgh, in her pure Virginity ... was ... Admitted Burgess and free-man of the Burgh' (Dunbar, 22 July 1730, B18/32/7).

29.4   The NAS holds the records of the following crafts either among the burgh or Exchequer records or in the GD collections:

Baxters (bakers) of Haddington (B30/18/1).

Carters in Leith (GD399).

Cordiners (shoemakers) of the Canongate (GD1/14); Edinburgh (GD 348); Haddington (B30/18/2 and GD302/62-66 and 128-129); Selkirk (GD1/13).

Dyers or Litsters of Aberdeen (E870/4).

Fleshers (butchers) of Ayr (E870/6); Haddington (B30/18/3).

Goldsmiths of Edinburgh and Glasgow (GD1/482).

Hammermen (metal workers) of Burntisland (B9/13/2); Hadding-ton (GD302/130-135); Linlithgow (GD76/390); Musselburgh (B52/8/4-6); Perth (GD1/427).

Tailors of Edinburgh (GD1/12); Linlithgow (GD76/385-391).

Weavers of Ayr (E870/5); Burntisland (B9/15); Haddington (B30/18/9).

Wrights and masons of Haddington (B30/18/4-8 and B30/22); Leith (GD1/943).

Wrights of Culross (GD1/977); Musselburgh (B52/8/1-3).

As with the burgesses or freemen of the burgh, lists of members of selected crafts have been published, for example the Hammermen of Burntisland, 1648-1873, along with other crafts, ed. A J Campbell (Fife Family History Society, 2000). Members of the Incorporation of Goldsmiths of Edin-burgh can be found in *Edinburgh Goldsmiths' Minutes, 1525-1700*, ed. H S Fothringham (Scottish Record Society, 2006), transcribed from GD1/482/1.

29.5   Some craft incorporation records kept elsewhere have been listed by the National Register of Archives for Scotland. Look in the catalogue of NRAS surveys under the names of the burgh, or in the classified paper index under 'Guilds and Incorporations'.

29.6   There are no such records of tradesmen who operated outwith the burghs. However, tradesmen and craftsmen may also be named in the records of mutual benefit societies associated with their trade and craft. The GD series include the records of the Society of Free Fishermen of Newhaven (GD265) and the Ancient Fraternity of Free Gardeners of East Lothian (GD420). The official series of friendly society records (FS) consist largely of rules and regulations of the societies. Only a very few include mid-nineteenth-century lists of members, eg the Strathaven Weavers Friendly Society (FS1/16/204). Such information is not noted in the FS catalogue but can be found in *Labour Records in Scotland* by Ian MacDougall (Scottish Labour History Society). Membership of such societies sometimes extended beyond those who were strictly of the stated trade.

29.7 Indentures of apprenticeship, whereby a boy became bound to serve a craftsman while he learned the craft, are noted in craft records. A few such indentures were registered in registers of deeds (see Chapter 13). Some survive in the GDs or similar collections, eg there is a series of indentures of Edinburgh apprentices referenced RH9/17/274-326. Some Edinburgh apprentices between 1695 and 1934 are recorded in the records of George Heriot's Trust (GD421, section 10). Do not expect an indenture to have survived: it is a bonus if it has done so.

29.8 From 1710, stamp duty was charged on indentures of apprenticeship. The collection of this tax was organised from London and no separate Scottish record seems to have been kept. Some Scottish apprentices are, however, recorded in the Stamp Board's Apprenticeship Books, 1710-1811, which are kept in The National Archives in London, reference IR1.

29.9 References to different trades and occupations can frequently be found in seemingly unrelated collections. Criminal court papers often record the occupations of those who were either charged with crime, or who were the victims of crime, or who served as jurors (see Chapter 15). During the First World War detailed information about tradesmen and small business owners in Edinburgh and Lothian can be found in the Military Appeal tribunal papers (see **18.24-26**). For online resources see **3.24**.

Business Records

29.10 Surviving business records sometimes include wages books or other records that name employees. There are some business records in the

GD series. For example, those of the Carron Company (GD58) and of Alex Cowan & Son Ltd, papermakers in Penicuik (GD311), include staff records. Business books, including wages books, are also to be found among the Court of Session records (see Chapter 14). Look also in the National Register of Archives for Scotland catalogue and classified index for records of business firms.

Dissolved and bankrupt companies

29.11 If your ancestor was involved in a business, or held shares in a limited company registered under the Joint Stock Companies Act 1856, you may find them in the files of dissolved companies (BT2). The files generally contain lists of shareholders and directors, including their occupation and address. Note that NAS only holds records of Scottish companies twenty years after they have been dissolved (wound up); the records of companies which are still active are retained by Companies House.

29.12 Information about the owners of businesses which have been sequestrated, or gone into bankruptcy, can be found among the Court of Session records (see **14.26**)

Board of Manufactures

29.13 If your ancestor was involved in fabric manufacture or the fishing industry from 1727 into the nineteenth century, you might want to examine the records of the Board of Trustees for Fisheries, Manufactures and Improvements in Scotland, which was established to assist economic development. Look at the catalogue referenced NG1. Among its projects, the Board awarded premiums to producers and appointed stampmasters and other inspectors to supervise the linen industry. Thus, in 1792, there were awards of £25 to William Douglas at Dalhousie for his Silesia Linen and of £15 to Donald McLeod in Arnol Island of Lewis, for oil produced from dog fish (NG1/42/2); while, in 1822, we are told that Thomas Faulds was growing 'mostly promising' flax on the farm of Lissens in the parish of Dalry (NG1/42/8). The regulation of the linen industry was ended in 1823, but there are superannuation records of the former inspectors up to 1859, sometimes giving their age or date of death (NG1/48/1).

29.14 From 1809, the responsibility for overseeing the fishing industry passed to the Fishery Board for Scotland. The names of some of the men involved in the fishing industry occur in its records, particularly the records of the local fishery offices (AF17–36), but it may take some trawling to find a name you want. Among the surviving records of fishery vessels are a few registers of establishment for the fishery cruisers the *Brenda* and the *Minna,* which include information about place and date of birth and service records of the crew, c.1898–1954 (AF6/65–8).

Licensees

29.15 From 1756, a person who sold ale or other excisable liquors, whether in an inn or a shop, was required to have a licence. If he operated within a burgh, then the licence was granted by the burgh court, and, if outwith a burgh, by the Justices of the Peace for the county. Look in the B or JP catalogue at the contents list of the relevant burgh or county for the licensing court records. Some such records are kept in local archives. Most of the surviving records start in the nineteenth century. We find, for example, that Mrs Isabella Laing, shipbuilder, was licensed in 1829 to sell ale in a house at the Shore of Dunbar (B18/12/1).

∽30∽
Electors and Elected

Electors until 1832

30.1 Before 1832 only a tiny minority of Scotsmen (but no women) elected representatives to Parliament, and the records of such elections are unlikely to add to the information you have about your ancestors. Representatives of the burghs were elected by the burgh council or by delegates of the councils: information is in the council minute books (B). Representatives of the counties were elected by freeholders, who were men who owned land or other heritable property in that county above a certain substantial value. The records of admission of landowners on to a roll of freeholders and of the election by the freeholders of a member of parliament are to be found among the sheriff court records. Look in the contents list of an appropriate SC catalogue to see if it contains the freeholders' records for that county. However, as, before a man was admitted to a roll of freeholders, the instrument of sasine which proved his ownership of sufficient land had to be recorded in the Register of Sasines (see **11.3–15**), the freeholders records may add nothing to what you have already found in that register. There may be points of interest where the admission or vote of a freeholder was disputed by his political opponents.

Electors since 1832

30.2 Since 1832, various Reform Acts have gradually expanded the electorate. By 1929, almost everyone over 21 was on the electoral register. Until 1918, parliamentary electors had to be male and proprietors or tenants of lands, houses or other heritable property or (since 1868) prosperous lodgers. *Electoral Registers Since 1832* by Jeremy Gibson and Colin Rogers (Federation of Family History Societies), though written from an English point of view, is useful in describing the background of electoral law. Its list of Scottish records is incomplete.

Register of Voters in North Berwick

	No.	Date	Name	Calling
7 Sept 1839. Expunge	1	30 Aug 1838	~~Adams Alex. Maxwell~~	Surgeon
	2	10 Sept 1833	Beglie George	Farmer
5 Sept 1840. Expunge	3	22 Sept 1832	~~Bertram Peter~~	Baker
	4	30 Aug 1838	Brash James	Mason
	5	22 Sept 1833	Brodie James	Baker
	6	"	Brown Revd George	Minister
Re Enrolled 7 Sept 1839	7	10 Sept 1833	Brown Wm Frederick Esq	Gentleman
	8	22 Sept 1832	Craven John	Butler
	9	"	Craven William	Farmer
	10	"	Crawford Alexander	"
	11	8 Sept 1834	Crawford John	Malster
	12	10 Sept 1833	Dall James	Merchant
	13	6 Sept 1836	Dalrymple Sir Hew	Gentleman
7 Sept 1839 Expunge	14	30 Aug 1838	~~Edington Peter~~	Grocer & Draper
	15	"	Eeles George	Tailor
	16	10 Sept 1833	Ferguson Robert Esq	Gentleman
	17	22 Sept 1832	Graham Revd R. M.D.	Minister
	18	8 Sept 1835	Handyside Peter	Farmer
	19	10 Sept 1833	Herkes Alexr	Weaver
	20	"	Hislop James	Shoemaker
	21	30 Aug 1838	Hood John	Farmer
	22	22 Sept 1832	Kemp Thomas	Baker
	23	30 Augt 1838	Low James	Wright
	24	22 Sept 1832	Ramage George	Farmer
Expunged 5 Sept 1862	25	30 Augt 1838	Ramage Henry	Baker
Re enrolled 7 Sept 1839	26	"	Richardson Andrew	Tenant in Abbey
	27	9 Sept 1837	Rime George	Parochial School Master
	28	22 Sept 1832	Smith George	Carrier
	29	30 Augt 1838	Somerville James	Clothy Merchant
	30			

Excerpt from the Register of Voters in North Berwick, 1838.

30.3   Until 1918, electoral registers had to record why an elector had the right to vote. Thus, they provide not only the name of the voter, but also his occupation, whether he is a proprietor or tenant, and a description of his property.

30.4   From 1882, provided they were proprietors or tenants, unmarried women and married women not living in family with their husband could vote for burgh councillors and, from 1889, for county councillors. From these dates, there are supplementary registers of female voters for use in local government elections.

30.5   Registers of voters survive intermittently. Those in the NAS are almost entirely nineteenth-century, when burghs were in separate constituencies from the counties that surrounded them. Therefore there are separate registers of voters in burghs and counties, though some registers of burgh voters survive among sheriff court records. Most burghs were grouped together, so that several burghs (sometimes in different counties) were combined to form one constituency. County registers are arranged by parishes. There are the following registers of voters in the burgh and sheriff court records in the NAS. Check the catalogue to obtain the exact reference.

Burghs: Culross, 1832-1851 (B12/7). Dunbar, 1832-1860 (B18/18). Dunfermline, 1868 (SC67/61). Earlsferry, 1902-1904 (SC20/46). Falkirk, 1840-1865 (SC67/61). Hamilton, 1864-1865 (SC67/61). Lauder, 1832-1861 (B46/9). Newburgh, 1833-1870 (B54/9). Newport, 1899-1900 (SC20/46). North Berwick, 1832-1915 (B56/12). Perth, 1876-1877 and 1892-1893 (SC49/58). Stirling, 1868 (SC67/61).

Counties: Caithness, 1832-1860 (SC14/64). Clackmannan and Kinross, 1832-1862 (SC64/63/26-36). Cromarty, 1832-1833 (SC24/21). Inverness, 1832-1872 (SC29/71). Kirkcudbright, 1832-1862 (SC16/68). Linlithgow, 1837 (SC41/99). Nairn, 1847-1873 (SC31/60). Peebles, 1832-1861 (SC42/44). Roxburgh, Hawick district, 1832-1846 (SC62/73). Selkirk, 1832-1861 (SC63/61). Stirling, 1832-1862 (SC67/61). Wigtown, 1832-1861 (SC19/64).

30.6   Some of these sheriff court records also include poll books and other records of voters. Similar records may occasionally be found in GD collections, most notably GD260, which includes electoral registers for the county of Dumbarton, 1873-1892 (GD260/4/1-5). Enquiries about records of voters should also be made to local archives and libraries.

Members of Parliament

30.7 Though the records described above will sometimes mention those elected, you should use printed sources if you are searching for an ancestor who might have been a representative in Parliament. These include the following:

The Parliaments of Scotland: Burgh and Shire Commissioners, edited by Margaret D Young (Scottish Academic Press, 1992-3) contains some 2,000 brief biographies, arranged in alphabetical order, of the men who represented the burghs and counties in the Scottish Parliament until 1707. It also contains an appendix, listing the constituencies alphabetically with names of the representatives of each.

Members of Parliament, Scotland, 1357-1882 by Joseph Foster.

The History of Parliament. The House of Commons. Four series of multi-volumes cover 1690-1820 (1964-2002), with further sections in preparation by the History of Parliament Trust

Who's Who of British Members of Parliament, 1832-1979 (The Harvester Press).

The Sick and Insane

The Sick

31.1   Records of patients in hospitals often supply the patient's age and some-times date of death. Hospital records are largely in the custody of the archivist of the Health Board within whose authority the hospital lies (see addresses in Appendix A). Records formerly in the NAS have been transmitted to the relevant Health Boards, except for a series of registers of out-patients of Dundee Royal Infirmary, 1851-1854 (CS96/2279-2304), and the records of the Kelso Dispensary and Cottage Hospital (HH71). The Kelso records include lists of patients in the hospital, since 1777, supplying the patient's name, parish, age, date of admission, disease and the outcome (mostly 'cured'). Thus, we learn that Margaret Cummins, resident in the parish of Eccles, aged 60, poisoned with laudanum, was admitted on 10 January 1828, was treated but died (HH71/44). There are also some records of out-patients and patients visited at home.

31.2   Those prevented by illness from earning a living might have received poor relief (see **32.1-11**). For example, in 1727, the parish of Inveravon supported 'John Fleeming a poor boy lyable to an epilepsie' (CH2/191/2, p244).

The Insane

31.3   The words 'lunatic' and 'insane' are used here to describe people suffering various grades of mental disturbance, which were sometimes not fully understood at the time. Records may survive if someone was appointed to administer the property of an insane person, or if he were put in the custody of an asylum or individual. Many records in NAS contain sensitive personal information and are restricted or closed for 100 years after they were written.

31.4   Obviously, only when the insane person owned property was there a need to go to law to decide who should be curator to administer that

Invalid and relation, late nineteenth century (GD254/1316/5).

property. Until 1897, such decisions might be 'retoured to Chancery' in the same procedure as heirs were proved. This is explained in **10.4–22**. Up to 1700, these decisions are to be found in the 'Inquisitiones de Tutela' in volume 2 of the *Inquisitionum Retornatarum Abbreviatio* (indexed in volume 3). After 1700, look in the 'Index to Tutories and Curatories in Record of Retours, 1701-1897'. The people indexed in this include insane persons, identifiable by being given a curator, not a tutor. To see the retour, order out by C22 and the volume number given in the index. The curator was usually the nearest male relative on the father's side aged at least 25 years.

31.5 The retour will tell you which sheriff court held the preceding inquiry. Where records of these inquiries survive, they may provide more details both of the condition of the insane person and of his relationship to his curator. Look in the relevant SC catalogue for 'Record of Services' or similar heading. For example, in 1830, James Mitchell, teacher, Kineff, was appointed curator to administer the affairs of William Gordon, bookseller, Aberdeen, his maternal uncle (C22/133, f.89). The related Aberdeen Sheriff Court records (SC1/27/20) supply the date of James's baptism and the names of his parents and William's father.

31.6 In the eighteenth century, an alternative procedure developed whereby a near relative petitioned the Court of Session for the judicial appointment of a 'curator bonis' to look after the affairs of an insane or otherwise incapable person. The records of such cases are among the records of the Court of Session (see **14.3** onwards).

31.7 After 1880, when the estate of an incapable person did not exceed £100 in yearly value, the appointment of a curator bonis could also be made by a sheriff court. A few sheriff courts kept a separate record of these appointments (perhaps in a 'Register of Judicial Factors'), but mostly they have to be sought among the ordinary court records (see **14.39-43**).

31.8 From 1849, the Accountant of Court (of Session) was responsible for supervising curators appointed to administer the estates of persons unable to administer their own affairs. Therefore, the Accountant of Court's records include information about better-off lunatics, including cases where the curator bonis had been appointed before 1849. Look in the catalogue for CS313-317.

31.9 Patients of all classes, but mostly paupers, were kept in asylums. Before the passing of the Lunacy (Scotland) Act 1857 there are few records of such asylums. Among the Aberdeen Sheriff Court records, there are registers of lunatics in asylums in Aberdeenshire, 1800-1823 and 1855-1857 (SC1/18/1-2).

31.10 A statutory licensing and inspection system was established for all public and private institutions in Scotland having 'the care or confinement of furious and fatuous persons and lunatics'. Inspection reports were submitted to the Royal College of Physicians in Edinburgh and the High Court of Justiciary. Within the JC records there have survived reports, accounts and returns on madhouses and lunatics, 1816-1857 (JC54). The reports (especially the early ones) contain detailed medical and social comment on named patients in public and private asylums and private houses, and observations on buildings and staff. In 1854 special reports were compiled giving the names and costs of maintaining lunatic paupers in each parish in Scotland for the years 1851-1853 (JC54/13-41).

31.11 From 1857, such asylums were regulated by the General Board of Commissioners in Lunacy. The Board's records are preserved in the NAS, listed under the Mental Welfare Commission for Scotland (MC). Access is restricted for 75 years for adult patients, and 100 years for children under the age of 16. The Board records include a general register of all lunatics in asylums (MC7). This lists and numbers the inmates chronologically, from number 1, Jean Morris, who was admitted to Newbigging House in 1805 (where she died 60 years later) to number 218,009 in 1962. Though this register apparently starts in 1805, it only records those who were still alive in 1858 or were committed since 1858. The register records name, date of admission, which asylum, date of death or discharge, and whither removed (if relevant). A partial index to the register is found at MC7/33: MC7/33/1 covers the period 1805-1962, letters O-Z only, and MC7/33/2 covers the period 1910-1955, letters A-G only. Access to these closed records is by data protection application to NAS. If the individual you are looking for falls outside either of these indexes, you will need to look through the registers or the Notices of Admission themselves (see **31.12**), and it therefore helps if you have an idea of when he might have been committed to an asylum.

31.12 Fuller details about those admitted to asylums since 1858 are contained in the Notices of Admission (MC2), which are arranged chronologically. The patient's number in the general register (MC7) is noted on his notice of admission. Information supplied, as well as their mental and physical health, includes full name, age, marital status, previous place of abode, nearest relative, and whether any member of his family had been insane. We find that Robert Primrose Paterson, aged 29, single, schoolmaster at Duddingstone, whose insanity was supposedly caused by 'Studying Some Educational Scheme', was admitted to the Royal Edinburgh Asylum on the petition of his mother in January 1858 (MC2/1).

31.13 There is no register of lunatics who were not put into asylums, though they may be named in the records of poor relief (see Chapter 32). However, in the Lord Advocate's papers, there is a 'Return of lunatics or idiots at large in the county of Edinburgh (Midlothian)' in 1850 (AD58/114). This provides the name and age of each patient, with whom he resides and by whom supported.

31.14 Some people accused of a crime were found to be insane. Court records, particularly the High Court of Justiciary (JC), will record that a person was 'Insane in bar of trial' and committed to prison. These persons are recorded in the Justiciary trials catalogue. The Home and Health Department records include casebooks, dating from 1846, and later files on criminal lunatics (HH17, 18 and 21/48). These are closed for 75 years.

The Poor

32.1 The poor are always with us and provision has to be made for them. Records relating to their maintenance can be valuable sources of information for the genealogist whose ancestors were paupers for all or part of their lives. Until recently the problematical nature of these sources has deterred the majority of genealogists. However, the advent of large indexing projects run by some local authority archives and family history societies has opened up poor relief records to thousands of researchers.

32.2 Before searching for pauper ancestors, the researcher should first grasp three aspects of poor relief in Scotland before the mid-twentieth century: there was a distinction made between 'deserving' and 'undeserving' poor; until the 1930s relief was largely organised by parish; and record-keeping was particularly concerned with a pauper's parish of birth or settlement.

32.3 From the sixteenth century until the Depression of the 1930s, able-bodied men and women were regarded as undeserving recipients of poor relief. Acts of parliament regulating the provision of poor relief repeatedly reserved the provision of relief to the deserving poor; in effect those who lacked funds or family support and who were unable, through age or infirmity, to maintain themselves. These included the elderly who lived without family support, the disabled and insane, orphans and destitute children, and the mothers of young children deserted by their husbands. The able-bodied unemployed were not entitled to relief, but were sometimes given relief if injury or illness temporarily prevented them supporting their family. So much the acts allowed, but in practice parishes often gave help to vagrant poor, usually unnamed in the records – 'a stranger', 'a poor man at the church door'.

32.4 Each parish was bound to support the deserving poor living within its boundaries, provided they had either been born there or had acquired settlement there. Settlement could be acquired by residing in a parish for seven years or, in the case of married women, by adopting their husband's parish of birth or residence. The onus on each parish to ascertain whether someone claiming relief was entitled to it and was legally settled in the parish, meant that parishes might investigate the circumstances of the claimant's family and his or her movements from one residence to another over several years.

32.5   An important date in the provision of poor relief is 1845, when what is often termed the 'New Poor Law' was introduced. However, for genealogical purposes it is best to consider poor relief records as belonging to three periods: the late seventeenth century until the 1820s, the 1820s until the 1880s and the 1880s until 1930. From 1930 onwards poor relief was no longer managed by parishes and surviving poor relief records from that era onwards will almost certainly be closed to public access, due to the sensitive nature of the information about individual claimants.

Poor relief records from the 1690s until the 1820s

32.6   Before the Poor Law Act, 1845, the responsibility for poor relief lay jointly with the heritors (see **11.41**) and kirk session of each parish, and records of payments to the poor may be found in the records of either (see **32.10-13** below). Burgh councils also made charitable payments to people in distress, but the burgh records (B) in the NAS are not very informative on this score, and searching through burgh minutes and accounts will, in general, be very time-consuming and unrewarding. Where local authority archives and libraries hold burgh records it may be worth enquiring whether local societies have carried out indexing.

Poor relief records from the 1820s until the 1880s

32.7   The Poor Law Act, 1845 set up parochial boards in Scotland's 878 parishes, and allowed them to fund poor relief from local property taxation rather than on church collections and contributions from heritors. The resultant transition from church authorities to what are termed 'civil parishes' took several decades. Only 230 parishes adopted the New Poor Law in 1845, but by 1865 only about 100 were still maintaining their poor as before. By the time parochial boards were replaced by parish councils in 1892 all Scotland's parishes operated under the same system.

32.8   In some parishes the parochial board continued to use the record-keeping practices of the heritors or kirk sessions, especially where registers of the poor had been compiled from the 1830s. After 1865 there was considerable standardisation in record keeping and registers compiled from then onwards often have information about paupers dating back to 1845 or earlier. Because of the overlap of responsibilities of kirk sessions, heritors and parochial boards, anyone searching for information about pauper ancestors in this transition period, therefore, should consult the records of kirk sessions and heritors (see **32.10–13** below), and the records of parochial boards (see **32.14–20** below).

Poor relief records from the 1880s until the 1930s

32.9 From the 1880s onwards you can be fairly certain that any surviving records relating to poor relief will be among civil parish records, which in most cases will be with local authority archives (see **32.14–20** below).

Poor relief catalogues in kirk session and heritors' records

32.10 Look in the indexes of parishes in both HR and CH2 repertories and then the relevant list of records for the particular parish. Some kirk session records are held under charge and superintendence by local authority archives, but most are held by the NAS. Almost all heritors' records are held by the NAS, but a few are held by local authority archives, often because these have begun life as heritors' minutes and become parochial board minutes. Poor relief accounts were occasionally kept as a separate record and as such will be specified in the HR or CH2 catalogue. For example, the heritors of Tranent kept a very detailed poor roll between 1827 and 1845, giving details such as '79, infirm, son silly' and, of a widow, '33, young children' (HR74/15/3). Much more commonly, payments to the poor are noted, in the midst of other business, in the minute books and account books kept by the heritors and kirk sessions. There is no shortcut to searching them, except in the few cases where the records have been indexed and/or published.

32.11 Income paid to the poor came from assessments on the heritors and collections at the church services. This 'poor money' was distributed to the 'Ordinary Poor' or 'Pensioners', who were paid at regular intervals and often appear in a list, and the 'Occasional Poor'. The latter category included payments in kind, such as supplying shoes or coal to a needy person; payments to the temporarily disabled, eg 10 shillings 'to one James Simpson who had his thigh bone broken' (Glencorse Kirk Session,

17 October 1700 – CH2/181/1); and payments to those who did not belong to the parish.

32.12 For the first decade after 1845 most kirk sessions and heritors continued for a time to provide for their poor from church collections and recorded payments in their minutes and accounts, eg Greenlaw kirk session distributed to named poor after the communion service twice yearly until 1881 (CH2/183/2). However, from the 1820s onwards the compilation of separate poor relief records became more common, and the information recorded therein more informative. The Dirleton heritors kept a roll of poor from 1825 until 1847 (HR42/4).

32.13 Though all infirm poor within the parish, whatever their denomination, were the responsibility of the established kirk session, the free churches also sometimes assisted their own poor. However, the names of their poor people are only occasionally reported in their records (CH3 and CH10-16).

Civil Parish Records

32.14 From 1845 onwards parochial boards kept minute books and accounts, but some boards also compiled more comprehensive registers of information on paupers. In 1865 record-keeping was standardised to a great extent by the body which supervised civil parishes at that time, the Board of Supervision, and from then on most parishes kept distinct types of registers (see **32.17-18** below). The records of parochial boards and parish councils are mainly held by local authority archives and libraries, but the NAS currently holds the records for 18 civil parishes in Wigtownshire (CO4/30-47), 24 civil parishes in East Lothian (CO7/7, DC4/4-11, DC5/4-5, and DC7/4) and 18 civil parishes in Midlothian (CO2/77-91). The Wigtownshire and East Lothian parish records contain minute books of parochial boards and parish councils, and registers of the poor. For the Midlothian parishes only minute books survive. In addition two volumes survive for the parishes of Forgan and Falkland in the County of Fife: a minute book for Forgan Parish Council, 1917-1929 (CO12/2) and the letter book of Falkland Parish's Inspector of the Poor, 1848-9 (CO12/1). Eventually all of these civil parish records are likely to be transferred to appropriate local archives.

32.15 Minute books and accounts of parochial boards and parish councils contain information on applications for poor relief, but the amount of information depends on the parish. Some parishes merely recorded the names of successful applicants and the amount or type of relief. Other parishes recorded more details of individual applicants, but in most minute books the information may only confirm what the researcher already knows, or else add nothing of substance. In some cases a parochial board minute book might begin life as the minute book of the heritors and contain information on poor relief back to the 1830s. As with all minute books and accounts, they will require time-consuming research, unless they have been indexed. Very few are indexed. The researcher should only turn to the minute books of a parochial board or parish council when no separate registers of the poor survive for that parish.

Registers of the poor

32.16 From the 1840s (and in some cases the 1830s) many parishes began compiling registers of the poor giving full details of the people who were aided. These records are particularly useful in recording the children of aged paupers and the parentage of orphans and illegitimate and deserted children. They can also be useful in showing the geographical movements of an individual. Each parochial board had to keep a roll of poor persons to whom it gave financial relief. Among the information recorded about each pauper was age, country and place of birth, whether married or single, name and age of wife and children living with the pauper, and name and age of husband or wife and children not living in family with the pauper. Thus, we find from the register of poor of Inch parish in Wigtownshire, that Sarah Ann Hawthorne or Caldwell, a washerwoman, who declined to go into the poorhouse in 1891, was 72, born in Ireland, and had 9 children, 5 of whom were in America (CO4/32/7, p408).

32.17 In 1865 the Board of Supervision imposed a greater degree of standardisation on record-keeping by parochial boards. From then on most parishes compiled what was known as a 'General Register of the Poor', which was in effect a record of successful applicants for relief. In some cases information about paupers on the parishes' books since the 1830s was included and researchers should be careful when considering the ages of individuals recorded, as these may be the ages in 1865, not at the time of the original application many years earlier. Likewise it is important to note that the information was added to these registers over time, but in most cases this is quite clear from the dating of the entries

GENERAL REGISTER OF POOR BELONGING TO

44

1865   Name   *Soones M: Master Margt. Walker.*

Residence	*Balenacy*	Earnings, Means, and Resources, besides Parochial Relief	*Earnings, about 4/- per week.*
Age	*29 years*		
Date of Minute of Parochial Board or Committee admitting Liability and authorizing Relief	*4. April 1860* *14. Nov. 1859*	Nature of Settlement	*Birth & Widow.*
Amount and Description of Relief authorized	*1/6 per week*	Name and Age of Wife, Child, or Children living in Family	*Children Beta Morrow 8 years. Alext Morrow 5 years - James Webster born 8 July 1865 - Margt. Walker, born 3rd July 1868 -*
Country and Place of Birth, and, if in Scotland, Parish of Birth	*Scotland. Glasserton*		
Religious Denomination, whether Protestant or Roman Catholic	*Protestant.*	Name, Age, and Weekly Earnings of Husband, Wife, Child or Children not living in Family and their Circumstances	
Condition—If Adult, whether Married or Single, Widow or Widower	*Single*		
If Child, whether Orphan, Deserted, or separated from Parent			
Trade or Occupation	*out door laborer*		
Wholly or Partially Disabled	*Partially*	Other Information not stated above	
Description of Disablement	*Children*		
Wholly or Partially Destitute	*Partially*		

Dates.	Change of Circumstances and subsequent Proceedings.	Dates.	Change of Circumstances and subsequent Proceedings.
20 May 1872	*Aliment withdrawn. Poorhouse offered, not accepted.*		
31st Octr. 1872	*Dr. certifies that this person is very ill. Inspector has visited and made himself acquainted with the circumstances, and has allowed necessary support and attendance.*		
28th Nov. 1872	*Recovered. and allowed 1/6 per week - 2 Chpd.*		
27 Feby 1873	*Aliment withdrawn - Poor House offered. (not accepted)*		

A page from a general register of the poor for Glasserton parish, Wigtownshire, 1865 (CO4/30/7).

and the changes in handwriting. Note that the term 'General Register of the Poor' does not mean that a central register was kept for the whole of Scotland. General registers were kept by individual parishes and their name differentiates them from other types of registers, such as children's separate registers (also introduced in 1865) and registers of able-bodied unemployed (introduced in the 1920s, when poor relief was extended to include workers made unemployed during the Great Depression).

32.18 Not everyone who applied for poor relief was added to the poor roll. Some information about failed applicants and those who were not added to the roll of regular poor may be found in parochial board/civil parish minutes. In 1852, the parochial board of Inch 'took up the case of Mrs Jean Finlay. The Board agree to pay the passage of her four children from Liverpool to America' (CO4/32/1), although there was no provision in the Poor Law (Scotland) Act for assisting emigration. From 1865 most parishes kept registers of applications for relief (some parishes had been keeping similar registers from the 1850s or even earlier). The value of such registers is that they contain information about all applicants for relief, not merely the successful ones whose details can be found in general registers etc.

32.19 Apart from the records for civil parishes in Wigtownshire, East Lothian, Midlothian and Fife held by the NAS (see **32.14**), most civil parish records are held by local authority archives and libraries. In many cases only minute books and accounts survive. In the case of the four largest cities, substantial runs of poor relief registers apparently survive only for Glasgow (in Glasgow City Archives). For the rest of Scotland the survival of registers of the poor is variable. Substantial sets of poor registers are held by Shetland Council Archives (Shetland), Orkney Council Archives (Orkney), the North Highland Archive at Wick (Caithness), Highland Council Archive (Sutherland, Ross & Cromarty, Inverness-shire, Inverness Burgh), Aberdeen City Archives (Aberdeen-shire), Angus Council Archives (Angus), Dundee City Archives (one parish in Angus), Glasgow City Archives (Glasgow City, Lanarkshire, Renfrewshire, Dunbartonshire), Renfrew Council Libraries in Paisley (Paisley Burgh), Ayrshire Archives (Ayrshire), and Dumfries & Galloway Libraries (Dumfriesshire and Kirkcudbrightshire). The Scottish Archive Network (*www.scan.org.uk*) can provide information about the location of most of these. There appear to be major gaps for several counties: most notably for parishes in Fife and Perthshire.

32.20 Access to poor relief registers for certain areas of Scotland has been greatly increased by large scale indexing projects carried out by archives and family history societies. The largest of these is the database at Glasgow

City Archives to poor relief registers compiled by parishes in Glasgow, Lanarkshire, Renfrewshire, Lanarkshire and Dunbartonshire. Indexing has also been carried out on poor registers for other counties, either by the local archive which holds the records or a local family history society. At the time of writing none of these is available online and enquiries should be directed to the archive concerned. One index of poor relief records which is online is a combined index to Liff & Benvie Parochial Board's Register of Poor (1854-1865) and Dundee East Poorhouse Register (1856-1878), compiled by Friends of Dundee City Archives and accessible at *http://www.fdca.org.uk/*.

Poor relief records in court records

32.21 An applicant who was refused relief by the inspector of poor for a parish could appeal to the sheriff of the sheriffdom in which that parish lay. An inspector of poor could apply to the sheriff for the removal from the country of a pauper who was not a native of Scotland, and also could raise an action in the sheriff court against a father who had deserted his wife and children or refused to support an illegitimate child. The sheriff court records (SC) therefore contain records of such cases.

32.22 A few sheriff courts kept separate records relating to poor relief appeals and related matters, but most of these cover only a limited period, such as the 'poor law minute books' compiled by Ayr Sheriff Court for 1846-1862 (SC6/82). These give the name of the appellant, the parish, and the date and decision of the case. In most cases, the records of appeal cases relating to poor relief have to be sought among the records of other Ordinary Court cases brought before the sheriff (see **14.39-43**). Identifying them may not be easy and the detail given may be minimal. If there is a register of summary applications, look there. Glasgow Sheriff Court's register (SC36/7) is particularly useful, as it starts in 1858, earlier than most. In such a register, look under 'Pursuer or Applicant' for a person appealing against refusal of relief and under 'Respondent' for a person who was to be removed to Ireland or England or had deserted wife and children.

32.23 For those whose ancestor appealed to a sheriff court after an unfavourable decision by a civil parish, a potential shortcut to information exists in the form of two published works. The first of these is Alexander McNeel Caird's *Poor Law Manual for Scotland* (1845 and later editions). In addition to summarising the statutes relating to the relief of the poor,

Caird provides a digest of over 60 selected cases relating to poor law in sheriff courts, the Court of Session and the High Court of Justiciary. For the period after 1851 anyone researching poor relief appeals should consult the *Poor Law Magazine*, which published a monthly digest of appeal cases. An edition of Caird is available in the West Search Room and digital copies of the pages in Caird relating to appeal cases are available in the Historical Search Room. Bound copies of the *Poor Law Magazine* are widely available in Scottish archives and reference libraries.

Destitution

32.24 The parish system of poor relief sometimes proved insufficient and had to be supplemented by private charity. To find the records of charitable foundations, sometimes called 'hospitals', which helped the poor of particular localities, you should first check the regional or district archive which serves that locality. The records of the King James VI Hospital, Perth, are in the NAS. Look in the GD79 inventory at section 7 for records of the deserving poor of Perth. In 1825, an application was made on behalf of the Widow Macphail, in South Street, aged 102 years (GD79/7/38/1).

32.25 In the cities, charitable institutions were established for the maintenance and education of orphans and other destitute children. Two such institutions whose records are held by the NAS are the Dean Orphanage (GD417) and Dr Guthrie's Schools (GD425), both in Edinburgh. Records which name children date from 1753 and 1854 respectively, but records less than 100 years old are closed to the public. Petitions for admission and admission registers can provide useful family information. James Ralston, admitted to Dean Orphanage in 1830, was the son of an army sergeant. His mother 'also followed the Camp since she was 11 years of age', suffering fatigue and exposure during the Peninsular Campaigns (GD417/175).

32.26 In response to the devastating failure of the potato crop in 1846, destitution boards were established to raise money to save the people of the Highlands and Islands from starvation. The records of these boards, listed in the Highland Destitution (HD) catalogue, name many of the people in the Highlands and Islands who between 1847 and 1852 were given meal or financial aid or were found work. Look at the registers listed as HD1. These registers vary in content but usually supply the name, age and occupation of each head of family, sometimes also the number of

Children at the Orphan Hospital of Edinburgh, later the Dean Orphanage, eighteenth century (GD417/255/9). Reproduced by courtesy of the Secretaries and Treasurers of the Dean Orphanage and Cauvin's Trust.

children in that family, and sometimes the names and ages of everyone in the family. Thus, we find that in May 1847, Mathew Jameson, a farmer and fisherman at Ollabury in the district of Northmaven in Shetland, was 35 and had one child above 12 and four under 12 (HD1/1). A register of the most needy families in Skye in 1850 (HD1/13) tells us that Donald McDiarmid, at Kilmuir in the district of Watternish, was aged 60 and his family consisted of Alice (45), Norman (7) and John (4). HD1 is not a complete series, but similar information can be found in meal distribution accounts (HD6/9–13) and in some of the papers relating to Shetland (HD17), Skye (HD20) and Wester Ross (HD21), particularly the abstracts of registry and applications for work. An equivalent record in the Tobermory Sheriff Court records is a register of meal distribution, 1848–1853, to paupers in and around Mull (SC59/15/5).

32.27 For a fuller summary of poor relief records in the NAS see Kirsty M Forbes and Robert H J Urquhart, 'Records in the National Archives of Scotland relating to Poor Relief, 1845-1930' in *Scottish Archives* volume 8 (2002).

∞33∞
Emigrants and Migrants

33.1   There is ample proof that Scotsmen migrated, both within the British Isles and overseas. Yet records of the actual movement of individual migrants are sparse. Most people searching for emigrant ancestors assume they will appear in a ship's passenger list: sadly this is not the case (see **3.21** for possible sources). Official ship passenger lists exist only from 1890 and these are held in The National Archives in London. Free movement within the United Kingdom has always been possible, but the evidence has to be dug out of records designed for other purposes, such as kirk session or parochial board records. There is no official record of the ordinary Scots who migrated to Northern Ireland in the reign of James VI, only of their well-to-do landlords.

33.2   There was similar freedom of travel abroad, generally unrecorded except for transported criminals (see **15.27**). Passports, as we know them, were not introduced until 1915. Previously, the Crown sometimes issued passes or letters of protection to people travelling in Europe, but these people were from the upper classes and intending to return. Before 1603, some of these letters were recorded in the Register of the Privy Seal (see **8.17**). Records of later passports are mainly in The National Archives in London.

33.3   If your ancestor emigrated to North America or Australia, look for him in the immigration records in the country of arrival or in the various published lists which are available such as:

Passenger and Immigration Lists Index – A Guide to Published Arrival Records of about 500,000 Passengers in the United States and Canada by P William Filby and Mary K Meyer (Gale Research Company, Detroit, 2nd edition,1988).

Directory of Scottish Settlers in North America, 1625-1825, 7 volumes, by David Dobson (Genealogical Publishing Company, Baltimore, 1984-1993), and his other similar works.

A Dictionary of Scottish Emigrants to the USA, 2 volumes, by Donald Whyte (Magna Carta Book Company, Baltimore,1972 and 1986).

A Dictionary of Scottish Emigrants to Canada Before Confederation, 3 volumes, by Donald Whyte (Ontario Genealogical Society, 1986-2002)).

A Directory of Scots in Australasia, 1788-1900, 3 parts (1994-98)

D Whyte, *The Scots Overseas: a Selected Bibliography* (Scottish Association of Family History Societies, 1995)

Ian Maxwell, *Tracing your Ancestors in Northern Ireland* (Stationery Office, 1997)

33.4 There are, however, two bodies of records in the NAS that deal specifically with short-lived nineteenth century schemes to assist emigrants from the western Highlands and Islands.

33.5 The Highland and Island Emigration Society was a voluntary association formed in 1851 to assist those affected by the potato famine. Its records are referenced HD4. They include lists of some 5,000 assisted emigrants who sailed to Australia between 1852 and 1857 (HD4/5). The emigrants are listed by ship and by family, giving the name and age of each person and where they had resided in western Scotland. An index of the names of these emigrants is available on-line at *http://www.scan.org.uk/researchrtools/emigration.htm*. See also **3.22**.

33.6 Files concerning a later scheme for state-aided emigration to Canada are listed in the AF catalogue under AF51. Files which provide family details of those who applied to emigrate are dated between 1886 and 1889. They include lists of applicants from some of the Western Isles and completed forms of application for assistance to emigrate. These record the members of the household of the applicant, stating each's age and relationship to the applicant. If any failed to embark, this is noted. Thus, we know that William Macleod (26), from Coll, emigrated with his wife and brother, but his cousin Donald MacDonald changed his mind and stayed behind (AF51/36). Some information about emigrants in Manitoba after 1889 is contained in the records of the Crofters and Cottars Colonization Board (AF51/188-211).

Slaves

34.1   The single most important record source is the British government's registry of slaves, 1813-1834, in The National Archives at Kew. Registers were kept on the islands of the West Indies in order to regulate the continuing trade in slaves in British dominions between the abolition in 1811 of the trade between the islands of the West Indies, and the final outlawing of slavery in 1834. The names and personal details of about 100,000 slaves are given, including their age and country of origin. It also details over 5,000 owners. See the TNA website for details, or Guy Grannum, *Tracing Your West Indian Ancestors* 2nd edition (Public Record Office [TNA], 2002).

34.2   Scottish merchants and landowners were early and active participants in the transatlantic slave trade, and in running plantations in the Caribbean using slave labour. Some of the records they have left are in NAS, and are described in a research guide on the transatlantic slave trade on the NAS website. When searching the NAS catalogue it is important to bear in mind that the language used in some entries to describe documents reflects the terms which their creators used, for example 'list of negroes', a term then commonly used to describe slaves. As well as illustrating aspects of the slave trade in general, and providing information about slave owners, the records in NAS can be a useful source of information about individual slaves at particular places and times. However, it is generally difficult to trace links between slaves, whose identities may not be well recorded, and their descendants.

34.3   Many of the best Scottish examples come from court cases, preserved among the records of the Court of Session and the Admiralty Court. The case of Horseburgh v Bogle, a dispute which yields not the names of the slaves, but of the African chiefs who were selling them to European slave traders on the Guinea Coast in 1727; this is believed to be the earliest such record (AC9/1042). It is likely that cases in the Court of Session (CS) contain lists of slaves and related information, but in order to find a relevant case you generally need to know the names of the parties, e.g. a slave owner or a business associate.

34.4   NAS also holds some records of plantations owned by Scots. Their correspondence, accounts and business papers mention, but do not always name, slaves. One exception is the detailed accounts for the years 1729-1735 left by Robert Cunnyngham, who owned a plantation on St Christopher (St Kitts). Heading a list of his Creole boy slaves in 1731 we find Jack, a valet, described as 'Piero and Violets son'. Piero is listed separately as a 45 year-old Creole, occupied as a carter, while Violet may be either a 40 year-old originating in Moccow, perhaps employed as a cook, or a 30 year-old cook also called Violet, who was born on a slave ship (CS96/3104, pp.4-6). The country of origin, age and occupation of each slave is recorded. A list of field slaves in 1733 also notes the country of origin and identifies many family relationships.

34.5   Slaves who worked in the plantation owner's household are sometimes mentioned in personal correspondence. If owners returned to Scotland, it was household slaves whom owners typically chose to accompany them. Thereafter the usual estate and household records may be used to trace their working lives in Scotland, while kirk session, parish registers and other records may also be helpful (see also **16.8**). In this situation slaves tended to adopt their master's family name. For example, in 1702 a slave called Scipio was brought from the West Indies, and from 1705 for a period of about twenty years served the Kennedy family at Culzean, Ayrshire. He was baptised, thereby obtaining his freedom in Scots law, but continued as a servant, now using the surname Kennedy. In 1728 he was disciplined by the kirk session of Kirkoswald for antenuptial fornication (CH2/562/1), and by his subsequent marriage had at least eight children according to the parish register.

34.6   Household slaves and former slaves working in households could be provided for in the wills of their masters. They could passed on like possessions, but the inheritance might involve a request for manumission. Similarly, the children and grandchildren of mixed-race relationships can be named in wills (Chapter 9), although less often in personal correspondence, as their existence or origins were usually discreetly guarded.

34.7   A handful of slaves in late eighteenth-century Scotland, for example Joseph Knight, were the subject of important legal cases which helped pave the way for the abolition of slavery. The NAS website provides information about these cases, of which NAS holds the original records.

34.8   Scots, like other Europeans, could also become slaves if they were cap-
        tured North African pirates and sold into slavery. Seamen sailing in the
        Mediterranean were vulnerable from the early seventeenth century until
        well into the eighteenth century. They are occasionally mentioned in
        the records. For example a letter of 1709 concerns the capture of the
        'Isabel' of Kirkcaldy by an Algerian vessel, and lists the Scots who were
        sold as slaves (B18/51/20). Papers relating to people from the British
        Isles who were enslaved can be found in The National Archives at Kew,
        especially in SP 71.

❦35❧
Genealogies

35.1 If you have been through even some of the records covered in this book, you will want to draw up your own family tree. Unless you are of the aristocracy or landed gentry, you are not likely find your own family tree ready-made. However, there is a chance that you might link your family tree to one already compiled. Published genealogies of Scottish families are listed in *Scottish Family History* by Margaret Stuart and Balfour Paul and *Scottish Family Histories* by J P S Ferguson. Manuscript genealogies of varying antiquity may be found in archives and libraries, such as those of the Scottish Genealogy Society and the Lyon Office (addresses in Appendix A).

35.2 Be aware that not every genealogy may be totally accurate. Check the details if you can.

35.3 There are some genealogies among the manuscripts in the NAS. RH16 is a collection of genealogies, indexed at the end of the RH16 inventory. Otherwise, seek for genealogies in the GD collections. A few of the GDs consist of papers gathered and compiled by people who did research. From our point of view, the most useful of these is the John MacGregor Collection (GD50), which, along with original papers and transcripts of documents, contains genealogies and genealogical notes, mainly of Highland families, especially MacGregors and Campbells. As the GD50 inventory is arranged in no logical order, you should examine it carefully. Some GD collections of the records of landed and noble families include genealogies and family narratives, usually but not exclusively of their own and related families. These genealogies may or may not be evident in the inventory contents list: try the miscellaneous section, if there is one.

35.4 You will no doubt have realised by now that family history research is an absorbing and potentially endless pursuit. Having started out with the intention of researching their family history, many people embark on related research, such as the local history of the area in which their ancestors lived. If you wish to do this, you may find our companion guide *Tracing Scottish Local History* of value.

35.5 Let us take as our final words on the ancestors we seek an observation by the American writer Oliver Wendell Holmes: 'Every man is an omnibus in which his ancestors ride.' In tracing your family history, you may discover more about yourself.

∽ Appendices ∽

ᴄᴏᴏ Appendix A ᴏᴏ
Useful Addresses

Please note that archive addresses and contact details may change. See SCAN
directory for up-to-date details – www.scan.org.uk/directory.

National Institutions

National Archives of Scotland
HM General Register House, Edinburgh EH1 3YY
Phone: 0131 535 1314   Fax: 0131 535 1360   *www.nas.gov.uk*

National Register of Archives for Scotland
The Registrar, HM General Register House, Edinburgh EH1 3YY
Phone: 0131 535 1403/5   Fax: 0131 535 1430   *www.nas.gov.uk/nras*

General Register Office for Scotland
New Register House, Edinburgh EH1 3YT
Phone: 0131 334 0380   Fax: 0131 314 4400   *www.gro-scotland.gov.uk*

Court of the Lord Lyon
New Register House, Edinburgh EH1 3YT
Phone: 0131 556 7255   Fax: 0131 557 2148   *www.lyon-court.com*

Museum of Scottish Lighthouses
Kinnaird Head, Stevenson Road, Fraserburgh AB43 9DU
Phone: 01346 511022   Fax: 01346 515879   *www.lighthousemuseum.org.uk*

National Galleries of Scotland
National Gallery of Scotland, The Mound, Edinburgh EH2 2EL
Phone: 0131 624 6200   *www.nationalgalleries.org*

National Library of Scotland
George IV Bridge, Edinburgh EH1 1EW
Phone: 0131 226 4531   Fax: 0131 226 4803   *www.nls.uk*

National Monuments Record of Scotland
Royal Commission on the Ancient and Historical Monuments of Scotland
John Sinclair House, 16 Bernard Terrace, Edinburgh EH8 9NX
Phone: 0131 662 1456   Fax: 0131 662 1477   *www.rcahms.gov.uk*

The National War Museum of Scotland
Edinburgh Castle, Edinburgh EHI 2NG
Phone: 0131 225 7534   Fax: 0131 225 3848   *www.nms.ac.uk/war*

Royal Scottish Academy of Art & Architecture
The Dean Gallery, 73 Belford Road, Edinburgh EH4 3DS
Phone: 0131 624 6277   E-mail: collections@royalscottishacademy.org
www.royalscottishacademy.org

Scottish Catholic Archives
Columba House, 16 Drummond Place, Edinburgh EH3 6PL
Phone: 0131 556 3661   *www.scottishcatholicarchives.org.uk*

Scottish Jewish Archives Centre
Garnethill Synagogue, 129 Hill Street, Glasgow G3 6UB
Phone: 0141 332 4911   *www.sjac.org.uk*

The National Archives
Kew, Richmond, Surrey TW9 4DU
Phone: 020 8876 3444   Fax: 020 8392 5286   *www.nationalarchives.gov.uk*

Public Record Office of Northern Ireland
66 Balmoral Avenue, Belfast BT9 6NY
Phone: (+44) 028 9025 5905   *www.proni.gov.uk*

The National Archives of Ireland
Bishop Street, Dublin 8, Republic of Ireland
Phone: +353 (0) 1 407 2300   Fax +353 (0) 1 407 2333   *www.nationalarchives.ie*

Local Archives

Aberdeen Council Archives
Old Aberdeen House, Dunbar Street, Aberdeen AB24 3UJ
Phone: 01224 481775   Fax: 01224 495830   *www.aberdeenshire.gov.uk*

Aberdeen City Archives
Town House, Broad Street, Aberdeen AB10 1AQ
Phone: 01224 522513   Fax: 01224 638556   *www.aberdeencity.gov.uk/archives*

Angus Archives
Hunter Library, Restenneth Priory, By Forfar DD8 2SZ
Phone: 01307 468644   *www.angus.gov.uk/history/archives/*

Argyll and Bute Council Archives
Manse Brae, Lochgilphead, Argyll PA31 8QU
Phone: 01546 604774   Fax: 01546 604769   *www.argyll-bute.gov.uk*

Ayrshire Archives
(transferring to new premises in 2009)
Phone: 01292 287584   Fax: 01292 284918   *www.ayrshirearchives.org.uk/*

Clackmannanshire Council Archives
Alloa Library, 26-28 Drysdale Street, Alloa FK10 1JL
Phone: 01259 722 262   Fax: 01259 219 469   *www.clacksweb.org.uk/culture/archives*

Dumfries and Galloway Archives
Archive Centre, 33 Burns Street, Dumfries DG1 2PS
Phone: 01387 269254   Fax: 01387 264126   *www.dumgal.gov.uk/lia*

Dundee City Archives Support Services
21 City Square, Dundee DD1 3BY (Callers please use 18 City Square, Dundee)
Phone: 01382 434494   Fax: 01382 434182   *www.dundeecity.gov.uk/archive*

East Dunbartonshire Information and Archives
William Patrick Library, 2 West High Street, Kirkintilloch G66 1AD
Phone: 0141 775 4541   Fax: 0141 776 0408   *www.eastdunbarton.gov.uk*

East Lothian Archive Service
Library & Museum Headquarters, Dunbar Road, Haddington, East Lothian EH41 3PJ
Phone: 01620 828200   e-mail: archives@eastlothian.gov.uk   *www.eastlothian.gov.uk*

Edinburgh City Archives
Level 1, City Chambers, High Street, Edinburgh EH1 1YJ
Phone: 0131 529 4616   Fax: 0131 529 4957   *www.edinburgh.gov.uk*

Edinburgh Room
Edinburgh City Libraries, Central Library, George IV Bridge, Edinburgh EHI IEG
Phone: 0131 242 8030   Fax: 0131 242 8035   *www.edinburgh.gov.uk*

Falkirk Council Archives
Falkirk Museums History Research Centre, Callendar House, Callendar Park,
Falkirk FK1 1YR
Phone: 01324 503779   *www.falkirk.gov.uk/services/community/cultural_services/
museums/archives/archive.aspx*

Fife Council Archive Centre
Carleton House, Balgonie Road, Markinch, Glenrothes KY7 6AQ
Phone: 01592 583352   Fax: 01592 417477   *www.fife.gov.uk*

Glasgow City Archives and Special Collections
Mitchell Library, 210 North Street, Glasgow G3 7DN
Phone: 0141 287 2999 or 2876   Fax: 0141 287 2815   *www.glasgow.gov.uk/en/
Residents/Library_Services/The_Mitchell/*

Highland Council Archive
Inverness Library, Farraline Park, Inverness IV1 1NH (until autumn 2009)
Phone: 01463 220 330   Fax: 01463 711 128   *www.highland.gov.uk/leisureandtourism/
what-to-see/archives/highlandcouncilarchives/*

Lochaber Archive Centre
Lochaber College, An Aird, Fort William, Inverness-shire PH33 6AN
Tel: 01397 701942 / 700946   E-mail: *Lochaber.archives@highland.gov.uk*

Midlothian Council Local Studies and Archives
Library Headquarters, Clerk Street, Loanhead EH20 9DR
Phone: 0131 271 3976   Fax: 0131 440 4635   *www.midlothian.gov.uk*

Moray Council Local Heritage Centre
East End School, Institution Road, Elgin, Moray IV30 1RP
Phone: 01343 569011   Fax: 01343 549050   *www.moray.gov.uk/LocalHeritage/*

North Highland Archives
Wick Library, Sinclair Terrace, Wick, Caithness KW1 5AB
Phone: 01955 606432   Fax: 01955 603000   *www.highland.gov.uk*

North Lanarkshire Archive
10 Kelvin Road, Lenziemill Industrial Estate, Cumbernauld G67 2BA
Phone: 01236 638 980   Fax: 01236 781 762   *www.northlan.gov.uk/*
leisure+and+tourism/museums+and+heritage/archive+centre/

Orkney Archives
The Orkney Library and Archive, 44 Junction Road, Kirkwall KW15 1AG
Phone: 01856 873166   Fax: 01856 875260   *www.orkneylibrary.org.uk/html/archive.htm*

Perth and Kinross Council Archive
AK Bell Library, 2–8 York Place, Perth PH2 8EP
Phone: 01738 477012   Fax: 01738 477010   *www.pkc.gov.uk/archives*

Scottish Borders Archive & Local History Centre
Heritage Hub, Kirkstile, Hawick TD9 0AE
Phone: 01450 360699   *www.scotborders.gov.uk/council/specialinterest/*
heartofhawick/18964.html

Shetland Museum & Archives
Hay's Dock, Lerwick, Shetland ZE1 0WP
Phone: 01595 695057   Fax: 01595 696729   *www.shetland-museum.org.uk*

South Lanarkshire Archives
South Lanarkshire Council Record Centre, 30 Hawbank Road, College Milton,
East Kilbride G74 5EX
Phone: 01355 239193   Fax: 01355 242365   *www.southlanarkshire.gov.uk*

Stirling Council Archives Services
5 Borrowmeadow Road, Springkerse Industrial Estate, Stirling FK7 7UW
Phone: 01786 450745   Fax: 01786 443005   *www.stirling.gov.uk/index/*
accessinformation/archives/archivevisiting.htm

West Lothian Council Archives and Record Management Centre
9 Dunlop Square, Deans Industrial Estate, Livingston, West Lothian EH54 8SB
Phone: 01506 773770   Fax: 01506 773775   *www.westlothian.gov.uk*

University Archives

University of Aberdeen
Special Libraries and Archives, King's College, Aberdeen AB24 3SW
Phone: 01224 272598   Fax: 01224 273891   *www.abdn.ac.uk*

Dundee University Archives
Archive Services, University of Dundee, Dundee DD1 4HN
Phone: 01382 384095   Fax: 01382 385523   *www.dundee.ac.uk/archives*

Edinburgh University Archives
Special Collections, Edinburgh University Library, George Square,
Edinburgh EH8 9LJ
Phone: 0131 650 8379   Fax: 0131 650 2922   *www.lib.ed.ac.uk/lib/resources/
collections/specdivision/*

Glasgow Caledonian University Archives
The Saltire Centre, Glasgow Caledonian University, Cowcaddens Road,
Glasgow G4 0BA
Phone: 0141 273 1188   *www.gcal.ac.uk/archives/index.htm*

Glasgow University Archive Services
13 Thurso Street, Glasgow G11 6PE
Phone: 0141 330 5515   Fax: 0141 330 2640   *www.gla.ac.uk/archives/*

Heriot-Watt University Archives
Riccarton, Currie, Edinburgh EH14 4AS
Phone: 0131 451 3218   Fax: 0131 451 3164   *www.hw.ac.uk/archive*

St Andrews University Library
Department of Manuscripts, North Street, St Andrews KY16 9TR
Phone: 01334 462339 (Special Collections Reading room)   Fax: 01334 462282
http://www.st-andrews.ac.uk/specialcollections/

Stirling University Library and Special Collections
Andrew Miller Building, Stirling FK9 4LA
Phone: 01786 467235   Fax: 01786 466866   *www.library.stir.ac.uk/libraries/
collections/spcoll/*

University of Strathclyde Archives
Andersonian Library, Curran Building, 101 St James Road, Glasgow G4 0NS
Phone: 0141 548 2497   Fax: 0141 552 3304   *www.strath.ac.uk/archives/*

Medical Archives

Dumfries and Galloway Health Board Archives
See Local Archives – Dumfries and Galloway Archives

NHS Greater Glasgow and Clyde Board Archive, 77-87 Dumbarton Road,
Glasgow G11 6PW
Phone: 0141 330 2992   Fax: 0141 330 4158   *www.gla.ac.uk/services/archives/nhsggca/*

Lothian Health Services Archive
Edinburgh University Library, George Square, Edinburgh EH8 9LJ
Phone: 0131 650 3392   Fax: 0131 650 6863   *www.lhsa.lib.ed.ac.uk/*

Highland Health Sciences Library (NHS Highland Archives)
University of Stirling, Highland Campus, Centre for Health Science, Old Perth
Road, Inverness IV2 3JH
Phone: 01463 255600, ext. 7600   Fax: 01463 255605

Northern Health Services Archives
Victoria Pavilion, Woolmanhill Hospital, Aberdeen AB25 1LD
Phone: 01224 555562   *www.nhsgrampian.org/*

Royal College of Nursing Archives
42 South Oswald Road, Edinburgh EH9 2HH
Phone: 0131 662 6122/6123   Fax: 0131 662 1032   *www.rcn.org.uk/development/*
library/archives

Royal College of Physicians and Surgeons of Glasgow
234–242 St Vincent Street, Glasgow G2 5RJ
Phone: 0141 227 3234   *www.rcpsg.ac.uk/*

Royal College of Physicians of Edinburgh
9 Queen Street, Edinburgh EH2 1JQ
Phone: 0131 225 7324   Fax: 0131 220 3939   *www.rcpe.ac.uk/library/*

Royal College of Surgeons of Edinburgh
Nicolson Street, Edinburgh EH8 9DW
Phone: 0131 527 1630   Fax: 0131 557 6406   *www.rcsed.ac.uk*

Genealogical Societies

Aberdeen and North East Scotland Family History Society
164 King Street, Aberdeen AB24 5BD
Phone: 01224 646323   Fax: 01224 639096   *www.anesfhs.org.uk*

Alloway & Southern Ayrshire Family History Society
c/o Alloway Library, Doonholm Road, Ayr KA7 4QQ
www.asafhs.co.uk

Association of Scottish Genealogists and Researchers in Archives (ASGRA)
259 Broad Street, Cowdenbeath, Fife KY4 8LG
Phone: 01383 515465   *www.asgra.co.uk*

Borders Family History Society
Membership Secretary,
35 Corbar Road, Stockport, Cheshire SK2 6EP
www.bordersfhs.org.uk

Family History Society of Buchan
Arbuthnot Museum, St Peter's Street, Peterhead, Aberdeenshire AB42 1QD
www.fhsb.org.uk

Caithness Family History Society
Membership Secretary
Smithy House, Castletown, Caithness KW14 8TY
www.caithnessfhs.org.uk

Central Scotland Family History Society
The Secretary
11 Springbank Gardens, Dunblane FK15 9JX
www.csfhs.org.uk

Dumfries and Galloway Family History Society
Family History Centre, 9 Glasgow Street, Dumfries DG2 9AF
Phone: 01387 248093   *www.dgfhs.org.uk*

East Ayrshire Family History Society
c/o The Dick Institute, Elmbank Ave, Kilmarnock KA1 3BU
www.eastayrshirefhs.org.uk

Fife Family History Society
Glenmoriston, Durie Street, Leven, Fife KY8 4HF
www.fifefhs.org

The Genealogy Society of Utah
Family History Support Office, 185 Penns Lane, Sutton Coldfield,
West Midlands B75 1JU
www.familysearch.org

Glasgow & West of Scotland Family History Society
Unit 13, 22 Mansfield Street, Glasgow G11 5QP
www.gwsfhs.org.uk

Guild of One-Name Studies
The Hon Secretary,
Box G, 14 Charterhouse Buildings, Goswell Road, London EC1M 7BA
www.one-name.org

The Heraldry Society of Scotland
25 Craigentinny Crescent, Edinburgh EH7 6QA
www.heraldry-scotland.co.uk

Highland Family History Society
Suite 4, Third Floor, Albyn House, 37A Union Street, Inverness IV1 1QA
www.highlandfhs.org.uk

Lanarkshire Family History Society
c/o Motherwell Heritage Centre, Local History Room, High Road,
Motherwell ML1 3HU
www.lanarkshirefhs.org.uk

Largs and North Ayrshire Family History Society
The Secretary

c/o Largs Library, 26 Alanpark Street, Largs, Ayrshire KA30 9AG
www.largsnafhs.org.uk

The Lothian Family History Society
c/o Lasswade High School Centre, Eskdale Drive, Bonnyrigg, Midlothian EH19 2LA
www.lothiansfhs.org.uk

Moray Burial Ground Research Group
secretary@mbgrg.org   *www.mbgrg.org*

North Perthshire Family History Group
www.npfhg.org

Orkney Family History Society
Orkney Library & Archives, 44 Junction Road, Kirkwall KW15 1AG
www.orkneyfhs.co.uk

Renfrewshire Family History Society
c/o Paisley Museum & Art Galleries, High Street, Paisley PA1 2BA
Tel: 0141 889 3151   *www.renfrewshirefhs.org.uk*

Scottish Association of Family History Societies
www.safhs.org.uk

The Scottish Genealogy Society
15 Victoria Terrace, Edinburgh EH1 2JL
Phone/Fax: 0131 220 3677   *www.scotsgenealogy.com*

Shetland Family History Society
6 Hillhead, Lerwick, Shetland ZE1 0EJ
www.shetland-fhs.org.uk

Tay Valley Family History Society
Research Centre, 179-181 Princes Street, Dundee DD4 6DQ
Phone: 01382 461845   *www.tayvalleyfhs.org.uk*

Troon@Ayrshire Family History Society
c/o M.E.R.C., Troon Public Library, South Beach, Troon, Ayrshire KA10 6EF
www.troonayrshirefhs.org.uk

West Lothian Family History Society
23 Templar Rise, Livingston, West Lothian EH54 6PJ
www.wlfhs.org.uk

∽Appendix B∽
Useful Books

Various published works are recommended at appropriate points in the text. The following list repeats some of the more useful of them and also suggests further publications which you may wish to consult. The names of publishers are placed in brackets.

Annual Report of the Keeper of the Records of Scotland (Copies may be purchased from the National Archives of Scotland, or viewed on *www.nas.gov.uk.*)

British Genealogical Microfiche by Stuart A Raymond (Federation of Family History Societies)

The Concise Scots Dictionary (Scottish National Dictionary Association/Polygon at Edinburgh)

The Genealogist's Internet by Peter Christian (The National Archives)

Genealogy for Beginners by Arthur Willis (Phillimore & Co)

Guide to the National Archives of Scotland (The Stationery Office/Stair Society)

In Search of Scottish Ancestry by Gerald Hamilton-Edwards (Phillimore)

Index of Scottish Place Names from 1981 Census (The Stationery Office)

Jock Tamson's Bairns: A History of the Records of the General Register Office for Scotland (General Register Office for Scotland)

My Ain Folk by Graham S Holton and Jack Winch (Tuckwell Press)

National Index of Parish Registers, Volume XII: Sources for Scottish Genealogy and Family History by D J Steel (Phillimore, for Society of Genealogists)

Netting Your Ancestors by Cyndi Howells (Genealogical Publishing Company Inc)

The New Statistical Account of Scotland (15 volumes, published 1845. Electronic version available at *http://edina.ac.uk/statacc/*)

An Ordinary of Arms contained in the Public Register of all Arms and Bearings in Scotland by Sir James Balfour Paul (Genealogical Publishing Company, Inc)

An Ordinary of Arms, Volume II, contained in the Public Register of all Arms and Bearings in Scotland, 1902-1973 by David Reid and Vivien Wilson (Lyon Office, Edinburgh)

The Parishes, Registers and Registrars of Scotland by S M Spiers (ed) (Scottish Association of Family History Societies)

Scotland. A Genealogical Research Guide (LDS, Family History Library)

Scottish Ancestry Research: A Brief Guide by Donald Whyte (Scotpress)

Scottish Family Histories by Joan P S Ferguson (National Library of Scotland)

Scottish Family History by Margaret Stuart and Sir James Balfour Paul (Oliver & Boyd; reprinted by Genealogical Publishing Company, Baltimore)

Scottish Family History by David Moody (Genealogical Publishing Company, Inc)

The Scottish Genealogist, the quarterly journal of the Scottish Genealogy Society (address in Appendix A)

Scottish Genealogy by Bruce Durie (History Press)

The Statistical Account of Scotland compiled by Sir John Sinclair (21 volumes, published 1791-1799. Electronic version available at *http://edina.ac.uk/statacc/*)

The Surnames of Scotland by George F Black (The New York Public Library)

The Scottish Family Tree Detective: Tracing Your Ancestors in Scotland by Rosemary Bigwood (Manchester University Press)

Tracing Your Ancestors in the Public Record Office by Jane Cox and Timothy Padfield (The Stationery Office)

Tracing Your Ancestors in Northern Ireland by Ian Maxwell, edited by Grace McGrath (The Stationery Office)

Tracing Your Army Ancestors by Simon Fowler (Pen and Sword)

Tracing Your Scottish Ancestry by Kathleen B Cory (Polygon)

Using Death and Burial Records for Family Historians by Lilian Gibbens (Federation of Family History Societies)

Wills and Where to Find Them by T W S Gibson (Phillimore)

Your Scottish Ancestry: A Guide for North Americans by Sherry Irvine (Ancestry Incorporated)

NAS publications are available in the ScotlandsPeople Centre shop in General Register House, and at West Register House. A selection of titles is listed on the NAS website at *www.nas.gov.uk*.

Many useful calendars and indices of Scottish records have been and are being published by the Scottish Record Society. For a list of available titles, see *www.scottishrecordsociety.org* or *www.nls.uk/print/index.html*. The Society's earlier publications are unfortunately out of print.

❧ Indexes ❧

⧉Index⧉
to Classes and Types
of Records

∽Index∾
to Categories of
Individuals